Ruba Totah, Jonas Tinius (eds.)
"PostHeimat" – Inquiries into Migration, Theatre, and Networked Solidarity

Ruba Totah is an anthropologist at the Johannes Gutenberg Universität Mainz. Her research interests and writing cover cultural activism, transnationalism and gender across Palestine, the Arab area, and Europe. Her PhD focuses on "Cultural Transnationalism and The Arab Uprisings: Migrating Artists from Syria to Europe." Together with Jonas Tinius, she was the director of the research section of the "PostHeimat Network".

Jonas Tinius is a socio-cultural anthropologist and teaches at the Humboldt-Universität zu Berlin. Together with Ruba Totah, he was the director of the research section of the "PostHeimat Network".

Ruba Totah, Jonas Tinius (eds.)

"PostHeimat" – Inquiries into Migration, Theatre, and Networked Solidarity

[transcript]

Bibliographic information published by the Deutsche Nationalbibliothek

The Deutsche Nationalbibliothek lists this publication in the Deutsche Nationalbibliografie; detailed bibliographic data are available in the Internet at https://dnb.dnb.de

2025 © Ruba Totah, Jonas Tinius (eds.)

transcript Verlag | Hermannstraße 26 | D-33602 Bielefeld | live@transcript-verlag.de

Printing: Majuskel Medienproduktion GmbH, Wetzlar
https://doi.org/10.14361/9783839462515
Print-ISBN: 978-3-8376-6251-1 | PDF-ISBN: 978-3-8394-6251-5
ISSN of series: 2700-3922 | eISSN of series: 2747-3198

Printed on permanent acid-free text paper.

Contents

PostHeimat Encounters

Essays and Talks

Annexes

Introduction

Ruba Totah

In the summer of 2015, while on a short visit to Germany, I passed by a central train station and saw shocked-looking groups of people with backpacks deboarding buses. I had a familiar irritation in my chest, and my feet felt heavy. I turned and saw more people in fear while many others approached to lend a hand. I asked around and learned that these were asylum seekers who had just arrived in Germany. The day passed with both ease and unease, ending in a "refugee-welcoming" performance space where a Syrian group sang and played music. The singing was in Arabic. While I could understand the lyrics, those standing near me did not seem to understand, but they danced with the rhythm and cheered.

A year later, May Skaf, a Syrian actress, stood on a podium at the Maxim Gorki Theatre in Berlin to perform *Letter from Tigers to Humanity*. This performance was a collaboration between the Centre for Political Beauty (CPB), May Skaf, and the Gorki. In this provocative political theatre piece, bearing some semblance to Christoph Schlingensief's *Ausländer Raus* container project *Bitte liebt Österreich* in Vienna in 2000, the CPB campaigned to have refugees be devoured by tigers in Berlin if the government were to forbid 100 Syrian asylum seekers from entry into Germany. The collective had planned to fly them illegally from Izmir into Berlin on a specially chartered plane on June 28, 2016. After Air Berlin cancelled the flight on Tuesday morning, the tiger feeding was scheduled for that same evening at the Maxim Gorki Theatre. The producer sought volunteers through the campaign's website, claiming to have found at least one refugee ready to be devoured. The refugee who allegedly prepared to sacrifice herself was Actress May Skaf. However, instead of jumping into the cage, she delivered a speech in the form of a monodrama about her story of seeking refuge in Europe.

I met Skaf two years later during my research. She described to me the process of collaboration with the writer and producer of the performance:

"It was my only chance to say what I wanted, to tell the whole world. I wanted to emphasise the word 'Europe' and its supremacy and politics toward refugees at borders. I did not want to beg. I wanted everything to be real. The tigers' part of the performance was the part I liked least because it was not real, and I wanted everything to be real. [...] When I saw the tiger in the cage, I realised I had the same white hair as it had on its body. They [the artistic team] liked the idea and planned the accessories to look tiger-like. The performance was about me being a refugee actress, talking about my journey. I call it a résumé; it tells my story. The performance delivered a political message and spoke of my refugee experience. I was not acting, and I meant every word I said from my heart. The audience could feel that I was not acting, either. I did not hear any clapping right at the end of the show. The audience took a while to realise it was a show where they would clap." (Skaf 2017)

Since this performance and the day at the station, I have seen theatres chasing migrants' realities. There has been a growing interest in performing arts productions involving refugees, migrants, and asylum seekers. Forms of verbatim and documentary theatre have become a political tool for solidarity (Flynn & Tinius, 2015). I kept Skaf's performance in mind whenever I attended a performance by an artist arriving in Germany. I tried to understand what was unique about these performing artists' cultural experiences in Europe. Who has the right to tell a personal story? Can such stories stand against the robust systems of hegemonic, statist narratives and representations?

As a Palestinian, I had several questions come to my mind. For instance, when would a Palestinian artist get to stand freely in a world-renowned theatre and say whatever she decides to say about (human) rights and Western standards? Or an Iraqi? Or a Native American? Am I discriminating on the basis of similar labels of nationality, too, or are meta- and micro-systems of powers and borders imposing them on me by being exclusive? I also wanted to know how these migrant artists' experiences differed from those of nomad artists or migrants, who were not artists, as Javeh Asefdjah questions in her essay contribution in the group profile section of this book. For years after 2017, policies were created in Europe to enhance artists' cultural participation, such as funding ensembles for migrant artists in Germany, governmental funding for artists in Austria, France and Belgium, and programmes in Sweden that kept the wheel of solidarity art rolling – and a Global Refugee Art market growing. In July 2018, Skaf passed away, but many other artists continued to find ways to perform. By 2019, I noticed that the intensity of artists' engagement was fading, and some of the newly established "refugee" or "migrant" ensembles had already been dissolved. During the global COVID-19 pandemic from 2020 onwards, the news barely mentioned any significant theatre programs related to exile, open borders, or collectives. Theatre buildings of all ideologies became vacant, and artists either stayed aside and waited or shifted their corporeal reality to virtual spaces. The news moved on, and digital theatre became the new thing, to put it cynically (Wihstutz, Vecchiato & Kreuser, 2022). The latest wave of refugees from Ukraine reactivated interest and debates on art by migrants. The rise of cancellations of theatre and artistic events with political backgrounds in Germany, such as at Gorki in 2023 and other European cities, raised further concerns about freedom of speech, democracy, and the question of whose voices are heard and whose are not. The fall of the Syrian regime at the end of 2024 reactivated again the status of Syrian refugees in Germany and brought new challenges and queries related to return migration and artist safety and cultural freedoms. This book provides a testimony of a five-year (2017–2021) collective journey among hundreds of art workers at more than six theatre institutions to call for and try to understand what diversity in theatre can mean. This took place under the umbrella of what we called the PostHeimat Network. It ploughs the "Refugees Welcome" soil to advocate for people's transnational cultural experiences and means of their representation, especially those considered "creative" as artists and workers in theatre.

Reflecting and writing about this journey is not an easy task; it is full of queries that contemplate the difficulty that Edward Said (2013) saw in the process: "to represent someone or even something has now become an endeavour as complex and as problematic as an asymptote, with consequences for certainty and decidability as fraught with difficulties as can be imagined" (2013: 285). The journey of this book is also a contemplation of preceding efforts by German-speaking theatre institutions against populist, white-centric, Eurocentric perceptions that dominate the perspectives around theatre and against patterns of urban economic, spatial, and temporal transformations resulting from capitalist and social systems. This testimony brings hope for a future of theatre that minds its past.

Theatre and Decolonisation

As a testimony, the book connects personal stories about migration, theatre practice, and ethnography to reveal entanglements with processes of decolonisation where conceptions about 'home' are negotiated. Meaning-making of theatre practice resembles stories about 'home' that are narrated, performed, and observed, bringing a plethora of explanations that are examined through anthropology, theatricality, and the performative, ontological and decolonial turns (Gluhovic et al., 2021; Bejarano et al., 2019; Balme, 1999). Focus on decolonising the concept of home through theatre provides arguments on practice and cases where indigenous communities, migrant and marginalised groups, and others are still under the mighty powers of colonialism, socialism, and capitalism (Tuck &Yang, 2021). For example, forms of decolonial anthropology, such as 'action anthropology' and 'practising anthropology', and methods which include participatory and collaborative approaches provide means that the discipline seeks to transcend Eurocentrism towards applied engagement and activism (Chávez & Skelchy, 2019; Bejarano et al., 2019; Alexander et al., 2021).

In theatre, decolonising research and practice evolved in the past decades in forms such as 'public' or 'native' engagements. They converse with and reverse the coloniality in Western paradigms of explanations by understanding confrontations with the intolerable academisation of the suffering of communities that are made an object of study (Sharifi & Skwirblies, 2022). While colonialism is a system of political, economic, and cultural domination in which one nation or people establish sovereignty over another, coloniality is what endures long after the formal systems of colonial rule have disappeared (Stoler, 2016). Discussions on the case of migration and theatre connected to it appeal to both notions, especially that migrants, once under the sovereignty of the host countries' formal political, economic and cultural systems, live under new colonial rules in addition to remnants of coloniality they bring with them from 'home', supposing that their home countries were not among those who still suffer under unended colonial rule. In other words, hosting implies, in Derrida's phrasing, always hostility and exclusion, or "hostipitality"; these are two sides of the same coin, and they are activated in the act of crossing the threshold of a nation, a host, a home, *Heimat* (Derrida, 2000; Agudio, Bueti & Ndikung, 2020).

Tuck and Yung's essay "Decolonization is not a metaphor" (2021) argues that current uses of decolonisation liquidise the violence of colonial and coloniality processes into a resolvable issue in the status quo by promoting reconciliation with it. In cases such as colonisation in Palestine and beyond, Khalidi (2021: 240) discusses three layers of confrontation that have historically marked indigenous people during their struggle for decolonisation: the elimination of the entire subjugation of indigenous people, the defeat and expulsion of the coloniser, and the reconciliation with the colonised. Decolonising practice and research in a migration context are also multi-layered by communities turning from objects into active participants in the meaning-making of cultural practices. They turn the practice into a resistive engagement tool and confrontational activism of both colonialism and coloniality. Here, theatre becomes the playground, which several scholars explained as a movement against discourses and absolutes, such as Turner's (1979) introduction of the concept of making, not faking, and Bhabha's (2012) political view of performance as breaking and remaking. Theatre-making as active participation is a type of self-ethnography that promotes the plurality of narratives and invites possibilities to practice open, flexible, adaptable, situation-sensitive, and nuanced meaning creation, all contained within a diversity perception (Bala, 2017). In this sense, theatre becomes what Conquergood explains, "the commonplace, the nexus between the playful and the political" (1992: 80).

That said, the discussion about diversity in contemporary German theatre scenes deals with decolonisation in ways that shift the confrontation with such systems away from being a mere metaphor. This book is one such serious attempt at exploring discourses, methodologies, and experiences grounded in the German-speaking theatre scene where independent theatre institutions and practitioners are in constant movement of resistance towards means for change in mentalities, procedures, and policies. In one of its sections, our interview with theatre scholar Azadeh Sharifi (2021) on contemporary theatre practices in Germany provides that decolonisation efforts made by German academia and art institutions are deeply rooted in colonial epistemology, where it is not very worthy to operate in the same old terms or insert new meanings to them. Beyond the book, Sruti Bala (2017) calls for decolonising theatre studies and practices by rethinking these as a "site of the collective pursuit of nurturing the free imagination" (335, see also Sharifi & Skwirblies, 2022). Through inviting an anecdotal story form as a reflexive approach to promote a view on how collectives can pursue free imagination, Bala aimed "to make as visible as possible the grounds from which perceived realities are discursively constructed" (2017: 336). This book provides inquiries about theatre and migration by putting into the readers' hands anecdotal stories, narratives, observations, debates, and scholarly examinations that discursively construct a PostHeimat imagined space in theatre practice.

PostHeimat Network

City theatre institutions of the network came together to respond to the conse-quences of migration to Germany after 2015, and each of the profiles provided in the book explains their motivations. A common feature is related to them being Ger-man-speaking ensemble theatres. Over decades, German-speaking cities' cultural landscapes, which include network members' activism, have been actively interact-ing with socio-political changes and creating meanings for migrant and refugee artists (see e.g. Tinius 2023). German theatre institutions perceive themselves as forums that host debates on the city's socio-political and economic developments, such as in the Theater an der Ruhr, Maxim Gorki Theater, Münchner Kammerspiele, and others. Those institutions have been trying to introduce collaborative practices with precarious, "free", and independent theatre scenes, working on thinking mi-grant and post-migrant theatre concepts to guarantee a third space of inclusion for diverse backgrounds (Sharifi, 2017), where theatre could allow decolonial con-frontations with socio-political systems that have been dominating theatre spaces such as nationalism, populism, and Eurocentrism.

The PostHeimant network has some roots in the cultural engagements with the urban change following the migration wave to Germany in 1940 onward and the Wende. Theatre institutions began to weigh migration and diversity topics consider-ably. As debate forums, theatre institutions interacted with changes and realised the demand for similar changes to theatre structures as part of the urban transforma-tion processes. Christopher-Fares Köhler provides in his essay how the term "post-migrant" society was coined from the post-migrant theatre movement and suggests how Germany is in a constant transformation where migration is a driving force, and theatre is a catalyst of change around it.

Change is mainly advocated by artists, practitioners, and people, as well as their means of commenting artistically on their lives amidst hegemonic reiterations of a *Leitkultur*, which we contest in our essay on problematising the term "PostHeimat". The change indicates two-sided transformation arrows in the theatrical scape, which are dependent on each other and are a reaction to each other. On the one hand, change at the level of conceptions of "Heimat" and "Belonging". On the other hand, change at the level of theatre aesthetics. Despite many failed attempts, such transformative contexts continue to emphasise the role of theatre in debating, protesting, and creating narratives about forms of city transformation. As such, there is a need for theatre studies and practice to examine further potentials and define theatre's role in dealing with the problematic site of transformation by tracing to understand landmarks of theatres' contributions to the debate around urban transformations during the past century (Tinius 2019). Emerging from this need, the PostHeimat network is a project that emerged from theatre practice to reflect on its structures and feed back into its landscape. It is for that reason that we speak of the attempt to create and think about "networked solidarity".

The PostHeimat network created a structure that enabled increasing debate through various encounters, organised almost four times a year at shifting locations but always connecting academics with theatre and civil society initiatives. These encounters were open to the public and comprised keynotes and contributions presented at various panels. Participants introduced diverse experiences to the discussion tables and exchanged opinions about theatre productions. The encounters also created working groups: the aesthetics working group, the research working group, and the cultural policies working group to enable in-depth, longer-term, and specialised discussions on various collective concerns of the network. The aesthetics working group focused on the performativity and practicalities of theatre practice, thinking about the important and also problematic developments of particular aesthetics in migrant and refugee theatre, while the research working group provided scholarly reflections and examinations related to work in practice, reviewing methodologies for collaborative, multimodal work between theatre, performance, and cultural policy. The cultural policy working group discussed an intersectional diversity act needed for a more diverse institutionalisation of theatre practice and how such a cultural policy proposal could be enacted, if at all. The working groups' documentations in this book are considered a work in progress, open to new findings resulting from practice, and therefore deliberately unfinished in certain parts. Through these groups, the network becomes an activism movement and a learning journey, in the reflexive nature of the field, of all members against rigid policies. Beyond, it is a constant constructor of solidarity practices which result from the ongoing relational dynamics among its members.

This book attempts to reverse the academisation of the struggle of communities experiencing migration processes in the German-speaking theatre. It advocates the role of anthropological research of activism by holistically examining the case of theatre and migration from a plurality of narratives, witnessing voices on a collective movement that uses theatre practice as a tool for activism against normative discourses around 'home', 'diversity', and 'inclusion'. The network and the book try to realise a double gesture in the activism movement. It is a reflection and an ethical proposal for creating good conduct.

Who Tells a Story?

Theatre groups and groups of artists, scholars, and activists within the PostHeimat network engaged in artistic debates during the multiple encounters, creative processes, and internal administrative and artistic processes to direct their approaches in ways that would actualise the right to tell a personal story and construct narratives. The role of story-telling is essential for standing against power systems that control narratives and representations. The discourses in the theatres' portfolios provided for this book form the basis of the network's labour in this direction. The portfolios build a collective consensus on the importance of narrative exchange to maintain theatre as a debate forum which infuses relational aesthetics with a transformative reality and agenda. For example, the Boat People project's portfolio implies content that primarily deals with "diversity-sensitive topics and representations within the production teams that would potentially counter structural racism in the institution and contribute to the migration debate." The Münchner Kammerspiele's portfolio suggests that their welcoming projects for the newly coming non-German artists to Germany encourage an aesthetically progressive opportunity and endeavour for the theatre scene that contributes to a transnational theatre, where different narratives are shared and negotiated in the German institutional theatre settings. Institutional support for the theatre groups' approaches depended on funding sought, primarily by the Theater an der Ruhr, to bring life to the network's various activities. Nevertheless, these fundings follow cultural policies, which the essay by Özlem Canyürek critically examines. Canyürek provides that independent performing arts initiatives and networks operate under severe financial constraints, subsidised almost solely through project-based funding, which demands support from these policies to help manifest the fairness-based discourse on cultural diversity.

While the network's participating groups followed German cultural participation policy to promote diversified narratives despite bureaucratic regulations, individuals within these institutions, among activists and artists affiliated with them, question these policies. A network member, actress Javeh Asefdjah, asks in one of the encounters panels, "Who is putting something into whose mouth? What is inexpressible to me? What speaks through me?" Actress Kenda Hmeidan asks herself while reflecting on her experience in one PostHeimat network encounter at the Maxim Gorki Theater, 'Who is this person in me talking? I feel it is not myself." Golshan Ahmad Haschemi, in another encounter, provides, "Now, while my wish would be that it is us, who shape, form and determine how and by whom these topics are tackled, the status quo tells a different story." In a self-reflexive approach, the essay by Christopher-Fares Köhler demonstrates a practitioner-based conclusion on styles of narrations in contemporary German theatre: the first is *telling the story* where artists speak about their experiences on stage, sometimes even connecting it to a parable, a mythological story. The second is *refusing to tell the story*, where the story is used as a counter-argument, mainly by negating a specific representation. Canyürek's essay explores a connection between individual artists' and policymakers' visions for developing and advocating a new non-discriminatory pluralistic discourse for the performing arts scene in Germany. The essay proposes criteria for ways of engaging with various axes of difference. One is concerned with narrating diverse experiences that would invite different types of stories not bound by a Western theatre canon.

Both the essays and artists' contemplative moments relate to a view on institutions' role in putting victim narratives on stage, which connects to Spivak's concern in 'Can Subaltern Speak?' (1988). Essentialist underpinnings of information provided through artists' representations on stage force narratives that reproduce relations of inequality and asymmetry, by homogenising migrant artists and leaving unequal power relations unaltered. The essays and artists' contemplations explain how information provided within a story becomes more important than the story artists provide on stage. To support their solidarity agendas, institutions and audiences who need the information may neglect the story itself, how the artists narrate it, and hence their subjective intentions. Information becomes the priority of the institution and the driver of its discourse. For Walter Benjamin, information within a story "does not survive the moment in which it was new" (1968: 366). For Bala (2017), information within the story "must reveal everything as completely and efficiently as possible for it to be disseminated and replicated without error" (336). From here, replicating certain information or discourse in stage narratives cannot alter power relations, and focusing on it ceases to be effective in solidarity plights. A story, on the other hand, is different. Benjamin continues: "It does not expand itself. It preserves and concentrates its strength and can release itself even after a long time" (366, see also Shibli 2024 on narration and the story-teller). Perceiving stories of migrants in such a way helps resume theatres' role in reproducing subjective stories rather than guiding the information in their narratives. The PostHeimat network continuously emphasised questioning who narrates and what a narrative is. It also advocated how theatre practitioners work together to share a narrative with the audience. This book practically investigates the need to examine what these produced narratives represent without cornering the reader with one defined answer.

Observing Observers

This book's guiding voices drive the PostHeimat network's activism towards an engaged ethnographic observation of what is observed in creative processes. In addition to artists' voices, the book comprises a variety of scholarly witnesses on the relational dynamics creating the conversation about diversity in theatre. These witnesses are complementary and decisive in imagining the network's mission. None of these voices is dispensable nor replaceable in creating the momentum of change and revealing system ruptures. Artists' witnessing confronts cultural policies and institutional mechanisms, including structures of racism and exclusion. Theatre institutions' witnesses are self-critical realities of harmonisation and attempts for change and inclusivity. Scholars' witnessing comprises processes of reflections on both.

Deep in this reflexive approach, essays by scholars in the book reflect on how cultural policies remain salient controllers of metanarratives that artists and institutions continuously re-examine and challenge, but often also need to operate with(in). Scholars' witnesses are mediating attempts to interpret and advocate artists' and institutions' practices towards their decolonising activism. Scholarship coinciding with network activism demonstrates that artists, including actors and actresses, dramaturgs, directors, and others, are activists who have engaged in intercultural interstices of the transnational space provided at theatre institutions. It provides that artists' engagement in intercultural spaces enables intersubjective relationships, creating strategies for constructing a third space of "beyondness" (Totah & Khoury, 2018). Whether through improvisations achieved or translation mechanisms, they developed these strategies for creating a third space that is comprised of moments of enduring-in-the-self being practised through various temporal and artistic scopes through improvisations. In these spaces, translating and interpreting intercultural and intersubjective dialogue enabled continuous solidarity construction in the relational dynamics of theatre (ibidem). These confrontational mechanisms to robust discourses are vital to realising what is beyond 'home' and Heimat.

Scholars also provide that home-making is a practical term for what artists endure during creative processes in a post-migrant theatre, opening space for discussions about Heimat. In addition to strategies that create a space of beyondness or "interstitial agency" (Tinius, 2019), artists' relational dynamics in transnational intercultural spaces include survival trajectories and strategies to re-establish a 'home' that can surmount the new national boundary, where they can find settlement and belonging (Totah, 2021a, 2021b). Some of their trajectories include identifying with migration systems, where artists' repeated patterns of compromise, maneuver, and patience cope with estrangement resulting from forms of exile. Their trajectories also include disentanglement from emotional connections to the home country's collective entity and confrontation with cultural affiliations. These trajectories are contradictory, but artists experience them in parallel. Their trajectories explain how they have struggled to identify past nation-states' connections that may forge possibilities of finding a new 'home.'

This book is both a witness document and a proposal for thinking about Heimat after migration, and currently about return migration, and after a hegemonic and normative repurposing of Heimat itself, which we witnessed in the years after 2017. It emerges from an experiment in networked solidarity between major German-speaking theatres and migrant actors and directors, funded by the Kulturstiftung des Bundes. It documents the emergence, frictions, and difficulties in establishing a federal network of public migrant theatre initiatives at public theatre institutions and establishing reflexive, research-based, and cultural-policy-developing components and working groups through such a network. After years of encounters, plays, and working meetings, this book critically examines the *status quo* of these theatres and is open to a frank reflection on why some groups and projects could not function, or ceased to exist. Failure, discontinuity, and fragmentation are part of the landscape of publicly-funded German theatre; this book makes these experiences visible. Nevertheless, it also goes beyond the documentation of this process by inviting practitioners, scholars, activists, and artists to work on what artistic work *after* Heimat could mean. Including interviews, essays, cultural policy drafts, utopian imaginations, and biographical narratives, this book offers a critical view of migration, theatre, and networked solidarity in German society. Reading this book will reveal that more than one language is involved, and more than single or native English expressions and abilities are present in such an experiment. In the content of keynotes, encounters, talks, and essays, the English language is left with light editing to involve the reader in the experience and dynamics of communication between network members. It invites the reader into a witness-like document, as an open file on the experience and an ethnographic text open for multiple interpretations, in the same way that the network lived its experience. The book helps the public understand how this network came about, and what may remain of it. As we leave it open to explanations, we realise contextual reasoning for its emergence and the desire to create a network of producing companies involved in migration and *Flucht* in the German-speaking context. Lastly, introducing the network can be best done by the spoken words of its members, as they comment on what comes to their mind when hearing 'PostHeimat'. Responses, gathered on the brink of the Covid-pandemic at the Maxim Gorki Theater in 2020, came in several languages:

- 'Ruhrgebiet'
- 'Denke ich an einen Ort, wo lebe kann ohne Hass.'
- 'Overcoming nationalists, racists, and othering structures?'
- "قدرة الوطنية على تحقيق ذاتها وبعد ذلك الانطلاق لما هو أبعد من ذلك، بما يشمل حفظ الحريات "في التعبير، والابداع والتنوع"
- 'Ruhrorter'
- 'Verantwortung'
- 'First of all, it goes beyond the term of Heimat, which has a very negative con-notation for me. So we do not need Heimat anymore. However, it also creates a different mindset for everyone to look at the terminology used in the present day.'
- 'Maxim Gorki'
- 'For me, it includes a vision for how we will shape the future.'
- 'Definition von Identität, jenseits von wo ich herkomme.'

Bibliography

Agudio, E. Bueti, F. & Ndikung, B. S. B. Eds. (2020). *Whose Land Have I Lit on Now? Contemplations on the Notions of Hostipitality*. Archive.

Alexander, P. Cannon, A. Stobart, H. & Wilkins, F. (2021) Editorial, *Ethnomusicology Forum*, 30(1), 1–3.

Bala, S. (2017). Decolonising theatre and performance studies: Tales from the classroom. *Tijdschrift voor Genderstudies*, 20(3), 333–345.

Balme, C. B. (1999). *Decolonizing the stage: Theatrical syncretism and post-colonial drama*. Oxford University Press.

Bejarano, C. A., Juárez, L. L., García, M. A. M., & Goldstein, D. M. (2019). *Decolonizing ethnography: Undocumented immigrants and new directions in social science*. Duke University Press.

Bhabha, H. K. (2012). *The location of culture*. Routledge.

Chávez, L., & Skelchy, R. P. (2019). Decolonization for Ethnomusicology and Music Studies in Higher Education. *Action, Criticism & Theory for Music Education*, 18(3).

Conquergood, D. (1992). Ethnography, rhetoric, and performance. *Quarterly journal of Speech*, 78(1), 80–97.

Derrida, J. (2000). Hostipitality. *Angelaki*, 5(3), 3–18.

Flynn, A. & Tinius, J. (2015). "Reflecting on Political Performance: Introducing Critical Perspectives". In Alex Flynn and Jonas Tinius (eds), Anthropology, Theatre, and Development: The Transformative Potential of Performance. Palgrave Macmillan, pp. 1–28.

Khalidi, R. I. (2017). Historical Landmarks in the Hundred Years' War on Palestine. *Journal of Palestine Studies*, 47(1), 6–17.

Rai, S. M., Gluhovic, M., Jestrovic, S., & Saward, M. (Eds.). (2021). *The Oxford Handbook of Politics and Performance*. Oxford Handbooks.

Said, E. W. (2013). *Reflections on exile: and other literary and cultural essays*. Granta Books.

Sharifi, A. (2017). Theatre and Migration. *Independent Theater in Contemporary Europe*, 321–416.

Sharifi, A. & Skwirblies, L. Eds. (2022). *Theaterwissenschaft postkolonial/dekolonial*. transcript.

Shibli, A. (2024). "Universalism & narration", in: Minor Universality Research Team. Ed. *Universalism(e) &... Conversations*. De Gruyter, pp. 159–180.

Spivak, G. C. (1988). "Can the Subaltern Speak?", in: Cary Nelson. Ed. *Marxism and the Interpretation of Culture*. University of Illinois Press, pp. 271–314.

Stoler, A. L. (2016). *Duress: Imperial durabilities in our times*. Duke University Press.

Tinius, J. (2019). 'Interstitial Agents: Negotiating Migration and Diversity in Theatre', in: Bock, Jan-Jonathan and Sharon Macdonald. Eds. *Refugees Welcome? Differences and Diversity in a Changing Germany*. Berghahn, pp. 241–264.

Tinius, J. (2023). *State of the Arts. An Ethnography of German Theatre and Migration*. Cambridge University Press.

Totah, R. (2021). Transnational Subjectivities of Arab Artists in Europe. *Critical Stages/Scènes Critiques. June*, 23. 1–16.

Totah, R. (2020). Negotiating "home:" Syrian and Palestinian Syrian artists in Borderlands. *Civil Society Review*.

Totah, R. (2020). Negotiating 'Home' Borders: Creative Processes Hosting Syrian and Palestinian Syrian Artists in Europe. *European Journal of Theatre and Performance*, (2), 424- 461.

Totah, R., & Khoury, K. (2018). Theater against Borders: 'Miunikh–Damaskus'—A Case Study in Solidarity. *Arts*, 7(4), 1–14.

Tuck, E., & Yang, K. W. (2021). Decolonization is not a metaphor. *Tabula Rasa*, (38), 61–111.

Turner, V. (1979). Dramatic ritual/ritual drama: Performative and reflexive anthropology. *The Kenyon Review*, 1(3), 80–93.

Wihstutz, B., Vecchiato, D. & Kreuser, M. Eds. (2022). *#CoronaTheater. Der Wandel der performativen Künste in der Pandemie*. Theater der Zeit.

I. Th eatre

boat people project

Gorki Exile Ensemble

Gro

Hajusom - Center for Transnational Arts

ups

Collective Ma'louba

por
tr

Open Border Ensemble

aits

Ruhrorter

The RUHRORTER group

How and why were you founded, and what is the group's status now that it is connected to the PostHeimat network?
We already had initial talks about this in 2016 together with the Münchner Kammerspiele (Anne Schulz & Krystel Khoury). In 2017, we succeeded in organising the first joint meetings and workshops. This is also where the idea emerged to organise ourselves better and set up our desire for networking and opening up structurally. The goal was to share experiences, exchange knowledge, and discuss aesthetic issues and their political implications. This is how PostHeimat came into being.
Ruhrorter was founded more than a decade ago from a desire to return political work in theatre back onto the stage, to step back from the enormous expectation built up around theatre as a form of therapy, and to focus on rehearsals, on building a collectivity, on working with sites, spaces, and archives embodied by people and institutions in the Ruhr region – hence also our name, borrowed from the Ruhrorterstrasse between Duisburg, Oberhausen, and Mülheim, and also the site of the rehearsal spaces of the Theater an der Ruhr.

How do you describe the aims of your group – Some groups started years ago; have there been changes in their aim?
The group RUHRORTER now looks back on eleven years of artistic work on the complex themes of migration, flight, administration and law. Initially conceived as a theatre project, RUHRORTER gradually combined more and more elements of theatre, film, radio play and artistic installations to create space for the post-migrant realities in Mülheim an der Ruhr and the Ruhr region. It was and still is important to us not to limit the artistic activity to biographical-documentary approaches alone but to use the potential of fiction and improvisation.
In 2022, we celebrated our 10th anniversary with 1) an audio walk through the city centre of Mülheim an der Ruhr. We followed the voices and traces where our projects once took place or met people important to us. 2) an art installation, and 3) the opening of our archive. Unfortunately, we are still trying to obtain institutional funding and still have no planning security. Currently, we are focusing on our children's theatre group as well as on supporting the projects of former participants, such as

Yazan Abo Hassoun, who is now realizing his second project entitled "We are here" in Bochum and Mülheim an der Ruhr.

How do you describe your strategies, priorities and work aesthetics?
RUHRORTER has realised theatre and installation works with refugees since 2012, which at times and especially at the beginning have been accompanied by anthropological research and includes a children's theatre program. Consequently, the working approaches differ depending on the project. As already formulated above, however, all works have a politically formal claim in common. We do not want to reduce art with refugees to authenticity and documented biographies but rather expand it to include the artistic dimension and the political role of fiction.
Generally, our works occur in spaces unrelated to theatre or art performances. In recent years, we have performed in various abandoned and occupied places. Be it the former women's prison, an empty factory building, or the municipal library/media centre of the city of Mülheim an der Ruhr. The respective histories and relationships that made up these and other places become part of our work whenever possible. In this way, the theatre productions and art installations address the interwoven nature of urban and migration history in the Ruhr region and add contemporary images, languages and ideas to the sometimes historically significant places.
Another unifying element is the duration of the project. To meet the various demanding tasks that we set for ourselves as a group, we plan with work and rehearsal processes lasting several months. We consider such patient and open-ended processes as a requirement for creative exchange between the respective participants, which can then lead to interesting performances and presentations. We work continuously in cooperation with the Theater an der Ruhr, which supports us ideally and infrastructurally as far as possible.

What are the biggest challenges to your group?
As mentioned above, further work approaches arise from direct contact with refugees and their interest in working together or exploring new artistic ways. We are at a point where further interested people from our environment should be supported by us in realising theatre and art projects. Also, some former participants have already taken on tasks in the context of RUHRORTER, such as creating costume designs or directing a children's theatre group.
The RUHRORTER team would happily provide further advice and support, such as taking over the technical infrastructure and a large part of the administrative tasks. In any case, it was and is a great concern for us to offer practical help in the field in which we have professionalised ourselves and could only do so thanks to the help of third parties. One goal here would be to hand over the entire project to former group members, either in its entirety or for the most part. However, these approaches have been in the making for years or have not yet received the attention

they need to have an intensive impact on the overall project. For this purpose, we have tried several times and for years to obtain long-term structural funding in sufficient amounts. So far, we have been unsuccessful.

Which performances did you organise as part of PostHeimat?
"The hum of the laws" – a radio installation by RUHRORTER, March 21st, 2019
How does the Constitution (Grundgesetz) sound? Maybe poetic, auspicious, menacing? The audio installation "DAS SUMMEN DER GESETZE" ("The Buzz of Laws") is devoted to the fundamental rights that secure the foundation of our coexistence. The Grundgesetz raises questions about dignity, freedom and personal development. It confidently states what seems natural these days: All human beings are equal before the law. The voices of newly arrived people and long-time residents, of international legal experts and translators, have their say. They talk about the beauty of the Constitution and its blind spots, about legal and injustice experiences. While the Grundgesetz was written for eternity, it tells of the continuous transformation of society. Together with the audience, RUHRORTER is conducting a major conversation at four locations in the Ruhr area, in which the effectiveness and limits of fundamental rights are discussed from different perspectives. Original sound recordings, audio and visual documents, as well as atmospheres of everyday togetherness, sounds of fear and dreaming, are condensing and swelling to a buzz of laws.

INSTALLATION Maximilian Brands & Wanja van Suntum | SOUND DESIGN Jan Godde | PRODUCTION MANAGEMENT Adem Köstereli | PHOTOGRAPHY Franziska Götzen | PR Ann-Kathrin Allekotte

OPEN BORDER ENSEMBLE

Krystel Khoury

How and why were you founded, and what is the group status now that it is connected to the Post Heimat network?
Back in 2015, the new direction of the Münchner Kammerspiele with Matthias Lilienthal wished to continue addressing diversity within the German institutional theatre on an aesthetical and a structural level. It set up a program collaborating with many non-Western directors, such as associés and German ones, to produce performances for the theatre repertoire. In line with this interest, the *Kammer4you* team with Anne Schultz was set to work on audience development and accessibility, organising topical campuses for students, focused workshops for kids, teenagers, women, and people of colour and presentations after talks and symposiums. Opening up to a broader, younger, socially and culturally more diverse audience than before, the theatre's artistic direction aimed to increase audience curiosity with artistic productions that reflected Munich's shifting demography and its culturally diverse social fabric more significantly.
In fact, in September 2015, Germany's borders were opened to welcome refugees. The city theatre felt concerned by these newcomers' massive arrival, living conditions, and new life in Munich – especially since their first stop was this city. In October 2015, it organised *The Open Border Congress* within the frame of a more comprehensive project, "Munich Welcome Theater". This congress gathered artists, scholars, activists, and "people who have come to Germany as refugees themselves or are simply interested in coping with the social challenges of worldwide migration movements". It called for a "society of the world that defends openness and diversity", a clear statement of solidarity. The theatre later continued its active involvement with the issue of migration and exile when Anne Schulz established the *Welcome Café* in April 2016. This format, away from an aesthetic positioning, leaned for more urgent social intervention. It made one of the theatre stages accessible as a cultural place for local inhabitants and newcomers to meet, share, and access practical information and participate in cultural events.
The ongoing collective commitment expressed a common need to build up alternative narratives. In December 2016, this culminated in the production of the Open Border Ensemble Festival with Arabic-speaking artists and theatre amateurs, fea-

turing lectures, stage plays, films, and concerts providing momentum to the Café initiative. After the first rush and solidarity urgency, the theatre decided out of this experience to give another configuration to The Open Border Ensemble project and develop it further. 2017 was thus a preparatory year, leading to its implementation as such. I was invited to participate in those conversations, facilitate the creation of the new group, coordinate the project and shape it artistically.

The asylum seekers' migration flow incited the theatres in Germany to work more towards inclusiveness and diversity and adopt transcultural approaches as a form of solidarity. Thinking globally, we questioned solidarity beyond the national scope yet still connected to it. Our interrogation revolved around how theatre can be in solidarity with other theater scenes, such as the Syrian one, for example, how to expand the connections beyond borders while answering the urges of the German context and which collaborative modality to trigger. Our perspective was embedded in postmigration discourses channeling the idea that the migration phenomena are a norm even though the heterogeneity they bring into society is still not reflected enough on German institutional theater stages.

After auditions in Munich and Beirut, the theatre was able to invite the Syrian performers Majd Feddah, Kinan Hmeidan and Kamel Najma — all of whom had completed their theatre studies at the High Institute of Dramatic Arts in Damascus, Syria—to be the permanent new members/actors of The *Open Border Ensemble*. This being said, the idea of the ensemble as a closed capsule of – in this case – male actors was challenged in each production by engaging a wide range of individuals: actresses, directors, translators, dramaturges, producers who were reshaping it into an expanding and mutant platform: May Al Hares, Lola Arias, Maja Beckman, Jessica Glause, Rabelle Ramez Erian, Ruba Totah, Ramy Al Borolosy, Dana Mikhail, Julia Zehl, Charlotte Hesse, to name a few. Looking back at this experience, I can say today that The Open Border Ensemble, throughout its existence, kept on redefining itself and its borders.

It was clear from the start that such a project longing to resist isolation would thrive to carve a space for discussing and questioning those issues with other groups and/or initiatives that had been created or were being implemented at that time in other cities in Germany. This was when Anna and I contacted like-minded colleagues and *Ruhrorter* to engage in further conversations and to co-organise a first encounter under the title of post-Heimat in 2018 as a working meeting in Munich, out of which the idea of an official network came to life. The group also hosted the third network encounter in 2019. In that sense, although *The Open Border Ensemble* adventure ended in 2020 with the newly appointed director and artistic team at the Münchner Kammerspiele, the group was connected to the post-Heimat network as an active founding member.

How do you describe the aims of your group – Some groups started years ago; have there been changes in their aim?
The Open Border Ensemble aimed to forge a new experiential, collaborative path by resisting borders and artistic isolation. The basic initial idea of the project was to encourage the theatre to regard the presence and participation of the newly coming non-German artists as an aesthetically progressive opportunity and endeavour for the theatre scene. It sought to contribute to transnational theatre, allowing different narratives from cultural and socio-political contexts to emerge, be shared, and be negotiated in German institutional theatre settings. While in the first season of 2017/2018, the Open Border Ensemble would be at the core of two theatre productions, the mid-term aim was to involve further and include its members in the operative structure of the theatre, experiment with the challenges that such an endeavour would mean, and on the long-term to establish the Open Border Ensemble artists as an integral part of the regular acting ensemble of the Münchner Kammerspiele or maybe vice-versa.

How do you describe your strategies, priorities and work aesthetics?
To set up such an initiative, it seemed clear at first that the theatre team needed to gather the best conditions possible for creating a welcoming and safe space, including calling for specific human resources dedicated to this project: an artistic director, a production manager, translators, etc. It also needed to face its own preconceptions regarding the OBE. Working constantly towards communication away from tokening the Syrian artists – in that specific context – has been a focal point, but also providing human relational support, inventing professional opportunities and triggering networking spaces. Regarding work aesthetics, the idea was to offer the artists different ways of working by participating in several projects. If their first season was based on documentary theatre aesthetics due to the overall political context, it quickly became clear that such an approach needed to evolve, include other genres and temporalities, face language problems, etc. Indeed, the project was meant to last only 8 months and eventually lasted 3 seasons, with constant learning and adaptations!

What are the biggest challenges to your group?
When the project was launched, the group faced many challenges, from communication to a feeling of instability, desperation, and blurriness regarding the overall Open Border Ensemble aims, their individual positions and agency in a group that they were forming but did not take part in its (hi)-story. Language issues were undoubtedly the most evident challenge at the beginning before turning them into possibilities. First on the level of professional and daily interactions, but later on an artistic level. Indeed, the focus that language gets in the German theatre tradition is central. Thus, not being able to communicate using it turned out to be frustrat-

ing with time – despite the presence of translation. How do you feel comfortable and welcomed when you do not speak the same language as the host? When do you start feeling more than a visiting guest? How do you connect organically with an already established group of artists? How do you make yourself heard as a theatre actor or actress, and by which audience in such a context? Moreover, even if you are familiar with the hosting language, the specificities of the working culture, its logic, and the production system can be hard to grasp. How does mutuality shape it in an institutional frame with well-anchored "ways of doing"? Obviously, there are more questions than answers.

Which performances did you organise as part of PostHeimat?
The PostHeimat network dynamics allowed the sharing of the theatrical works produced by the Münchner Kammerspiele in which the Open Border Ensemble played. In May 2018, when the first working meeting of the Post-Heimat Network meeting was held in Munich, the first project of the Open Border Ensemble, "Miunikh-Damaskus: Stories of a City" directed by Jessica Glause, with Syrian refugee and Syrian and German non-refugee cast, was part of the program and performed to the participants with an after-talk. The performance's aim, set on a mobile stage, was an attempt to minimise stereotypes, deconstruct essentialist cultural identity prejudices and invite the audience to shift their common perspective. The PostHeimat network allowed the reinforcement of ties between some group members and others. Later in the year, Kamel Najma joined the Collective Maalouba to participate in *"Days in the Sun"*, directed by Mudar Alhaggi in Mülheim. It was also an opportunity for artists to show their work to the "community". In 2019, for encounter # 3, a video projection of the performance "For The Last Time" by Kinan Hmeidan was meant to be presented. This performance installation dealt with the idea of the ongoing psychological process of destruction and construction one goes through when changing the environment and going from one place to another. For the program, Kinan Hmeidan wrote:

> "Why all this effort in striving for change and wanting to colour the images stored in our memory? Why all this strain in figuring out answers, in trying to fit and reshape spaces and memories that might vanish in one instant? I build up and destroy. I am building up to destroy. One more time. Why do all this weariness and quest for new surroundings appear to be one when, in the end, all appears to be one? Yes, One. Syria, Germany, Ghana, Afghanistan, Switzerland... (...) "I will not be where I was and where I will always be. I will hide in huge spaces, in a hole, and I will lie to myself, and I will mock myself. I am on a visit."

Collective Ma'louba (founded 2017)

How and why were you founded, and what is the group's status now that it is connected to the PostHeimat network?

The project was initiated by Rolf C. Hemke and Sven Schlötcke of Theater an der Ruhr in Mülheim an der Ruhr in late 2016. The goal was to give artists in exile a new place to live and work. Initially, the group's core consisted of the director Omar Abusaada, the author Mohammad Al Attar, the stage and costume designer Bissane Al Charif and the producer and dramaturge Immanuel Bartz. The trio of Abusaada, Al Attar and Al Charif left the project before its first production to realise an IPHIGENIE production at Volksbühne Berlin with its then-new artistic director, Chris Dercon. Working on the theatre production YOUR LOVE IS FIRE for Ruhrfestspiele Recklinghausen at the beginning of 2017, the actress Amal Omran, the author Mudar Alhaggi and the director Rafat Alzakout joined the project and gave it its name COLLECTIVE MA'LOUBA (Ma'louba translates to upside down). Today, the core collective includes Amal Omran, Mudar Alhaggi, Immanuel Bartz and Omar Mohamad, who is in charge of public relations and developing an audience network. The group has been in residence at Theater an der Ruhr for the past five years. The artistic directors of Theater an der Ruhr decided not to prolong the residence beyond the year 2021. In 2022, COLLECTIVE MA'LOUBA became an independent artistic group without the support of a theatre institution in Germany.

The first meeting of groups which would shape the PostHeimat network in May 2018 came about because of the initiative of the independent artistic group RUHRORTER and the Munich Kammerspiele. COLLECTIVE MA'LOUBA and four other groups were invited to the first meeting in Munich, the first Encounter (#1). And it became evident that if the network wanted to continue, it would need a long-term financial base. With its application for renewed three-year funding, COLLECTIVE MA'LOUBA included the PostHeimat network in its application form and its artistic productions in 2019, 2020, and 2021. The application was granted by the Kulturstiftung des Bundes and the Ministerium für Kultur und Wissenschaft des Landes Nordrhein-Westfalen and for the groups, individual members and associates of the network two Encounters (Encounter #2 -Encounter #7) per year for three years could be realised.

How do you describe the aims of your group – Some groups started years ago, have there been changes in their aim?
In its theatre productions, COLLECTIVE MA'LOUBA questions the political and social condition of the Arab world against the background of recent rebellions and penetrates the taboos of Arab and European society. Further artistic projects of thematic relevance, such as installations, exhibitions, concerts and workshops, accompany the theatre productions. They are shown in North Rhine-Westphalia, Germany, and abroad, thus creating transnational meeting places.

How do you describe your strategies, priorities and work aesthetics?
An external priority of the project over the past five years has been to be very successful artistically in a very short time to justify the extensive funding over five years. An essential internal priority of the project over the past five years has been to build mutual trust, form a group and its ways of working, and find its own artistic core.

What are the biggest challenges to your group?
Sustainability: In 2016, the Federal Cultural Foundation funded three flagship projects at three German theatre institutions, which was certainly also a cultural policy reaction to the ongoing wave of refugees. The Exil Ensemble is at the Maxim Gorki Theatre, the Open Border Ensemble is at the Kammerspiele in Munich, and the Collective Ma'louba is at the Theater an der Ruhr.
From the point of view of the sustainability of the projects, the Maxim Gorki Theater has created the best perspective for its group and taken over parts of the group into its ensemble. The Open Border Ensemble ceased to exist at the end of Matthias Lilienthal's directorship. The Collective Ma'louba will lose its artistic home at the Theater an der Ruhr at the end of 2021 and face an unknown future. In the project-related funding logic of cultural institutions, the focus changes every few years. Today, it's artists in exile; tomorrow, digital projects that come about because of a pandemic; the day after tomorrow, projects dealing with climate change. This makes it impossible to work from a perspective and in a long-term manner.
Time: Projects connected with the themes of flight and migration require a lot of time and space because they occur in unknown and unfamiliar contexts, languages and environments. In addition to artistic decisions, artists living in exile must make extensive and sometimes serious personal decisions. The question of exile, when and if it will end and how and where one's life will take place is a very central.

Mudar Alhaggi: "I don't think we create a new audience. Since I've been working in Germany, I've been constantly trying to understand better the audience as well as the theatre in general. It's not an easy task, but I like the challenge. In the end, we may realize that the whole thing is not about a new audience but a new kind of theatre. "

Amal Omran: "We must not underestimate how deep the shock waves triggered by European culture are for some of the people who had to flee. Through the theatre, they can access this culture; at the same time, it represents an opening of society to the migrant part of the population. Theatre is always a secular public sphere that does not wall itself off but, on the contrary, attempts to make society transparent. The fact that taboos are breached in the context of the theatre or that things are talked about that are censored in the Arabic world is a major challenge. "

Immanuel Bartz: "The theatre creates friction, which in turn triggers transformation. The aesthetic mirror held up to patriarchal power structures and the associated ways of expression engender immense dynamism and a great need for discussion within a heterogeneous audience. Equality between men and women is a huge topic because the hierarchical relationships between the sexes have not been overcome in the West either. The #MeToo discussions and even a glance at theatre structures, which men in many areas still dominate, provide ample evidence for it. Theatre and life – and indeed living together – constitute an indissoluble unity in this respect."

Omar Mohamad: "For the people who attend our events, it makes a huge difference whether Arabic-speaking projects exist or not. When you are in exile, culture – and the theatre – assume a profoundly relevant social function. Public attention has increasingly shifted away from the theatre due to the new media and social networks – and because it has become more apolitical. But in these contexts, it again takes on an essential and indispensable role, meaning no other medium can replace that. And that means a lifelong meaning and role. We now have audiences who engage with the art form of theatre because it is an art that generates a public sphere that is inextricably associated with conversation and communication: audiences for whom theatre have become a vital factor in their individual lives."

Which performances did you organise as part of PostHeimat?
Since the beginning of the network, we created two projects within the context of PostHeimat:

REINE FORMSACHE (2019),
In the play, REINE FORMSACHE, two Syrian theatre actors have lived in Europe for a few years. They share a room and a story as time goes by. What do we do now, and what are we going to represent? Can we continue acting? They take advantage of their presence on stage and include the audience in their space – the play unfolds and starts with the question WHAT IF. It premiered in November 2019 and was presented at Maxim Gorki Theatre as part of Encounter #4 in March 2020.

OVERDOSE. The Unfinished Show of Pain and Joy (2021),
A vast stage inhabited by a group of people: A writer, a composer, a painter and a narrator. They all serve the oracle in the centre of the room. Three travellers arrive on the scene. All are occupied with their concerns. All are coming from their very personal experience of isolation. Will the oracle be able to help them? Will it provide answers to their questions? And will it show them who they really are? Seven performers, three languages, and some pains and joys – boat people project, Collective Ma'louba and kainkollektiv created a theatre journey of voiceless singers, torn actors and non-performers. The project was developed over 12 months in collaboration between the three collectives of which two are part of PostHeimat and a diverse group of theater makers from Syria and Germany.

COLLECTIVE MA'LOUBA (gegründet 2017)

Wie und warum habt Ihr Euch gegründet und wie steht es heute um die Anbindung der Gruppe an das PostHeimat-Netzwerk?
Das Projekt wurde Ende 2016 von Rolf C. Hemke und Sven Schlötcke vom Theater an der Ruhr in Mülheim initiiert. Ziel war es, Künstler*innen im Exil einen neuen Ort zum Leben und Arbeiten zu geben. Der Kern der Gruppe bestand zunächst aus dem Regisseur Omar Abusaada, dem Autor Mohammad Al Attar, der Bühnen- und Kostümbildnerin Bissane Al Charif und dem Produzenten und Dramaturgen Immanuel Bartz. Das Trio Abusaada, Al Attar und Al Charif verließ das Projekt noch vor der ersten Produktion, um eine IPHIGENIE-Produktion an der Volksbühne Berlin unter dem damals neuen Intendanten Chris Dercon zu realisieren. Während der Arbeit an der Theaterproduktion YOUR LOVE IS FIRE für die Ruhrfestspiele Recklinghausen stießen Anfang 2017 die Schauspielerin Amal Omran, der Autor Mudar Alhaggi und der Regisseur Rafat Alzakout zu dem Projekt und gaben ihm den Namen COLLECTIVE MA'LOUBA (Ma'louba bedeutet übersetzt „auf dem Kopf stehend"). Zum Kernkollektiv gehören heute Amal Omran, Mudar Alhaggi, Immanuel Bartz und Omar Mohamad, der sich um die Öffentlichkeitsarbeit und den Aufbau eines Publikumsnetzwerks kümmert. Seit fünf Jahren ist die Gruppe am Theater an der Ruhr zu Gast. Die künstlerische Leitung des Theaters an der Ruhr hat beschlossen, die Residenz nicht über das Jahr 2021 hinaus zu verlängern. Mit dem Jahr 2022 wird COLLECTIVE MA'LOUBA eine unabhängige Künstler*innengruppe ohne die Unterstützung einer Theaterinstitution in Deutschland werden.

Das erste Treffen von Gruppen, die das PostHeimat-Netzwerk formen sollten, kam im Mai 2018 auf Initiative der freien Künstler*innengruppe RUHRORTER und der Münchner Kammerspiele zustande. COLLECTIVE MA'LOUBA wurde zusammen mit vier anderen Gruppen zum ersten Treffen in München eingeladen, das der erste Encounter (#1) war. Und es wurde klar, dass das Netzwerk, wenn es weitermachen will, eine langfristige finanzielle Basis braucht. Mit dem Antrag auf eine erneute dreijährige Förderung hat COLLECTIVE MA'LOUBA das Netzwerk PostHeimat neben seinen künstlerischen Produktionen in den Jahren 2019, 2020 und 2021 in den Antrag aufgenommen. Der Antrag wurde von der Kulturstiftung des Bundes und dem Ministerium für Kultur und Wissenschaft des Landes Nordrhein-Westfalen bewilligt und für die Gruppen, Einzelmitglieder und Partner*innen des Netzwerks konnten zwei Encounter (Encounter #2 -Encounter #7) pro Jahr für drei Jahre realisiert werden.

Wie beschreibt Ihr die Ziele Eurer Gruppe – Einige Gruppen haben vor Jahren begonnen, hat sich Euer Ziel verändert?
In seinen Theaterproduktionen hinterfragt COLLECTIVE MA'LOUBA vor dem Hintergrund der jüngsten gesellschaftlichen Veränderungen die politische und soziale Verfasstheit der arabischen und europäischen Welt. Weitere künstlerische Projekte von thematischer Relevanz, wie Installationen, Konzerte, Lesungen und Workshops, begleiten die Produktionen. Diese werden in Nordrhein-Westfalen, Deutschland und dem Ausland gezeigt und stiften transnationale Begegnungsräume.

Wie beschreibt Ihr Eure Strategien, Prioritäten und Arbeitsästhetik?
Eine externe Priorität des Projekts in den letzten fünf Jahren bestand darin, in sehr kurzer Zeit künstlerisch sehr erfolgreich zu sein, um die umfangreiche Finanzierung über fünf Jahre zu rechtfertigen. Eine interne wesentliche Priorität des Projekts in den letzten fünf Jahren war es, gegenseitiges Vertrauen aufzubauen, eine Gruppe und ihre Arbeitsweise zu formen und den eigenen künstlerischen Kern der Gruppe zu finden.

Eine Beschreibung von HAJUSOM – Zentrum für transnationale Künste, des Ensembles „Hajusom" und der Geschichte mit PostHeimat

Legende Typographien in der Reihenfolge der Beiträge:
Julia zur Lippe / Koordination Zentrum, Geschäftsführung
Ella Huck / Künstlerische Co-Leitung Ensemble
Dorothea Reinicke / Ex-Künstlerische Co-Leitung; ouside eye
Katalina Götz / Performerin, Koordinatorin Ensemble
Josep Caballero García / Künstlerische Co-Leitung Ensemble

How and why were you founded, and what is the group's status now that it is connected to the Post Heimat network?

Hajusom e.V. ist ein Zentrum für transnationale Künste in Hamburg. Entstanden ist es 1999 aus einem Theater-Ferienworkshop für minderjährige unbegleitete Geflüchtete in einer Erstversorgungseinrichtung, für den die beiden Performance-Künstlerinnen Ella Huck und Dorothea Reinicke angefragt wurden. Gemeinsam mit den Jugendlichen entschieden sie, dass die Arbeit nach der ersten erfolgreichen Premiere weitergehen sollte: sie entwickeln (bis heute) große Performance-Formate auf Kampnagel, gehen als junges Ensemble auf Tournee und laden internationale Künstler*innen für nachhaltige Kollaborationen ein. 2009 wurde aus dem Projekt Hajusom ein eigenständiger Verein, unter dessen Dach neben dem Ensemble vier weitere Gruppen für junge Menschen mit Flucht- und Migrationserfahrung künstlerisch arbeiten. Seit diesem Zeitpunkt ist Hajusom e.V. zu einem Zentrum herangewachsen: es gibt nun auch ein professionelles mentoring-Team und den Bereich Transfer, der die Erfahrungen Hajusoms in Workshops und Lectures weitergibt und externe Expert*innen ins Haus einlädt. Bis zu 80 Menschen wöchentlich sind im Zentrum künstlerisch aktiv.

Als Dorothea Reinicke und ich zum ersten Mal 1999 vor 19 jungen Menschen standen, um einen dreimonatigen Performance-Workshop mit unbegleiteten

Jugendlichen mit Fluchterfahrung durchzuführen, habe ich mehr gefühlt als gedacht, dass dies womöglich ein Urknall für ein größeres Unterfangen sein könnte – für das Transnationale Zentrum HAJUSOM. Als junge Performance-Künstlerin setzte ich die Performance-tools ein, die ich in der internationalen Theaterschule von Jacques Lecoq in Paris kurz zuvor erlernt hatte, mit dem Ziel professionelle Performances zu kreieren, in denen sich die Autor*innenschaft der einzelnen Performer*innen im Tanz wie im szenischen Spiel, in der Musik wie im Text abbildet.

Performance-Konzepte der „Gießener Schule" (Kolleg*innen von She ShePop und Showcase beat le mot waren über Jahre im künstlerischen Leitungsteam), trugen mit zur Schärfung des ästhetischen und politischen Profils bei. Heute beschreiben wir das Konzept unserer Arbeiten als fluide, offen, es hatte und hat zum Ziel, dass alle über die Jahre wechselnden Beteiligten sich in den Produktionen «zu Hause» fühlen können und insbesondere die jungen Performer*innen eine neue Verortung – eine «Post-Heimat» bei Hajusom und in der Kunst finden.

Anfang 2018 bekam unsere damalige Gastspielmanagerin Lea Connert eine Mail von Wanja van Suntum von den RUHRORTERN mit einer Einladung zum ersten Encounter an den Münchner Kammerspielen. *„Diese Veranstaltung hat künstlerischen Austausch und eine kulturpolitische Vernetzung zum Ziel"* so heißt es in der Mail.

Daraus entstand wieder einmal bei Hajusom die Frage, wer aus dem Team Hajusom „repräsentiert" und in diesem Fall nach München fährt. Aufgrund der Fragestellung, die verhandelt werden sollte, hätte die künstlerische Leitung fahren müssen: Ella Huck und Dorothea Reinicke, zwei *weiße* Frauen, Künstlerinnen, Initiatorinnen von Hajusom, deren jahrzehntelange Erfahrungen genau diesen gewünschten künstlerischen und kulturpolitischen Austausch hätten bereichern können. Einmal mehr wurde das Dilemma der Hajusom-Struktur sichtbar: Ein ausschließlich *weißes* Leitungsteam baut und steuert ein Theaterzentrum für Menschen mit Flucht- und Migrationserfahrung. Ein Transformationsprozess musste dringend angeschoben werden, was aber zu dem Zeitpunkt noch nicht gegeben war. So wurden Lea Connert und das langjährige Ensemblemitglied Farzad Fadai gebeten, nach München zu fahren, um auch die Perspektive des Ensembles und eines Menschen mit Migrationserfahrung in dieses Meeting einzubringen.

Wer spricht für wen? Eine Frage, die Hajusom mittlerweile in einen gigantischen Transformationsprozess gestürzt hat. Wir haben viel gelernt über tokenism, Rassismus und fehlende Transparenz. Über Mitbestimmung, Verantwortung und Hierarchie. Der Wunsch, mit einem diversen Team ein Zentrum wie Hajusom zu lenken, ist nach wie vor groß, aber wir haben verstanden, dass es ein sensibler

Prozess ist, dorthin zu gelangen und dass Diversität nicht nur behauptet werden darf.

Der Prozess der tiefgehenden strukturellen Transformation, den Hajusom als Zentrum für transnationale Künste dann begann und seit mehr als einem Jahr durchläuft und der als kontinuierlicher Prozess alle Arbeitsbereiche auch in Zukunft begleiten wird, ist eine große Herausforderung für alle Beteiligten – auch auf persönlicher Ebene. Die lang produktiv eingespielten, jedoch häufig intransparenten Abläufe in unserem *weißen* Leitungsteam haben ausgedient, mit ausgelöst durch meinen Abschied von der fast 25 Jahre eingenommen Position einer Künstlerischen (Co-)Leitung. Es gibt Raum für eine neue Generation motivierter, kompetenter Menschen, die das „decolonize!" mit vorantreibt.

Wer spricht für wen? Diese Frage haben wir uns auch im letzten online Encounter #5,5 gestellt. Denn auch das Netzwerk ist weit entfernt davon, divers zu sein. Von den sechs Gründungsensembles sind drei nicht mehr existent. Es ist mehr ein Netzwerk von Einzelpersonen geworden, die noch immer über die Themen der erwähnten allerersten Mail von Wanja diskutieren:

a) strukturelle Positionierung (wie arbeiten Gruppen und Projekte in verschiedenen Häusern und welche institutionellen Kontexte und Strukturen haben sich dabei entwickelt? Wie integrieren wir auf struktureller Ebene Geflüchtete, bzw. wie öffnen wir Theaterinstitutionen für nachhaltige Veränderungen im Bereich Diversität und Migration?), b) ästhetisch/künstlerische Entwicklungen (welche Herangehensweisen, Methoden und künstlerische Dimensionen entwickeln sich in diesem Feld? Welche Probleme, Potenziale, Synergien entstehen hier?)

c) kulturpolitischer Austausch und Netzwerk (wie können wir die Themen Flucht, Migration, Diversität langfristig und nachhaltig auf die kulturpolitische Agenda stellen und verankern?)

Corona hat auch hier mit eisernem Besen gefegt – diejenigen, die künstlerisch arbeiten, haben kaum noch Kapazitäten, an den Encountern teilzunehmen, den Diskurs mit voranzutreiben. Die Researcher*innen übernehmen mehr und mehr. Das Netzwerk scheint weg von den Fragen der Praxis, des künstlerischen Alltags hin zum theoretischen Diskurs zu rutschen. Auch hier ein Prozess, der vielleicht eine der größten Schwierigkeiten kulturpolitischen Handelns aufzeigt – die Gefahr, die Praxis aus den Augen zu verlieren. Wer spricht für wen?

How do you describe the aims of your group – Some groups started years ago, have there been changes in their aim?
When I first joined Hajusom ten years ago, it was a place where I could be myself, try new artistic ways of expression, meet diverse/different new people and have a lot of fun. This hasn't changed, though Hajusom has grown into a transnational Art

Center and we performers feel more entitled to identify ourselves as artists and have grown confident to claim our place in the art world.

> I started to collaborate with Hajusom as a choreographer five years ago. What touched me at first, was the special relation between the artistic work and the social empathy. In Hajusom it is very important to create a social safe space in which everybody has their space to be, to share their points of view and ideas and to experiment in artistic ways.

How do you describe your strategies, priorities and work aesthetics?
Communication is a very important aspect of our work. We talk a lot! For example, after every rehearsal, we sit together and give each other feedback. However, these instances are not restricted to our work process. Also, for our art, it is very important for everyone involved to have a voice and be heard. Even more, it is an important feature in our performances, which we like to describe as «many-voiced» (vielstimmig)

> The main strategy, I would say, is to always talk and to feel where it needs to change things or to become better. It is never perfect and I see the aim of Hajusom working for a safe and diverse safe space more as a practice. It is a constant connection with all the members of the group.
>
> Feed-back and creating spaces for it, is very important in Hajusom practice, as well as the respect of many diverse ideas and to talk about artistic content.
>
> In Hajusom, there are always guest artists who come to give an input. So Hajusom is always confronted with different ways of working and different esthetics. This asks for an extreme openness and curiosity to experiment with new ideas, approaches and people.

Priorität hat der lange künstlerische Prozess, die Recherche nach einer „dekolonialen Ästhetik", die kollektiven Arbeitsweisen in Hinblick auf Entscheidungsstrukturen immer wieder kritisch zu hinterfragen. Wir im (derzeitigen) künstlerischen Team erkennen unsere eigene Prägung durch dominant westliche Konzepte und Ästhetiken und es ist uns ein großes Anliegen, entsprechende Bewertungsmechanismen in jeder Phase der Arbeit aufzubrechen. Die Qualität unserer Arbeit macht sich auch an der Qualität dieses gemeinsamen Reflexionsprozesses fest und daran, inwieweit es gelingt, uns gemeinsam mit den Performer*innen dieser neuen Ästhetik anzunähern, ein Theater der Zukunft mit zu entwerfen.
What are the biggest challenges to your group?

> As performers we face many challenges. As migrants and refugees we are often not granted full participation in the art world and our perspectives are only considered as an exceptional non-representative view. Although many of my colleagues are very passionate about their work, they often lack the time necessary to be more

engaged. We see ourselves as professional performers, yet many of us have a full-time job, go to school and/or study. We do not only have to sustain ourselves, but for many of us this is a condition linked to our residential status, too. In addition some of us also have to face criticism and opposition from our own families and friends, because as women we are not supposed to stand on a stage or because wearing tights is not masculine. However we still show up for rehearsal every Friday – even on our vacation.

The main challenge is time. The performers have their jobs or studies. To coordinate all these different lives can be sometimes challenging and hard work. It needs a very constant contact between the coordination team and the performers. This as well demands from each one to have a strong motivation in being part of a project and to work together.

The constructive side of it is that the artistic processes of a project can be quite long, between 1,5- 2 years. And this gives the time to develop each project slowly and with dedication.

Die größte Herausforderung für das Ensemble ist es die vielen Perspektiven zusammen zu führen, die den Kosmos Hajusom ausmachen – die jüngste Performerin ist 9 Jahre alt, die älteste Ehrenamtliche 82, es arbeiten unterschiedliche Künstler*innen im Team mit (Bühnenbildner, Kostümbildnerin, Musiker, Videokünstlerin) und Performer*innen auf der Bühne. Der Kosmos Hajusom ist komplex. Es gibt sehr verschiedene Ausgangspositionen, von denen aus das gemeinsame Ziel, zusammen künstlerisch zu arbeiten, anvisiert wird. Dank des starken solidarischen Spirits hat uns die dieser verrückten Vielheit innewohnende Kraft stets inspiriert und ist in unsere künstlerische Arbeit geflossen.

Das Exil Ensemble am Maxim Gorki Theater

Ludwig Haugk

Das Exil Ensemble wurde im Jahr 2016 gegründet, die Pläne dazu wurden 2015 am Gorki entwickelt. Ausgangspunkt war zum einen die politische Situation, zum anderen eine konkrete künstlerische Arbeit: Für die Produktion THE SITUATION untersuchten die Regisseurin Yael Ronen und die Dramaturgin Irina Szodruch Berlin als Ort, an dem sich die komplizierte Gemengelage der Konflikte des Nahen Ostens spiegelt. Die Autorin entwickelte das Stück gemeinsam mit den Spieler*innen, die zum Teil dem Ensemble des Gorki angehörten (Orit Nahmias, Dimitrij Schaad) zum anderen Teil als Gäste hinzukamen: Maryam Abu-Khaled, Karim Daoud, Ayham Majid-Agha, und Yusuf Sweid.

Durch die erfolgreiche und produktive Arbeit, die unter Anderem zum Theatertreffen eingeladen wurde, entstand der Wunsch mit allen Kolleg*innen weiterzuarbeiten, zugleich war einigen von ihnen eine Rückkehr nach Syrien/Palästina nicht möglich oder sehr gefährlich. Der Impuls der Intendantin Shermin Langhoff, das Gorki-Ensemble um die Spieler*innen zu erweitern fiel zusammen mit der Krise der europäischen Humanität 2015, als die reichsten Länder der Welt offensichtlich nicht willens waren, einem humanitären Notstand professionell zu begegnen und mitten in der EU tausende Geflüchtete ohne Perspektive und Zuflucht Repression, Menschenverachtung und Gewalt ausgesetzt waren. Langhoff beschloss in dieser Situation den ungewöhnlichen Schritt, sich als Theater nicht auf verbale Kritik bzw. Solidaritätsbekundung zu beschränken, sondern aktiv zu werden. In kürzester Zeit gelang es, über Drittmittelakquise den finanziellen Grundstock für sieben neu zu schaffende Ensemblestellen und einen organisatorischen Overhead erfolgreich zu beantragen. So konnte das Exil Ensemble gegründet werden, das Menschen, die an der Ausübung ihres künstlerischen Berufs gehindert werden, eine Möglichkeit geben sollte, diese Tätigkeit auch im Exil ausüben zu können.

Auch wenn das Exil Ensemble eine institutionelle Gründung war, wurde von Beginn an versucht, eine künstlerische Kommunikation auf Augenhöhe zu führen. Mit Ayham Majid-Agha wurde ein künstlerischer Leiter benannt, der zuvor Dozent am Institut für Drama und Kunst in Damaskus und nunmehr selbst Teil des Ensembles war. Neben Sprachkursen und künstlerischen Workshops erarbeitete das Exil Ensemble Produktionen, darunter die Uraufführung eines Stücks von Ayham Majid-Agha, das im Rahmen der ein-Jahr-langen Schreibwerkstatt „*Flucht, die mich bedingt*" am Gorki entstanden war und das er selbst inszenierte (*SKELETT EINES ELEFANTEN IN DER WÜSTE*). Unmittelbar nach der Konstituierung des Ensembles entstand mit Yael Ronen das Projekt „Winterreise", das auf einer gemeinsamen Bustour des Exil Ensembles durch das winterliche Deutschland 2017 basierte. Weitere Projekte waren *ELISAVETA BAM* nach Daniil Charms in der Inszenierung von Christian Weise sowie *HAMLETMASCHINE* von Heiner Müller in einer Inszenierung von Sebastian Nübling, in die auch poetische Kommentartexte von Ayham Majid-Agha eingingen und zur Venedig – Biennale Teatro eingeladen wurde.

Zudem erhielten die Mitglieder des Exil Ensembles, das zunächst für zwei Jahre aus Mitteln der Lotto-Stiftung und der Kulturstiftung des Bundes finanziert wurde, Deutsch- und zum Teil auch Englischunterricht. Ein Workshop-Programm sollte Schauspielpraxis (Workshops mit Ensemblemitgliedern), Dramaturgie (geleitet von Jens Hillje), Tanz (Workshop mit Isabel Schaad) und anderes vermitteln.

Das Format des Exil Ensembles als autonome Einheit innerhalb des Theaterbetriebs, die aber gleichzeitig mit eingebunden ist in die dramaturgische Gesamtprogrammierung – verwaltet selbstverwaltet gewissermaßen – ermöglichte die vielen starken Inszenierungen des neugegründeten Ensembles, die ein begeistertes Publikum fanden und auf Gastspielen überregional und auch international gefeiert wurden. Die Konstellation stellte sich aber auch als stark konfliktanfällig heraus. Denn auch wenn die Leitung des Gorki alles daransetzte, aus der paternalistischen Geste herauszukommen, konnte dies nicht vollständig gelingen, da diese in der Systematik angelegt war. Gleichzeitig war dieser Prozess der Annäherung, des Grenzen Kennenlernens eine wichtige Erfahrung, die weder das Theater noch die beteiligten Künstler*innen bereuen.

Konfliktlinien ergaben sich z.B. auch aus der Frage, wie die Idee des Exil Ensembles zu kommunizieren sei. Sollte es ein eigener Brand sein, mit eigenem Logo, ein Ensemble, empowert durch seine Eigenständigkeit? Sollte die Geschichte des Ensembles und seiner Mitglieder publik gemacht werden, ging es um Lautstärke erzeugen, um die Ensemblegründung als politisches Zeichen? Oder war es vielmehr angezeigt, eine neue Selbstverständlichkeit zu etablieren, eine Forcierung von Mehrsprachigkeit und Diversität der Narrative, ohne große Proklamation und Markierung? Der Konflikt ist nicht ganz aufzulösen oder wenn dann nur insofern, als anstelle der Alternativsetzung eine Chronologie gesetzt wurde. Noch ist es uns nicht erlaubt, als selbstverständlich zu behaupten, was von der Mehrheitsgesellschaft nicht als selbstverständlich akzeptiert wird. Und so wurde das Projekt zunächst zum Gegenstand der im Gorki auf allen Ebenen vorangetriebenen Repräsentationsdebatte. Das Exil Ensemble war zunächst sehr klar ein politisches Projekt. Das führte zu einer wichtigen Stärkung der Thematisierung der Situation geflüchteter Künstler und geflüchteter Menschen überhaupt. Zum anderen aber führte es auch zu den Fragen: Sind wir gemeint oder geht es um unseren Status? Ab dem zweiten Jahr veränderte sich das stark zugunsten der künstlerischen Arbeit. Die Reibungen fanden mehr und mehr hier statt und das war gut, denn hier konnten sie produktive Wärme erzeugen. Vor allem die sich durch die Zusammenarbeit ergebende Kommunikation unter den Schauspieler*innen „beider" Ensembles, ließ sie zu einem Ensemble werden.

Zugleich ergab sich auch dank der Förderung des Landes Berlin ein Prozess, der als das wichtigste Ergebnis des ganzen Vorhabens gelten kann: das Aufgehen des Exil Ensembles im Gorki Ensemble. Im Wissen um die voraussehbaren Schwächen hatte Shermin Langhoff das Projekt von Anfang an als eines angelegt, das sich selbst abschaffen sollte. Einige der ersten Mitglieder gingen nach zwei Jahren andere Wege. Vier der ehemals sieben sind geblieben und heute Ensemblemitglieder des Gorki wie alle anderen auch.

POSTHEIMAT-ENCOUNTER #4 am Maxim Gorki Theater

Monica Marotta

Die vier Tage POSTHEIMAT- ENCOUNTER #4 am Maxim Gorki Theater, organisiert von Christopher-Fares Köhler und Monica Marotta, sollten es eine klare Richtung haben – es wurde sich für den Titel THE ART OF (EN)COUNTERING entschieden. 2018 trafen sich die sechs Theatergruppen des PostHeimat Netzwerks zum ersten Mal und widmeten sich den Fragen von Migration, Repräsentation, Identität und Flucht. Wie können intersektionale und gerechtere Formen der (transnationalen) Zusammenarbeit im Theater und in den Künsten stattfinden? Beim 4. Encounter dieses sich kontinuierlich entwickelnden Netzwerks wurde auf einen künstlerischen Austausch mit dem Publikum durch ein viertägiges öffentliches Programm aus Diskussionen, Künstlergesprächen, Lesungen und Performances, mit dem Fokus auf zukünftige Möglichkeiten und Modelle gesetzt.

Das Programm war in 4 Formate unterteilt:

1. Performances als Theaterpraktiken mit und von Ensembles des PostHeimat Netzwerks

In SALTY ROADS, Teil der Performance-Reihe *Mythen der Wirklichkeit*, untersuchen der palästinensische Regisseur Bashar Murkus und sein Team, das zum Teil aus den aus Palästina stammenden Mitgliedern des Gorki Exil Ensembles besteht, das Meer als Quelle der Mythologie von gestern und heute. Es sind nicht nur religiöse und romantische Geschichten, die dem Meer entsprungen sind. Seit der Antike sind seine Ufer auch Ort politischer Debatten über Grenzen, Heimat und Teilung.

DIE VERLOBUNG IN ST. DOMINGO – Ein Widerspruch von Necati Öziri gegen Heinrich von Kleist ist eine dramatische Liebesgeschichte im Umfeld der Revolution. Öziri hinterfragt vermeintlich eindeutige Positionen und fügt der Geschichte eine neue Ebene der Opposition hinzu, die eine heutige Diskussion über Gewalt und Gegengewalt anregt.

In REINE FORMSACHE des Kollektivs Ma'louba fragt die fantastische Schauspielerin Amal Omran mit theatralischer Dialektik "Was wäre, wenn …?" Was wäre, wenn sie, berühmt in ihrem Land, sich entschließen würde, nach Syrien zurückzukehren, an der Grenze verhaftet und von einem Offizier verhört würde? Wäre dieses Verhör wirklich möglich?

2. Diskussionen mit dem Publikum im Anschluss an die Performances sowie Panels zum Thema Sprache, zu anderen ähnlichen, bereits existierenden Realitäten oder Plattformen in Deutschland, zu eingewanderter Literatur:

LANGUAGE POLITICS mit Yvonne Griesel, Oliver Kontny und Bashar Murkus, ein Gespräch über die Sprache in Übersetzungen und Translationen zwischen dem verbalen Kodex verschiedener Kulturen, Erlebnissen und Theaterformen, eine Diskussion über die Bedeutung von Mehrsprachigkeit, die Politik der Sprache(n) und Möglichkeiten für die Zukunft.

(EN)COUNTERING THE FUTURE, eine Panel-Diskussion mit Emre Akal, Lara-Sophie Milagro, Kenda Hmeidan und Elena Agudio, in der es darum ging, mögliche Konzepte und Gedanken zu identifizieren, die den Weg für transkulturelle, vielfältige, mehrsprachige Zukunftsräume für Kunst und Denken ebnen könnten.

In READING RESITANCE lasen und präsentierten drei Autoren (Özlem Özgül Dündar, Raphael Amahl Khouri und Liwaa Yazji) ihre Texte und stellten sich der Diskussion mit dem Autor und Moderator Deniz Utlu. Aus unterschiedlichen Blickwinkeln und thematischen Perspektiven setzten sie sich mit Queerness, Migration, Politik, Geschichte(n), Identitäten und Erinnerungen auseinander und beleuchteten in ihren Texten die widerständige Kraft des Schreibens.

3. Angewandte Kunst als Form des Widerstands, während der gesamten Zeit des Encounters. Das Archivprojekt der postkolonialen Berliner Galerie SAVVY Contemporary, COLONIAL NEIGHBOURS ist auf dem Netzwerktreffen zu sehen. Lizza May David stellt ihr Projekt, das Teil der Fragmente-Reihe des Kunstraums ist, vor.

4. Interne Workshops und Come-togethers, bei denen die sechs Theatergruppen eingeladen waren, nicht nur gemeinsame Schritte nach vorne zu machen, wie die

Website oder weitere Kooperationen, sondern auch die Realitäten der deutschen Theaterszene zu untersuchen und neue Initiativen anzustreben. Hier entstand ein erster Entwurf des Statements: *Problematising PostHeimat*.

The Exile Ensemble

Monica Marotta and Ludwig Haugk

The Exile Ensemble was founded in 2016, the plans for which were developed at the Gorki in 2015. The starting point was, on the one hand, the political situation and, on the other, a concrete artistic work: for the production THE SITUATION, director Yael Ronen and dramaturg Irina Szodruch examined Berlin as a place in which the complicated mix of conflicts in the Middle East is reflected. The playwright developed the piece together with the players, some of whom were members of the Gorki ensemble (Orit Nahmias, Dimitrij Schaad) and others who joined as guests: Yusuf Sweid, Ayham Majid-Agha, Maryam Abu-Khaled and Karim Daoud.

Due to the successful and productive work, the desire to continue working with all the colleagues arose, but at the same time a return to Syria/Palestine was not possible or very dangerous for some of them. The impulse of the artistic director Shermin Langhoff to expand the Gorki Ensemble to include the players coincided with the crisis of European humanity in 2015, when the richest countries in the world were apparently unwilling to professionally address a humanitarian emergency, and in the middle of the EU thousands of refugees without perspective and refuge were exposed to repression, contempt for humanity and violence. In this situation, Langhoff decided to take the unusual step of not limiting himself as a theater to verbal criticism or expressions of solidarity, but to become active. In a very short time, the financial basis for seven new ensemble positions and an organizational overhead was successfully applied for through the acquisition of third-party funds. Thus, the Exile Ensemble could be founded, which should give people, who are prevented from practicing their artistic profession, an opportunity to practice this activity in exile.

Even though the Exile Ensemble was an institutional foundation, an attempt was made from the beginning to conduct artistic communication at eye level. With Ayham Majid-Agha, an artistic director was appointed who was himself part of the ensemble. In addition to language courses and artistic workshops, the Exile Ensemble developed productions, including the world premiere of a play written by Ayham Majid-Agha, which had been created in the context of a yearlong creative writing workshop "Flucht, die mich bedingt" at the Gorki and which he himself directed (SKELETT EINES ELEFANTEN IN DER WÜSTE). Immediately after the constitution of the ensemble, the project "Winterreise" was created with Yael Ronen, based on a joint bus tour of the Exile Ensemble through Germany in the winter 2017. Other projects were ELISAVETA BAM after Daniil Charms directed by Christian Weise as well as HAMLETMASCHINE by Heiner Müller in a production by Sebastian Nübling, which also included poetic commentary texts by Ayham Majid-Agha and was invited to the Venice – Biennale Teatro.

In addition, the members of the Exile Ensemble, which was initially funded for two years by the Lotto Foundation and the German Federal Cultural Foundation, received German and, in part, English lessons. A workshop program was designed to teach acting practice (workshops with ensemble members), dramaturgy (led by Jens Hillje), dance (workshop with Isabel Schaad), and more.

The format of the Exile Ensemble as an autonomous unit within the theater company, but at the same time integrated into the overall dramaturgical programming – administered self-managed, so to speak – made possible the many strong productions of the newly founded ensemble, which found an enthusiastic audience and were celebrated at guest performances nationwide and also internationally. However, the constellation also turned out to be highly prone to conflict. For even though the management of the Gorki made every effort to get out of the paternalistic gesture, this could not succeed completely, since it was inherent in the system. At the same time, this process of rapprochement, of getting to know each other, was an important experience that neither the theater nor the artists involved regret.

Lines of conflict also arose, for example, from the question of how to communicate the idea of the Exile Ensemble. Should it be its own brand, with its own logo, an ensemble empowered by its independence? Should the history of the ensemble and its members be publicized, was it about generating volume, about the ensemble's founding as a political sign? Or was it rather indicated to establish a new self-evidence, a forcing of multilingualism and diversity of narratives, without much proclamation and marking? The conflict cannot be completely resolved, or if so, then only insofar as a chronology was set in place of the alternative setting. We are not yet allowed to assert as self-evident what is not accepted as self-evident by the majority society.

And so the project initially became the subject of the debate on representation, which was pushed forward at all levels in the Gorki. The Exile Ensemble was initially very clearly a political project. This led to an important strengthening of the thematization of the situation of refugee artists and refugees in general. But on the other hand, it also led to the questions: Are we meant or is it about our status? From the second year on, this changed strongly in favour of the artistic work. The frictions took place more and more here, and that was good, because here they could generate productive heat. Above all, the communication among the actors of "both" ensembles, which resulted from the collaboration, allowed them to become one ensemble.

At the same time, a process emerged that can be considered the most important result of the whole project: the dissolution of the Exile Ensemble. Aware of the predictable weaknesses, Shermin Langhoff had designed the project from the beginning as one that was to abolish itself. Some of the first members went other ways after two years. Four of the former seven have remained and are now ensemble members of the Gorki like everyone else. For the ENCOUNTER #4 – Station Gorki organised by Christopher-Fares Köhler and Monica Marotta, we decided to give a precise direction for the 4 days, and we entitled it THE ART OF (EN)COUNTERING. In 2018 the six theatre groups that composed the network PostHeimat held their first meeting, dedicated to questions of migration, representation, identity and seeking refuge. How can intersectional and more equitable forms of (transnational) cooperation take place in the theatre and the arts? This continually developing network's fourth encounter engages in an artistic exchange with the audience through a four-day public programme of discussions, artist talks, readings and performances, with a focus on future possibilities and models.

The program was divided in 4 formats comprehending:

1. Performances as theatre practices, created with and by Ensembles belonging to the groups of PostHeimat SALTY ROADS as part of the Myths of Reality performance series, the Palestinian director Bashar Murkus and his team, composed partially by Gorki Exile Ensemble from Palestine, investigate the sea as a source of yesterday's and to- day's mythologies. It's not religious and romantic stories that have emerged from the sea. Since ancient times, their shores have also been the place for political debates about borders, homelands and divisions. DIE VERLOBUNG IN ST. DOMINGO – An Objection of Necati Öziri against Heinrich von Kleist, which is a dramatic love story in the setting of the revolution, questioning supposedly clear positions and adding a new layer of opposition to the story. REINE FORMSACHE of Collective Ma'louba in which the fantastic actress Amal Omran, questioned with the theatrical dialectic "What if . . .?" What she, famous in her country, decided to return to Syria, was arrested at the border and interrogated by an officer? Would this interrogation really be possible?

2. Debates with the audience after the performances as well as panels about the language topic, about other similar already existing realities or platforms in Germany, about immigrated literature: LANGUAGE POLITICS with Yvonne Griesel, Oliver Kontny and Bashar Murkus, a talk about the languages with translators and other interpreters between the language of different culture, experiences and theatre forms, a discuss about the significance of multilingualism, the politics of language(s) and possibilities for the future. (EN)COUNTERING THE FUTURE, a panel-discussion with Emre Akal, Lara-Sophie Milagro, Kenda Hmeidan und Elena Agudio in which was aimed to identify potential concepts and thoughts that could pave the way for transcultural, diverse, multi- lingual future spaces for art and thought. In READING RESITANCE three authors (Özlem Özgül Dündar, Raphael

Amahl Khouri and Liwaa Yazji) read and presented their texts and engaged in discussions with the author and presenter Deniz Utlu. From different angles and thematic perspectives, they dealt with queerness, migration, politics, histor(ies), identities and memories and shed light on the resistant power of writing in their texts.

3. Applied Arts as form of resistance, during the whole time of the Encounter. The archive project of the post-colonial Berlin-based gallery SAVVY Contemporary, COLONIAL NEIGHBOURS has been to participate in the network meeting. Lizza May David presents her project, which is part of the art space's Fragments series.

4. Internal workshops and come-togethers, where the six theatre groups were invited not only to create mutual step forwards, like the website or further collaboration, but also to examine the realities of the German theatre scenario and aim new initiations. From that moment they edited the statement: Problematising PostHeimat.

Boat People Project

2009 haben Luise Rist und Nina de la Chevallerie, beide im Stadttheater arbeitend beschlossen sich hauptsächlich politischen Themen zuzuwenden, eigenverantwortlich zu produzieren und stärker im öffentlichen Raum tätig zu sein. Sie verließen das Stadttheater und gründeten eine GbR. Zu Beginn probten und führten wir in improvisierten mobilen Orten im Stadtraum auf, 2015 – 2018 bespielten wir ein ehemaliges Tonstudio im ehemaligen Institut für wissenschaftlichen Film, das in der Zeit auch als Unterkunft für Geflüchtete genutzt wurde. Seit 2018 bespielen wir eine eigene Spielstätte, in der im Normalfall bis zu 100 Menschen Platz finden. Diese rasante und stetige Entwicklung spiegelt sich inhaltlich, in der Künstler:innenzusammensetzung und der Außenwahrnehmung wieder. Wir sind als Kollektiv organisiert, ein fester Kern besteht aus 7 Künstler:innen vor Ort, daneben gibt es viele assoziierte Künstler:innen, mit denen wir regelmäßig und je nach Produktion arbeiten.

Unser Hauptfokus und der inhaltlicher Diskurs beschäftigt sich in möglichst radikaler Konsequenz und mit ehrlicher Reflektion um die Fragen, wie wir eine „vielfaltssensible Öffnung" erreichen, was Diversität überhaupt bedeutet, welche Repräsentant:innen in den Produktionsteams vorhanden sind, wie wir strukturellen Rassismus in unserer Arbeit verhindern und entgegentreten. Wie kann politisches Theater wirksam sein? Welchen Beitrag können wir zur „Migrationsdebatte" leisten?

Des Weiteren beschäftigen uns (auch bereits vor der Corona-Pandemie) die Fragen der Digitalisierung und der Barrierefreiheit. Von Beginn an ist Mehrsprachigkeit und Perspektivenvielfalt in den Projekten durchgängig Programm, daher spielt Übersetzungsarbeit immer schon eine große Rolle. Uns interessiert, wie sehr wir Digitalisierung dafür einsetzen können, erste Versuche gab es in diese Richtung bereits. Dabei versuchen wir bewusst mit dem Dilemma umzugehen, dass Digitalisierung Barrieren abbaut und gleichzeitig andere aufgebaut werden.

Die Frage, inwieweit Migration per se ein Objekt oder das Thema für Theaterstücke sein kann und welche Konsequenz dies für die künstlerische Zusammenarbeit hat, ist von Beginn an ein Thema in jedem Vorhaben. Der Impuls, die Arbeit jenseits der gewohnten Stadttheaterarbeit zu beginnen, kam 2009 durch die Schlagzeilen über Lampedusa und die vermehrten Schiffsunglücke dort zustande. Die beiden Gründerinnen von boat people projekt begannen zu recherchieren, inwieweit auch in Göttingen und in Niedersachsen Geflüchtete „angekommen" waren, wie die Lebenssituation der Menschen ist, welche Biographien sich hinter den Schlagzeilen verbergen. Im ersten Stück LAMPEDUSA standen Geflüchtete aus Äthiopien neben Studierenden aus Kamerun und Eingewanderten aus Ghana auf der Bühne – einem Stadtbus, der die mitfahrenden Zuschauenden an vertraut geglaubte Orte in Göttingen brachte.

Sowohl in LAMPEDUSA als auch in den späteren beiden Jahren mit den Stücken MIKILI und KEINSTERNHOTEL (2010 und 2011) haben wir Migration und Flucht als Thema fokussiert. In den Schauspielproduktionen bestand das Ensemble jeweils aus professionellen Schauspieler:innen aus Deutschland und der Schweiz und geflüchteten, meist jungen Menschen, aus afrikanischen Ländern. Wir bildeten intime, einander zugewandte Gruppen, erfuhren voneinander und übereinander. Lernten viel über deutsches Asylrecht und die politische Situation in den Herkunftsländern der neuen Kolleg:innen und machten diese zum Thema der Stücke. Gemeinsam Theater machen über Migration bedeutete damals wie heute auch das Grenzen verschwimmen, Professionelles nicht immer von Privatem zu trennen ist. Der Kontakt mit Ausländerbehörden und Sozialarbeiter:innen blieb nicht aus. Während der Proben wurde in vielen Sprachen diskutiert: wie können wir komplexe Sachverhalte wie die Gründe für Flucht möglichst ohne Worte ausdrücken, welche Bilder werden von wem auf welche Art gelesen? Wir weißen deutschen Theatermacher:innen wurden mit unserer eurozentristischen Sichtweise und Lesart und unserem bis dahin oft unbewusstem, strukturellen und individuellem Rassismus konfrontiert und haben viele schmerzhafte Erfahrungen gemacht, die bis heute nicht aufhören. Das Dilemma zeigte sich z.B. in der Öffentlichkeitsarbeit: wir wollen die Künstler:innen nicht labeln, ihre Herkunft, ihre Migrations- oder Einwanderungsgeschichte nicht ausstellen oder thematisieren, dies passierte aber oftmals per se durch unser Tun und auch durch eine eher konservative Berichterstattung. Auch der Name der comagny ist nicht ganz unschuldig an diesem Problem; daher steht der Name des Freien Theaters immer wieder zur Diskussion. Durch den zunehmenden Bekanntheitsgrad der Arbeit der Gruppe und den noch ergebnisoffenen Gesprächen im Kollektiv über eine Alternative ist diese Frage immer noch nicht abgeschlossen.

Wir haben gelernt und lernen noch, unsere Perspektive (die der weißen Theatermacher:innen) als solche wahrzunehmen, unsere Privilegien, Perspektiven, und eigenen Sozialisationsprozesse zu sehen und sie als solche zu benennen bzw. sie kritisch zu beleuchten. Nach 2011 haben wir auch verstanden, wie wichtig es ist Positionen konkret abzugeben und haben verstärkt professionelle Künstler:innen die nicht-weiß und/oder nicht-deutsch sind in die Leitungsebene und ins Ensemble eingeladen. Unser Anliegen ist es in einen Austausch zu kommen, zu debattieren, mehrere Positionen nebeneinander und gegenüberzustellen, gemeinsam Themen – unbedingt auch jenseits der Themen Migration und Flucht – zu generieren.

Die Auseinandersetzungen mit den Mitgliedern aus dem Post-Heimat Netzwerk hat uns auch in diesen Fragen immer wieder zum Reflektieren und zur Weiterentwicklung angeregt.

Schließlich konnten wir diese Fragen auch praktisch miteinander erproben: In der Kooperation mit Collective Ma´louba und Kainkollektiv haben wir nach einem Impuls von Mudar Alhaggi (Hörspiel OVERDOSE) eine digitale Theaterperformance entwickelt, in der es u. a. um die Frage ging, wie pandemisches Theater – wie Theater heute überhaupt – funktionieren kann. Die Zusammenarbeit zwischen den insgesamt 13 Theatermacher:innen dauerte, auch aufgrund der Pandemie, insgesamt 1,5 Jahre.

OVERDOSE – The unfinished show of pain and joy steht für uns für den erneuten Versuch mit vielen, sehr unterschiedlichen Theaterkünstler:innen die Frage auszuhandeln, wie die Grenzen zwischen Genres, Arbeitsweisen, Sprachen und Stile überwunden werden können. Wie aus diesen Grenzüberschreitungen Theater und Kunst entstehen kann. Wie wir die gemachten Erfahrungen in die nächsten Projekte und Zusammentreffen produktiv mitnehmen können.

OVERDOSE hatte als Online-Stream Premiere am 9.4.2020.

TEXT: Nina de la Chevallerie

O Töne:
Luise Rist, Mitbegründerin von boat people projekt über die Frage, warum sie als weiße Autorin über Migration schreibt:

Als Schreibende habe ich, bevor ich die erste Seite beginne, bereits mehrere Prozesse der Annäherung an Themen und Menschen durchlaufen. Im Moment, in dem ich den ersten Satz formuliere, bin ich aber allein. Ich lasse auch Menschen sprechen, in denen von Erfahrungen die Rede ist, die ich nicht gemacht habe. Jede Autorin, jeder Autor kann über Erfahrungen schreiben, die sie oder er nicht gemacht hat, denn es liegt im Wesen der Kunst, dass sie frei ist, und frei sein muss; Literatur, Theater, Musik und Malerei entstehen, weil sich Menschen zwischen Welten bewegen und als Beschreibende immer eine etwas randständige Position einnehmen. Einerseits. Andererseits gibt es Kunstschaffende, die aufgrund des weltweiten strukturellen Rassismus gegen People of Colour nicht zu Wort kommen, nicht gehört, gelesen oder gesehen werden, die aufgrund ihrer Hautfarbe oder Zugehörigkeit zu einer bestimmten Ethnie nicht die Möglichkeit zu einer künstlerischen Entfaltung bekommen haben. Ihnen den Vortritt zu geben, wenn es um die Einladung zu einem Podium oder zu einer Lesung geht, finde ich in diesem Kontext richtig. Als weiße, deutsche Autorin trage ich beim Schreiben zum Beispiel eines antirassistischen Theaterstücks eine besondere Verantwortung den Menschen gegenüber, die von Rassismus betroffen sind.

Die Schauspielerin Javeh Asefdjah zu der Frage, ob die Kunst einer migrantischen Künstlerin gleich migrantisch ist.

Die Frage, ob eine migrantische Künstlerin migrantische Kunst machen muss, beziehungsweise ob ihre Kunst per se migrantisch ist, weil sie selbst migrantisch ist – kann ich direkt mit einem NEIN beantworten.

Dies würde bedeuten, dass man die Künstlerin beziehungsweise den Künstler lediglich auf ihre bzw. auf seine Herkunft reduziert. Eine solche Reduktion würde dieser Person absprechen, dass sie sich dafür entscheidet, z.B. ein Bild zu malen, das „lediglich" ästhetisch etwas zum Ausdruck bringen will. Es würde bedeuten, dass eine Künstlerin mit migrantischem Hintergrund auch nur Blumen mit migrantischem Hintergrund malen darf, um es humorvoll zugespitzt zu formulieren, sprich exotische Blumen auf deutschem Boden. In meiner Familie gibt es viele Künstler*innen, die ganz unterschiedlichen Wege gegangen sind, um ihren Kunstwerken Ausdruck zu verleihen. Natürlich kann eine Künstlerin sich dafür entscheiden, ihre Herkunft und eigene Geschichte einfließen zu lassen, die Künstlerin kann sich dafür entscheiden, mit ihrer Kunst sozialkritisch und politisch zu sein, aber MÜSSEN tut sie das natürlich nicht. Als Schauspielerin spiele ich die bildende Künstlerin Irina Baryalei aus dem von Luise Rist geschriebenen Theaterstück GOLD, und gleich zu Beginn des Stücks stelle ich Fragen in den Raum, bzw. lässt mich die Autorin fragen: „Wer legt wem etwas in den Mund? Was ist unaussprechlich für mich, was spricht durch mich? .... Wer ist das Ich, das da vor ihnen steht?" Ich bin eine Schauspielerin, die sich dieser starken Frauenfigur mit all ihren Unsicherheiten zur Verfügung stellt, zwar habe ich persönlich ebenfalls einen Migrationshintergrund, jedoch nicht den gleichen Hintergrund der Figur Baryalei. Mir sind also einige ihrer Gedankengänge sehr vertraut, wir teilen ähnliche Erfahrungswerte bezüglich der Reduktion auf Nationalität und Kultur, aber es reicht nicht, sich auf diese Gemeinsamkeiten auszuruhen. Somit liegt es in meiner Verantwortung, mich tief mit ihrer speziellen Geschichte, mit ihrem Werdegang auseinander zu setzen, im Prinzip wie bei jeder anderen Figur auch – nur dass es bei Figuren mit einem Migrationshintergrund oft mehr, viel mehr zu entdecken gibt.

The Boat People

In 2009, Luise Rist and Nina de la Chevallerie, working at the Stadttheater, decided to turn mainly to political issues, to produce independently and be more active in the public space. They left the City Theatre and founded an independent group. In the beginning, we rehearsed and performed in improvised mobile venues in the city space. In 2015 — 2018, we played at a former sound studio in the former Institute for Scientific Film (IWF), which was also used as accommodation for refugees during that time. Since 2018, we have been performing in our venue, which usually seats up to 100 people. This rapid and constant development is reflected in the content, the composition of the artists and the external perception. We are organised as a collective, with a fixed core of 7 artists on site and many associated artists with whom we work regularly and depending on the production.

Our primary focus and the discourse on content deals as radically as possible and with an honest reflection on the questions of how we achieve a "diversity-sensitive opening", what diversity actually means, which representatives are present in the production teams, and how we prevent and counter structural racism in our work. How can political theatre be effective? What contribution can we make to the "migration debate"?

Furthermore, we are concerned (even before the Corona pandemic) with the questions of digitisation and accessibility. From the very beginning, multilingualism and diversity of perspectives have been part of the programme in the projects, so translation work has always played a significant role. We are interested in how much we can use digitisation for this, and there have already been initial attempts in this direction. In doing so, we consciously try to deal with the dilemma that digitalisation breaks down barriers and simultaneously creates others.

The question of the extent to which migration per se can be an object or the theme for theatre pieces and what consequence this has for artistic collaboration is a topic in every project from the very beginning. The impulse to start working beyond the usual municipal theatre work came about in 2009 through the headlines about Lampedusa and the increased number of shipwrecks there. The two founders of the boat people project began to research the extent to which refugees had also "arrived" in Göttingen and Lower Saxony, what the living situation of the people was like, and what biographies were hidden behind the headlines. In the first play, LAMPEDUSA, refugees from Ethiopia stood on stage next to students from Cameroon and immigrants from Ghana – a city bus that took the audience to several places in Göttingen.

Both in LAMPEDUSA and in the successive two years with the plays MIKILI and KEINSTERNHOTEL (2010 and 2011) we focused on migration and flight as a theme. In each of the drama productions, the ensemble consisted of professional actors from Germany and Switzerland and refugees, mostly young people, from African countries. We formed intimate groups that turned towards each other and learned about each other and from each other. We learned a lot about German asylum law and the political situation in the new colleagues' countries of origin and made this the theme of the plays. Making theatre together about migration meant then, as now that boundaries have become blurred, that the professional cannot always be separated from the private. Contact with foreign authorities and social workers did not go unnoticed. During rehearsals, there were discussions in many languages: how can we express complex issues like the reasons for flight without words, which images are read by whom and in which way? We white German theatre-makers were confronted with our Eurocentric view and reading and our often unconscious, structural and individual racism and had many painful experiences that continue today. The dilemma became apparent, for example, in our public relations work: we do not want to label the artists, we do not want to exhibit or thematise their origin, their migration or immigration history, but this often happened per se through our actions and also through rather conservative reporting. The company's name is also not entirely innocent of this problem; hence, the name of the Free Theatre is always up for discussion. Due to the increasing awareness of the group's work and the still open-ended discussions in the collective about an alternative, this question is still not closed.

We have learned and are still learning to perceive our perspective (that of white theatre-makers) as such, to see our privileges, perspectives, and own socialisation processes, and to name them as such or examine them critically. After 2011, we also understood how important it is to give concrete positions and have increasingly invited professional artists who are non-white and/or non-German to join the management and the ensemble. Our aim is to enter into an exchange, debate, juxtapose and contrast several positions, and generate themes together – by all means also beyond the topics of migration and flight.

The discussions with the members of the Post-Heimat Network have always inspired us to reflect on these issues and to develop them further.

Finally, we were able to test these questions in practice with each other: In cooperation with Collective Ma'louba and Kainkollektiv, we developed a digital theatre performance based on an impulse by Mudar Alhaggi (radio play OVERDOSE), which, among other things dealt with the question of how pandemic theatre – like theatre today in general – can function. The collaboration between the 13 theatre-makers lasted a total of 1.5 years, partly because of the pandemic.

For us, OVERDOSE – The unfinished show of pain and joy stands for a renewed attempt to negotiate the question of how the boundaries between genres, working methods, languages and styles can be overcome with many very different theatre artists. How theatre and art can emerge from these transgressions. How can we productively take the experiences we have made into the next projects and collaborations?

OVERDOSE premiered as an online stream on 9.4.2020.

TEXT: Nina de la Chevallerie

O tones:
Luise Rist, co-founder of boat people project on why she writes about migration as a white author:

As a writer, before I start the first page, I have already gone through several processes of approaching topics and people. But at the moment I formulate the first
sentence, I am alone. I also let people speak, talking about experiences I have not
had. Every author can write about experiences he or she has not had because it is
in the nature of art that it is free and must be free; literature, theatre, music and
painting come into being because people move between worlds and, as descrip-
tors, always occupy a somewhat marginal position. On the other hand, there are
artists who, because of the worldwide structural racism against people of colour,
do not have their say, are not heard, read or seen, and have not been given the opportunity for artistic development because of the colour of their skin or because
they belong to a particular ethnic group. In this context, I think it is right to give
them priority when it comes to invitations to a podium or a reading. As a white
German author, when I write, for example, an anti-racist play, I have a special responsibility towards the people who are affected by racism.

The actress Javeh Asefdjah on the question of whether the art of a migrant artist is migrant.

The question of whether a migrant artist has to make migrant art, or whether her
art is migrant per se because she herself is migrant – I can directly answer with a
NO.
       This would mean that the artist is reduced only to his or her origin. Such a re-
duction would deny that this person decides, for example, to paint a picture that
"merely" wants to express something aesthetically. It would mean that an artist
with a migrant background is only allowed to paint flowers with a migrant background, to put it humorously, i.e. exotic flowers on German soil. In my family there
are many artists who have taken very different paths to express their works of art.
Of course, an artist can choose to incorporate her origins and her own history, the
artist can choose to be socially critical and political with her art, but of course she
doesn't HAVE to. As an actress, I play the visual artist Irina Baryalei from the play
GOLD written by Luise Rist, and right at the beginning of the play I put questions
into the room, or rather let the author ask me: "Who is putting something into
whose mouth? What is inexpressible to me, what speaks through me? .... Who
is the me standing there in front of them?" I am an actress who makes herself available to this strong female character with all her insecurities, although I personally
also have a migrant background, I do not have the same background of the character Baryalei. So some of her thought processes are very familiar to me, and we
share similar experiential values regarding the reduction to nationality and culture, but it is not enough to rest on these commonalities. Thus, it is my responsi-

bility to delve deeply into her particular story, into her career, in principle as with any other character – except that there is often more, much more to discover about characters with a migrant background.

**25.-27.05.2018
ENCOUNTER #1
Münchner
Kammerspiele**

München

**23.06.2018
Premiere
NORA, boat
people projekt,
Theater im
ehemaligen IWF**

Göttingen

**21.-24.03.2019
ENCOUNTER #2
Theater an der
Ruhr**

Mülheim a.d.R.

30.05.2018
Premiere
INMITTEN DER
DUNKELHEIT
RIEF ICH DICH,
Ruhrorter, Innen-
stadt

Mülheim a.d.R.

27.03.2019
Premiere
AZIMUT
DEKOLONIAL,
Hajusom,
Kampnagel

Hamburg

31.05.2019
Premiere
DENN STILL-
STEHEN KANN
WEDER DER
FLUSS NOCH
DIE FLÜCHTIGE
STUNDE,
Ruhrorter,
St. Mariae
Rosenkranz/
Dorfkirche Saarn

Mülheim a.d.R.

25.-27.10.2019
ENCOUNTER #3
Münchner
Kammerspiele

München

02.10.2019
Premiere
HAARE, boat
people projekt,
Werkraum

Göttingen

09.11.2019
Premiere
REINE
FORMSACHE,
Collective
Ma'louba,
Theater an der
Ruhr

Mülheim a.d.R.

21.02.2020
Premiere
DER TITEL
IST FREI ÜBER-
SETZBAR,
boat people
projekt,
Werkraum

Göttingen

05.-08.03.2020
ENCOUNTER #4
Maxim Gorki
Theater

29.-30.10.2020
ENCOUNTER #5
Hajusom

16.-17.03.2021
ENCOUNTER
#5.5

Berlin

Hamburg
(digital)

(digital)

09.04.2021
Online-Premiere
OVERDOSE,
boat people
projekt,
Collective
Ma'louba,
kainkollektiv,
Ringlokschup-
pen Ruhr

Mülheim a.d.R.

11.-14.07.2021
ENCOUNTER #6
boat people
projekt

Göttingen
(live+digital)

27.08.2021
ENCOUNTER
#6.5 Hajusom

Hamburg
(live+digital)

20.06.21
Online-Premiere
THE RETURN
OF DANTON,
Collective
Ma'louba,
Shubbak Festival

London

10.09.2021
Premiere
GEISTER,
Ruhrorter,
Friedrich Wil-
helms-Hütte

Mülheim a.d.R.

**23. - 26.09.2021
ENCOUNTER #7
Theater an der
Ruhr**

Mülheim a.d.R.

18.09.2021
Premiere
ANFASSEN!,
boat people
projekt, vier.D,
Depot

Dortmund

24.11.2021
Premiere
MORGEN
GRAUEN, Haju-
som, Kampnagel

Hamburg

03.12.2021
Live-Premiere
THE RETURN
OF DANTON,
Collective
Ma'louba,
Münchner
Kammerspiele

München

to be
continued

II. W ork ing

Research Group
Documents

Cultural Policy Group
Documents

Gr
ou
ps

Cultural Policy Working Group

Özlem Canyürek, on behalf of the Cultural Policy Working Group[1]

Why Intersectional Diversity?

PostHeimat is concerned with accomplishing an "accessible" performing arts scene for all artistic workforces. *PostHeimat* focuses on systematic exclusion and discrimination and pursues an inclusive diversity discourse. Hence, the Network adopts an intersectional approach to diversity.

Intersectionality, coined by legal scholar Kimberlé Crenshaw, acknowledges that identity consists of various layers; it is never singular and fixed. Conversely, intersectionality recognises identity as dynamic and multiple. Not only do some of the components of identity (e.g. race, ethnicity, nationality, gender, sexual orientation, faith/religion, class, education, socio-economic milieus) converge, but also modes of oppression, discrimination, and racism often operate along intersecting markers of difference.

To address the unequal access conditions for accommodating diversity in the German performing arts scene, *PostHeimat* proposes that diversity discourse should deal with power dynamics and hierarchies within institutions that maintain the structural exclusion of some performing arts professionals who are marked as "the other" with overlapping labels (e.g. Black people, POC, immigrant, refugee/exile, queer, non-European, non-Western).

The Network considers itself a learning space where performing arts collectives, ensembles, artists, researchers, and cultural activists discuss overcoming structural barriers within institutions to democratise the performative practice. Thus, the Network embraces an intersectional diversity perspective to explore the prerequisites of an "equality-based" performing art scene and a cultural policy framework to diversify knowledge production, circulation and reception.

---

1   Immanuel Bartz, Özlem Canyürek, Nina de la Chevallerie, Christopher Fares Köhler, Ruba Totah, Julia zur Lippe, Wanja van Suntum

What is a Diversity Access Point (DAP)?[2]

PostHeimat focuses on anti-discrimination and anti-racism to understand diversity beyond a pure management concept. It is concerned with creating a space where diversity is recognised as a continuously developed process enriched by the perspectives of individuals and initiatives/groups with different realms of experiences and knowledge. In internal meetings of the cultural policy group, generating a learning space was identified as essential for raising awareness about intersectional diversity among ourselves and beyond as a network and opening this space to other performing arts practitioners, groups, and researchers. This search is ultimately related to introducing intersectional diversity as an inclusive concept to address structural inequalities preventing or limiting access conditions for marginalised and excluded artists and performing arts professionals.

In this regard, *Diversity Access Point (DAP)* is suggested as a learning lab for introducing and developing the concept of intersectional diversity and identifying its fundamental engagement areas for the pluralisation of the German performing arts scene. In other words, the *DAP* is envisioned as a space that seeks to pinpoint what intersectional diversity should achieve when it is implemented.

The below-mentioned points were extracted from the various working group sessions of *PostHeimat* as some of the foundations of a learning space in line with the intersectional diversity concept:

- The *DAP* acknowledges that we are a post-migrant[3] society living in a transnational world. Performing arts advocates for this society; hence, a political actor reflects the reality of society.
- To breach the construction of "otherness" and address unequal opportunities, the *DAP* deals with misusing "cultural diversity".
- The *DAP* recognises the individual elements of identity and perceives it as a dynamic, interactive and intersectional entity that cannot be encapsulated into national and ethnic frameworks.
- The *DAP* is concerned with achieving an equality-based plural performing arts scene and advocates for developing the discourse on intersectional diversity.

---

2   The name is suggested only as a tentative title for an imaginary learning space for the development of an inclusive diversity discourse.

3   The cultural policy group acknowledges the necessity of the term "post-migrant" in the first two years of the Network, but it ponders over whether or to what extent the concept of post-migrant appropriately reflects the features of the intersectional diversity concept.

Intersectional Diversity Act (IDA): *Working Draft*[4]

A. RECITAL CLAUSE

On the 27th of May 2018, the artistic groups BOAT PEOPLE PROJEKT (Göttingen), COLLECTIVE MA'LOUBA (Mülheim an der Ruhr), EXIL ENSEMBLE (Berlin), HAJUSOM (Hamburg), OPEN BORDER ENSEMBLE (Munich) and RUHRORTER (Mülheim an der Ruhr) established the network PostHeimat at Münchner Kammerspiele. Long term and sustainable goals of the initiative sponsored by the Kulturstiftung des Bundes and the Ministerium für Kultur und Wissenschaft NRW are to influence the structural deficits of the German theatre landscape, to reduce discrimination and racism within the theatre institutions as well as to shape the programs and productions of German theatres in a more multifaceted, intercultural and socially more representing way. The network invites artists, artistic groups, theatre institutions and academics to cooperate, steadily enrich the network with more members, and increasingly connect with related initiatives.

The idea behind establishing a network envisions the dissolution of the network if its goals have been realised in a permanently changed transcultural theatre landscape in Germany. The network has put this INTERSECTIONAL DIVERSITY ACT (IDA) into place to reach its goals. It is to be put into action by the cultural policies of all sixteen federal states in Germany. The IDA contains a set of demands, needs and recommendations towards a shift within the cultural policies in the following four sectors:

CULTURAL EDUCATION

In 1986, Kimberlé Crenshaw coined the term "Intersectionality." Since then, it has become one of the most influential terms of gender studies in the discourse of social justice and terms of identity politics. Countless intersectional parameters, such as social status, ethnicity, faith, gender, sexual orientation, age, spoken languages, and

---

4   This draft was developed by the working group "Cultural Policy" within the framework of Encounter #2 – Encounter #6 of the PostHeimat network, in which in particular Immanuel Bartz, Özlem Canyurek, Nina de la Chevallerie, Marie Drath, Christopher-Fares Köhler, Ruba Totah, Wanja van Suntum, Pakkiyanathan Vijayashanthan and Julia zur Lippe participated. The points do not claim to reflect the stance and opinions of all participants in the network. This draft is unfinished, just as the discourses, social, artistic and cultural-political processes at stake are still in motion. We hope we can support other initiatives in similar search movements by transparentizing our working draft. The discussions will continue, among others, in the working group "Diversity" of the Federal Association of Performing Arts (Bundesverband Freie Darstellende Künste).

cultural background, shape each person. The IDA acknowledges the intersectional parameters and devices the following demands, based on these ideas of intersectionality:

1.1 Training

Obligatory training in anti-discrimination literacy in all cultural institutions. Discrimination is understood in its broad definition: "The use of categorial, that is supposedly unambiguous and selective distinctions for the production, motivation and justification of unequal treatment with the consequence of social disadvantage." (Albert Scherr, Diskriminierung/Antidiskriminierung – Begriffe und Grundlagen, 26.2.16, bpb, link: https://www.bpb.de/apuz/221573/diskriminierungantidiskriminierung-begriffe-und-grundlagen?p=all)

The training should be held at least once a year for all staff members and in all hierarchies of power.

Workshops

1. Basic foundational training for the Institution / Theater (once a year).

- long-term, progressive concept.
    (b) Empowerment workshops.
    (c) One One-day workshop for the Artistic (Guest) Team (before each production).
    (d) "Critical Whiteness" workshops.

// Putting in the Manifesto the term of "failure" / things can fail
// Workshop → "Case Scenarios" (Best Practice) → Using Theater itself as a tool.

Language

...

CONSULTATION AND ADVICE

Everyone needs advice when it comes to the topics of intersectional diversity. The IDA gives the following demands in the section on consultation and advice.

2.1 Legal consultation

For employer and client:
Obligatory one-off, external professional legal advice to the production management (workshop) on specific labour law situations on topics such as residence status, tax law, and social law.

Draft contract: Before the draft contract begins, there should be a joint discussion between the employee and employer about the residence status and other legally relevant details of the employee's life situation. The contract should be adapted to this situation.

When the contract is concluded: Ensuring the contract is comprehensible at both the legal and linguistic levels. An interpreter may be involved if requested by the contractor.

Psychological services

Mandatory seminar/workshop for clients, especially on psychological consequences of war traumas, war and flight, and intersectional experiences of discrimination. Provision of a tried and tested network of institutions and counselling centres specialising in the psychological effects of experiences of discrimination and post-traumatic stress disorders.

Coverage of costs as well as provision of contacts and establishment of contacts for necessary counselling interviews, coaching and consultation hours for psychological stress arising during the work process.

Shaping artistic direction, boards and juries

In the IDA, we are interested in ensuring a multi-perspectivity in all areas (on stage and behind the scenes as well as at the management level) and in securing representations of marginalised groups and the general average society. In doing so, we should refrain from instrumentalising marginalised groups.

To ensure this, leadership positions, juries, and committees should be filled in an intersectional, diverse manner.

Transparency in Information

Ensure the transparent and democratic flow of information regarding job seeking, employment opportunities and funding processes. Ensure it through a programme of mentorship. Also, theatre institutions should be mentored in the area of non-acknowledged professional biographies.

"Anti-Diskriminierungs-Klausel"/ Anti-Discrimination Clause

To protect all employees and freelancers from discrimination and to empower them within their structures of work, an "Anti-Diskriminierungs-Klausel", based on the "Anti-Rassismus-Klausel" developed by Sonja Laaser and Julia Wissert, should be applied in every contract.

Actual Clause

//Klausel Nr. 1: Für alle Vertragsarten (deu/eng) – Stand Januar 2019: https://www.kanzlei-laaser.com/wp-content/uploads/2019/07/Anti-Rassismus-Klausel_deu-eng.pdf

//Klausel Nr. 2: Für Gastspielverträge mit Häusern (deu) – Stand Juni 2019: https://www.kanzlei-laaser.com/wp-content/uploads/2019/07/190715_Anti-Rassismus-Klausel_DAC_sl_ln.pdf

PRODUCTION

International, intercultural, and multilingual productions have specific needs within their creative processes, and these needs should be taken care of in the following ways:

3.1 Additional producer

Every production with an "international design" should have an extra producer responsible for the whole process, keep the overview of the process and have competencies such as language skills and knowledge of cultural backgrounds involved in the production. The producer should not be the translator of the production at the same time.

Documentation of productions

Less documentation or it needs to be implemented in a production's time/financial planning.

3.2 Translator

...

CAPACITY BUILDING AND FUNDING

To ensure long-lasting changes in the cultural policy sector, the following topics and alterations need to be taken into consideration:

4.1   Audience development

Representation: what kind of projects are presented?
Spaces: Where do we show theatre? Welcoming. Engaging with all audience. Inviting spaces. Intimacy.
Social Politics: Support the audience in coming to the theatre. Communication to all parts of society.
Format: Creating a community. Open spaces.

Resources

Not only by distributing money but what are the needs, how can we produce resources for creating jobs with lasting perspectives within the artistic field of theatre? Demanding the transparency of criteria in jury decision-making processes.

4.2   Potential funders

Institutions should proactively look for potential funders.

4.3   Prolongation of funding cycles

Prolonging the funding cycles, at least three years and the standard production time of half a year to a year. – counter-movement against the "economization of culture".

4.4   "Eigenanteil"

We don't need "Eigenanteil" (own contribution) within productions. The costs for documentation must also be reduced. A policy is missing that acknowledges or rewards the work of part-time theatre makers.

Research Working Group

Group Statement[1]

The research group explores the PostHeimat network through interdisciplinary and practice-relevant scholarship. The group critically reflects on and troubles possible modes, meanings, and implications of a PostHeimat becoming.

We understand the network as a processual and long-term inquiry into new meanings of post-migrant, intersectional and multi-perspectival approaches to societies and theatre. We accompany, document, and engage the relationship between artistic work, cultural policy proposals, and knowledge production from diverse contexts in and beyond the network.

Each encounter of the PostHeimat network produces situations that we consider as learning experiences about current dynamics and problems in and beyond the German theatre and, ultimately, society in transition. We emphasise the complementarity of participation, contemplative analysis, and urgent action.

Many of us are engaged in multiple ways of making theatre – as translators, dramaturges, writers, directors, artists, actors, activists, ethnographers, and audiences. We propose research as a performative co-witnessing field in which institutionalised and non-institutionalised, academic and para-academic knowledge production, activism and artistic practice can merge.

The research group is an open platform that invites collaboration.

Wir befassen uns mit dem PostHeimat-Netzwerk durch interdisziplinäre und praxisrelevante Forschung. Wir reflektieren und problematisieren mögliche Modi, Bedeutungen und Implikationen eines PostHeimat-Werdens. Wir verstehen das Netzwerk selbst als eine prozessuale und langfristige Untersuchung neuer Bedeutungen von post-migrantischen, intersektionalen und multiperspektivischen Zugängen zu Gesellschaften und Theater.

---

1   This statement was drafted by the research group of the PostHeimat network during and after Encounter #04 at the Maxim Gorki Theater in March 2020. Diese Erklärung wurde von der Forschungsgruppe des PostHeimat-Netzwerks während und nach dem Encounter #04 im Maxim Gorki Theater im März 2020 verfasst.

Wir begleiten, dokumentieren und beschäftigen uns mit der Beziehung zwischen künstlerischer Arbeit, kulturpolitischen Vorschlägen und Wissensproduktion aus verschiedenen Kontexten innerhalb und außerhalb des Netzwerks.

Jede Begegnung des PostHeimat-Netzwerks bringt Situationen hervor, die wir als Lernerfahrungen über aktuelle Dynamiken und Probleme in den Feldern der darstellenden Künste und letztlich in Gesellschaften im Wandel betrachten.

Wir betonen die Komplementarität von Partizipation, reflektierender Analyse und dringendem Handeln.

Viele von uns sind selbst auf vielfältige Weise in der Produktion von Theater impliziert – u.a. als Übersetzer*innen, Dramaturg*innen, Autor*innen, Regisseur*innen, Künstler*innen, Schauspieler*innen, Aktivist*innen und Zuschauer*innen. Wir schlagen Forschung selbst vor als ein Feld des "performative co-witnessing", in dem institutionalisierte und nicht-institutionalisierte, akademische und para-akademische Wissensproduktion, Aktivismus und künstlerische Praxis zusammenkommen können.

Die Forschungsgruppe ist eine Plattform, die allen offen steht.

Problematising PostHeimat[2]

Prompted by recurring nationalist appropriations of the term *Heimat* and its enduring colonial connotations in the German context, we felt the urge to re-open the notion, trouble it collectively, and shift its meaning *beyond* singular interpretations. Beyond Heimat, in this case, PostHeimat does not mean abandoning the possibility of connecting to the term but going through it, across it, and finding other and new meanings that signal a pluralistic *re*-appropriation of the notion.

PostHeimat, then, is a departure point to reflect on concepts like identity formation, nation, racism, and colonialism – and to move to an understanding of *home* that is non-discriminatory, does not equate nation with ethnicity or language, and profoundly recognises a post-migrant social theory. PostHeimat becoming points towards an emergent and, as of yet, incomplete idea. It stands for a heterogeneous process that resists forming a new canon, a new *Leitkultur*. PostHeimat proposes itself more as a conversation that does not shy away from admitting less uttered experiences. In doing so, it seeks to form part of a critical social imagination, a new ethic for a diverse common.

---

2   This reflection was drafted by the research group of the PostHeimat network during and after Encounter #04 at the Maxim Gorki Theater in March 2020. Diese Überlegungen wurden von der Forschungsgruppe des PostHeimat-Netzwerks während und nach dem Encounter #04 im Maxim Gorki Theater im März 2020 verfasst.

Theatre and the performing arts have long been a site and practice for imagining collectivity, sociality, individuality, and the relation of individuals to society. It can be a mode of thinking and enacting identities in a queer, plural and shifting way. It is constituted by and concerns relations between persons – between actors and actors, actors and audiences – but also functions by way of multiple further mediations through and across bodies, languages, materials, and the sonic. We want to build on this potential and reality of theatre as a collective practice to imagine Heimat post-Heimat. Or, as Dwight Conquergood put it, theatre is a form of 'co-performative witnessing' that brings about and imagines collectivities otherwise.

PostHeimat proposes an *Umleitkultur* (detour culture) rather than a *Leitkultur*, in which Christianity, Whiteness, and Masculinity are not guiding unmarked principles for social norms; instead, we let ourselves be accompanied by a distracting, queer, non-normative culture. Accepting detours rather than straight roads.

PostHeimat understands that the term *Heimat* played a significant role in the German colonial imagination and its racist ideologies (Kolonie und Heimat), and that it reverberates in the post-colonial present. As such, PostHeimat takes an anti-racist stance that grapples with the enduring neo-colonial heritage of the past.

Heimat comprises *Heim* and is linked directly to ideas and practices of hospitality, welcoming, giving refuge, and making a home. PostHeimat recognises the privileged and oftentimes asymmetrical, patronising, and even hostile character of guest-host relations. It seeks to reconsider *creating home* as a shared concern that prioritises the inalienable rights of safety and transnational citizenship over the not-quite logic of temporary asylum.

We advocate a move away from projecting migrants and refugees as 'to-be-integrated' members of a society, whose linguistic abilities, habits, and resources are regarded as 'lacking'; PostHeimat rethinks the concept of post-migrant citizenship not from the perspective of integration, lack, and hierarchy, but recognises plurality as potential, multiperspectivity as richness, and diversity as value.

Heimat has been mobilised to design public cultural institutions, such as museums, archives, and theatres, that instantiate the ties between culture, citizenship, and nation, and it has been preserved through such institutional traditions. PostHeimat recognises the ambivalent power of institutions to perform, represent, and institute visions of society; PostHeimat efforts problematise and enact a pluralising politics also within and through institutions without seeking to reproduce hegemonising institutional agency.

We recognise the performativity of discourse and consider these reflections as the first iteration of a PostHeimat *Umleitkultur*.

Angeregt durch die immer wiederkehrenden nationalistischen Vereinnahmungen des Begriffs Heimat und seine anhaltenden kolonialen Konnotationen im deutschen Kontext, verspüren wir den Drang, den Begriff neu zu öffnen, ihn kollektiv zu problematisieren, seine Bedeutung über singuläre Interpretationen hinaus zu verschieben. Jenseits von Heimat, in diesem Fall: PostHeimat bedeutet nicht, die Möglichkeit aufzugeben, an den Begriff anzuknüpfen, sondern durch ihn hindurchzugehen, ihn zu durchqueren und andere und neue Bedeutungen zu finden, die eine pluralistische Wiederaneignung des Begriffs signalisieren.

PostHeimat ist also ein Ausgangspunkt, um über Begriffe wie Identitätsbildung, Nation, Rassismus und Kolonialismus nachzudenken – und sich zu einem Verständnis von Heimat zu bewegen, das nicht diskriminierend ist, Nation nicht mit Ethnizität oder Sprache gleichsetzt und eine postmigrantische Gesellschaftstheorie zutiefst anerkennt. Das PostHeimat-Werden verweist auf eine aufkommende und noch unvollständige Idee. Sie steht für einen heterogenen Prozess, der sich der Bildung eines neuen Kanons widersetzt, einer neuen Leitkultur. PostHeimat versteht sich vielmehr als ein Gespräch, das sich nicht scheut, auch weniger geäußerte Erfahrungen zuzulassen. Damit will sie Teil einer kritischen sozialen Imagination sein, einer neuen Ethik für ein vielfältiges Gemeinwesen.

Das Theater und die darstellenden Künste sind seit langem ein Ort und eine Praxis für die Vorstellung von Kollegialität, Sozialität, Teilhabe und der Beziehung des Einzelnen zur Gesellschaft. Es kann ein Modus sein, um Identitäten auf merkwürdige, pluralistische und sich verändernde Weise zu denken und zu verwirklichen. Sie konstituiert sich durch und betrifft Beziehungen zwischen Personen – zwischen Akteuren und Akteurinnen, Akteuren und Zuschauerinnen- aber sie funktioniert auch durch eine Vielzahl weiterer Vermittlungen – durch und über Körper, Sprachen, Materialien und Klänge. Wir wollen auf diesem Potenzial und der Realität von Theatre eine kollektive Praxis aufbauen, um uns Heimat post-Heimat vorzustellen. Oder, wie Dwight Conquergood es formulierte, Theater ist eine Form der „ko-performativen Zeugenschaft", die kollektive Aktivitäten hervorbringt und anders imaginiert.

PostHeimat schlägt eine Umleitkultur statt einer Leitkultur vor, in der Christentum, Weißsein, Männlichkeit keine unmarkierten Leitprinzipien für soziale Normen sind, sondern wir uns von einer ablenkenden, queeren, nicht-normativen Kultur begleiten lassen. Umwege in Kauf nehmen, statt gerader Wege.

PostHeimat versteht, dass der Begriff Heimat in der deutschen kolonialen Imagination und ihren rassistischen Ideologien (Kolonie und Heimat) eine bedeutende Rolle spielt und in der postkolonialen Gegenwart nachhallt. PostHeimat nimmt daher eine antirassistische Haltung ein, die sich mit dem anhaltenden neokolonialen Erbe dieser Vergangenheit auseinandersetzt.

Heimat umfasst Heim und steht in direktem Zusammenhang mit Ideen und Praktiken der Gastfreundschaft, des Willkommens, der Zufluchtnahme und des Heimischwerdens. PostHeimat erkennt die privilegierten und
oft asymmetrischen, herablassenden und sogar feindseligen Charakter der Gast-Gastgeber-Beziehungen. Sie versucht, die Schaffung von Heimat als ein gemeinsames Anliegen zu überdenken, das den unveräußerlichen Rechten auf

Sicherheit und transnationale Staatsbürgerschaft Vorrang vor der nicht ganz einfachen Logik des vorübergehenden Asyls einräumt.

Wir plädieren dafür, Migranten und Flüchtlinge nicht mehr als „zu integrierende" Mitglieder einer Gesellschaft zu betrachten, deren sprachliche Fähigkeiten, Gewohnheiten und Ressourcen als „fehlend" angesehen werden. PostHeimat überdenkt das Konzept der postmigrantischen Staatsbürgerschaft nicht unter dem Gesichtspunkt der Integration, des Mangels und der Hierarchie, sondern erkennt Pluralität als Potenzial, Multiperspektivität als Reichtum und Vielfalt als Wert an.

Heimat wurde mobilisiert, um öffentliche Kultureinrichtungen wie Museen, Museen und Theater zu schaffen, die die Verbindung zwischen Kultur, Staatsbürgerschaft und Nation herstellen, und sie wurden durch solche institutionellen Traditionen bewahrt. PostHeimat erkennt die ambivalente Macht von Institutionen an, um Visionen von Gesellschaft darzustellen, zu repräsentieren und zu instituieren; PostHeimat versucht, eine pluralistische Politik auch innerhalb und durch Institutionen zu problematisieren und zu verwirklichen, ohne zu versuchen, hegemonisierende institutionelle Macht zu reproduzieren.

Wir erkennen die Performativität des Diskurses an und betrachten diese Überlegungen als die erste Iteration einer PostHeimat Umleitkultur.

III. Encounters

Between Sprachlosigkeit
and Constant Screaming.
Some Thoughts on
Working Post-Heimat

Hardcore
Confrontations

Lecture at PostHeimat
Encounter#2

ta

A Reflection

lk

s

Colonial Neighbours –
On How to Boil Rice
with a Pot Full of Air/
On the Wickedness of
Imagination

Hardcore Confrontations

Nora Amin

In the first decades of the twentieth century, German society was confronted with questions of otherness, elimination and exclusion for the sake of an illusion of purity of race. The horrors of the Nazi regime, and the Holocaust, have never left the memory and the trauma of German society. Such a systematic act of annihilation to a massive amount of people was conducted not only by the regime but by all the people who served the regime and believed in it through a pedagogy of obedience and order. This pedagogy justified mass killings under the pretext of functionality; it terminated lives because they were not considered functional or productive for German society and for the purity of the white race. It specifically terminated all those who did not fit into the model that was set by the dictatorship for how a German citizen should be. Therefore, it erased people who could not work because they were old or sick, people of different religions, people of different sexual orientations or from different origins, and people who were disabled, among others.

The pedagogy of the regime facilitated such criminal acts of dehumanisation while resting on the forced and deformed notion of identity of a certain Nazi German-ness. Now, after so many years and transformations, German society has to continue being alert towards new transformations and the emergence of that old ugly pedagogy. Although we live in a democratic regime with a lot of space for expression, criticism and change, we still need to pay attention towards any potential divergence from the foundations of human rights and equality. The great opportunity given to Germany with the recent waves of migration can actually enrich the culture and the economy, provide a better future for society, and guarantee the renewal of a country that may otherwise age very soon. The youth generation of recently migrated families will fuel the workforce and social fabric. It will create a new face for Germany within the next 15 years, a Germany that will no longer be primarily white. It is because of this coming generation, and because of migration as an opportunity for German society and not as a threat, that we need to change our cultural policy as part of an overall change in the value system, constitution and legislation to accompany the transformation of realities in Germany and the new era that it is stepping towards. Change in the performing arts sphere and its legislation would be part of a bigger change in the notions of citizenship and identity. Such change should be founded on equality above all and on up-rooting racism in all its forms and practices.

It is time now to review some notions and terms that are no longer reliable for change, whether because they have gradually fitted into the system instead of changing it or because the pace of manipulation and alteration is too fast for them to remain significant in their initial meaning and way. Among those concepts is "diversity". "Diversity," which started as a goodwill expression, could have gradually been transformed by the instrumentalisation of the ruling order and authority to become another expression of otherness. The German society has formulated its new terminology regarding "the inclusion of others", as expressed in the term "diversity". Therefore, "diversity" has been used to point out a certain non-uniformity while pointing all the way to a certain definition of German identity. "Diversity" has been carrying the connotation of "not German", "alien", "other", therefore contributing to the disconnection between today's German cultural sphere and its social fabric, focusing on difference as an exception to German identity, an exception that the German order is so charitably containing under the label of diversity. Today's cultural policy cannot be examined without consideration of the German concepts of identity and the Other, which stand in the core concepts of culture, policy, and state politics. To re-understand equality, equity, and social justice is also to examine citizenship and its constituents and go back to the constitutional definitions and the human rights laws and conventions.

If cultural legislations and policies are dividing and distributing cultural services and rights, and -initially- creating a space for typical German citizens (what is a typical German?) and another space for those who are not defined as such (like diversity funds, and migrant artists grants), those very legislations and policies are following a specific concept that guides them towards identifying who is a "typical German" and who is not (meaning who fits under the umbrella of "diversity"). For how can one define what is diverse without defining what is uniform, and how can one decide what is "other" without defining what is "same". The guidelines or concepts that define what needs to be "included" stipulate as well what is the norm. To think of what one can "include" is also to think of what is "inside" and what is "outside" and to define oneself as a stipulator/legislator of identity and otherness.

The Universal Declaration on Human Rights stipulates that everybody has the equal right to participate in culture. This participation can take the shape of either the right to produce culture or the right to receive cultural services. The concept of cultural justice is the foundation of such equality of rights when it comes to cultural creation and reception. The constitutional legislations of culture in each country should go hand in hand with the foundations of human rights conventions and declarations, which clearly stand against any discrimination based on race, gender, religion or ethnicity. Therefore, it is not acceptable to see that censorship still exists in some countries as an official department of the Ministry of Culture, just as it is equally strange to see that some societies that adopt the concepts of equality still discriminate between certain forms of cultural production and cultural actors. Considering some forms of art and cultural production as inferior to others, or as "not modern enough", as "undeveloped", or as "folklore" could be seen as a kind of cultural discrimination that is embedded in a specific vision that entitles itself to decide what art is and what identity is. This specific vision is not far away from racism.

When the legislator takes extraordinary measures to define the hierarchy within artistic production, he/she also decides what art is from a position of political power. While art is very relative and subjective, arts' legislations and policies should remain relative and with a big distance towards absolute thinking and the categorisation of human creativity. The other facet of such strict categorisation is the divisions and labelling of citizens. Thinking of a German citizen of Turkish origin as only belonging to a specific/special community can somehow be a pretext to "exclude" this citizen from the social fabric and, therefore, make the deformed attempt of bringing him/her back under the label of "inclusion". Inclusion is primarily based on exclusion. Labelling cultural productions, arts and artists as part of "inclusion" is equally labelling them as "others" or "Othering" them. Instead of confronting the major phenomenon that Europe and Germany are dealing with now -which is the decline of white uniformity and conformity in their societies- legislators are creating new labels and categories to encourage everybody who is outside of their concept of whiteness and identity. While German society is potentially living in one of the richest opportunities for growth and transformation - economically and culturally - a discriminatory system of thinking within the political power forms a major threat to such opportunity, basically reversing it into a weakness, a danger to white supremacy that has to be contained.

It is necessary to look at the cultural policy of Germany today through the lens of knowledge decolonisation, where the old notions of "same" and "stable" cultures can no longer survive.

There is no same, and there is no stability anymore. The core of culture now is that it is continuously transforming and totally open. This core can be extended to our world's human, social and societal conditions today. The notions of supremacy and nationalism will no longer hold in today's world. Today, we live in a world where identities are hybrid and transformative. Binary terms of identity, thought, and knowledge are fading away. The essence of equality and humanness within the Universal Declaration of Human Rights must create the foundation anew to understand today's world of armed conflict and displacement, to understand it as a world for which everybody is responsible. This egalitarian essence of humanness would enable us to re-think the notions of victimhood and humanitarian actions from an egalitarian perspective and to reverse them from being charitable actions of white supremacy into being a globally shared responsibility where the economic hierarchy of wealth is instead an economic and human debt to those who suffered wars and paid the price for the economic richness of the others, of the colonisers. Suppose we rely on this humanising foundation and its philosophy of decolonisation. In that case, we may be able to see that no one can "own" the culture now, nor define its parameters; no one can stipulate that this is the "owner/dweller" and that is the "other/newcomer". After all, human identity has become so incredibly complex and multi-layered to the extent that it is impossible to look at concepts of "otherness" except as part of the domain of coloniality and its extended history.

It is worth noting that when it comes to discussing cultural policy today, many of us focus on arts organisations, producers, artists, and public and private sectors. Therefore, we focus on the service providers and tend to neglect the public, the audiences and the overall beneficiaries. By doing so, we seem to create an unhealthy imbalance that impacts the policies that are being created -or not created- to support the beneficiaries/audiences. To place the focus on one end of the cultural operation and service and diminish the attention given to the other end is to think in unequal terms, considering the "receiver" as a mere passive entity. Although some recent attention has been given to outreach and audience development in the theatre world, we still lack a solid policy that addresses all the residents of Germany at large. Such a policy would put much effort into welcoming and attracting audiences from all ages, social and educational backgrounds, and economic status. It would be driven by a will to celebrate togetherness and led by an understanding that cultural services are a right for all. A right that challenges the prejudices, stereotypes and cliches of the so-called regular type of arts' beneficiaries or the traditional image of theatregoers being the white economically privileged persons. To change and expand the scope of our understanding and expectation of theatregoers is to change and develop our art production and knowledge sharing. Hence, balancing the focus on cultural policy-making between service providers and service receivers is also a healthy procedure to support the development of artistic productions and break their stigmatisation. To work towards a policy of open doors is to create a creative process of producing performances and concerts that can grow, transform and connect to everybody.

The ideal is not to see that one position in a specific arts organisation is reserved for a person from a "migrant background" but rather to see that racist and colonial thinking has been erased from today's value system and behaviour, whether through clear legislation, by-laws, regulations, or through long-term training, education and pedagogy. The labelling of "inclusion" and "diversity" may have been initiated in the first place to amend past failures and to force change. Yet, those special measures can quickly help the colonial and racist thinking to get comfortable because there would be no pressure to make radical changes since there is now a specific position dedicated to "diversity" and, therefore, no need for significant or fundamental change. Change needs to be implemented on a legislative and structural scope to protect any individual initiative otherwise the unjust system of discrimination would keep going. Let's opt for radical and fundamental change so that we do not find ourselves confronted again and again by the new countertactics that extend the life of racism instead of dismantling it.

Personal questions... in theatre... Here and now...

But what kind of theatre is considered eligible for consideration, funding and promotion?
Is it the theatre that looks similar to Western and European theatre concepts?
A theatre that re-produces a specific artistic identity set by the coloniser?
A theatre of imitation?
Or would it be a theatre that can be easily labelled as import, exotic, folkloric and alien?
Who defines what theatre is and what a good quality performance is?
And how do they define it?
According to which norms and aesthetics?
Because this debate is also about aesthetics and the forced borders of creativity and imagination, as well as it is about the rights to imagine and freely create art away from prejudice and away from the restrictions of the theatre venues and their preconceived notion of performance and scenography and rapport between the performers and the spectators.
This debate could also be about the new forms of censorship, one that is not set by a dictatorship but rather by a seemingly liberal system that employs categorisation to rule the market in a way that is already economically established and should not be shaken.
How can we, as artists, create without adhering to or listening to the categories and labels of the system?
How can I present myself as an artist with more than 25 years of experience in theatre and dance instead of presenting myself as an Arab woman?
How can artistic merit win over box-ticking?
How can my art be trusted enough to be qualified to be presented to an imaginary German audience?
How can my mind and professional creativity be accepted as equal and not inferior and less developed?
How would theatre venues and production systems welcome my topics and aesthetics if they do not adhere to the formula of speaking about my own Heimat and the suffering that exists there? And while we are supposed to be in the post-Heimat era? And without speaking of myself as a victim? And an alien?
How can I explain that despite all identity fragmentation, I still can belong?
Although it could be here or elsewhere, it could also exist as a nostalgic illusion of romanticism but with a practical sense of togetherness.

How can I explain that the stage can be a place for retrieving dignity and humanness, as long as it is a stage that respects my autonomy and does not invite me to
perform out of charity or solely political correctness?

I would like to be in the program because I am a good artist who has succeeded in
creating spectatorship over the years, and not because there is a slot available for
migrant women!

I guess one could say that the German stage could have a different future. A future
where the ownership of the stage goes to anybody and spectatorship goes to everybody, just as German soil can belong to those who plant it and make it flourish no
matter their skin colour (this is almost an Egyptian metaphor).

A future with no stage ownership and no systematic power structures defining performance, censoring creativity and eliminating the unwanted because of the sur-
plus.

In a future where every public space can become a stage outside the institutional
theatre venues and structures, different communities can create their cultural and
entertainment programs outdoors or in any communal space they design for themselves.

I guess the size of the yearly program would have space for everybody, and everybody
would re-appropriate and re-claim knowledge, sharing and creativity.

Encounter#2

Golschan Ahmad Haschemi

Dear organizers and attendees, thank you for inviting me to this inspiring gathering coinciding with the beginning of spring. To those of you who celebrate Nouruz, I would like to say: Nouruz Piruz, Happy New Year, Eyd Mobarak![1]

My name is Golschan Ahmad Haschemi, and I am a performer, a political educator and a cultural scholar. My work oscillates at the interface between artistic, political and scientific theory & practice and includes the intersectional topics of Queer-Feminism, Anti-Racism, Postcolonialism and Anti-Antisemitism.

My primary means of expression are performance art, music and theatre, through which I examine ways of Empowerment on both theoretical and practical levels, blending arts, politics and science. One of my engagements at the moment is with the Performance Collective Technocandy, with whom we are currently playing two performances at Theater Oberhausen. I will be talking more about that later.

The topic I will be discussing today revolves around structural racism, arts and cultural education and what we, as BIPOC[2], experience within these topics:

The experience of *being* – as I am currently living in Germany – and at the same time *not being* part of the German mainstream society is one that I share with quite some of the people in the audience today, as well as with the two people I will be sharing the panel with[3].

We have a *situated knowledge* that makes us understand quickly in which surroundings we are welcome, in which we, our bodies, are treated like aliens and in which ones we can simply be. Oftentimes, we can read a room and its atmosphere within minutes: is this a hostile environment? Are we being seen as the Other? Are we being treated as a token? Do we have to play the role of the counterpart to an otherwise paternalistic setting? Or is this really a space where we can do whatever it is that we want to do and what we are good at, without being stopped, slowed down

---

1   This lecture was part of the conference POST-HEIMAT – Encounter#2 which took place at the Theater an der Ruhr in Mülheim an der Ruhr from 21 – 24 March 2019.

2   BIPOC = Black, Indigenous and People of Colour

3   Panel-talk with Nora Amin, Golschan Ahmad Haschemi and Fatima Çalışkan

or distracted since distraction is – according to Toni Morrison – the severe function of racism?[4]

Also: who is this "We" I am referring to? When I say "We", I am not talking about a homogeneous group of so-called „Menschen mit Migrationshintergrund". I am not talking about having one uniform identity, nor do I claim that every BIPOC, every Migrant, and every racialized Person has to deal with the same kind of racism. Also, there are a lot of other terms and different (self-)identifiers surrounding people who experience racism. Hence, the "We" I am talking about is not *One* but multifaceted.

Within our many dimensions of being, we can connect through shared experiences. Experiences of racism, sexism, and antisemitism, amongst others, and their intersections. But also experiences of solidarity and empowering one another. I am talking about the acknowledgements we can give each other while sharing our manifold experiences and perspectives.

Now, while my wish would be that it is us who shape, form and determine how and by whom these topics are tackled, the status quo tells a different story:

I constantly observe our society's different discourses and dialogues, dealing with terminologies such as cultural diversity, multi- and transculturalism, integration, and assimilation. It is quite telling that a lot of times, these discourses are led without those having a say who actually are the ones affected most by structural and societal oppression. This imbalance in *who participates how* in social life and *who gives shape to society* also determines who shapes the landscape of arts, culture and theatre in Germany.

If we take a look at the ensembles and casts in most German theatres, we stumble upon a gap: We are barely there. The act of *not appearing* in German school books, not being mentioned in what is called German literature, arts and culture, being replaced on stage by white actors, e.g. in blackface, in racialised costumes or blandly white-washed, and then being told that the lack of our representation is due to a shortcoming in Black artists and artists of Colour – all these examples make quite clear who is part of the play, whose stories are told and what does and does not belong to the normative society we live in.

The problem is that it is not just a play but that these acts construct realities. They produce a status quo which does not offer a place for all members of society. The assertion of a norm leads to the exclusion of many who live in this reality but have no

---

4   "[…] the function, the very serious function of racism is distraction. It keeps you from doing your work. It keeps you explaining, over and over again, your reason for being. Somebody says you have no language and you spend twenty years proving that you do. Somebody says your head isn't shaped properly so you have scientists working on the fact that it is. Somebody says you have no art, so you dredge that up. Somebody says you have no kingdoms, so you dredge that up. None of this is necessary. There will always be one more thing."; Toni Morrison's Keynote at Portland State University, May 30th 1975; last visited July, 1st 2021. https://www .mackenzian.com/wp-content/uploads/2014/07/Transcript_PortlandState_Tmorrison.pdf.

space for identification or not one that they can choose. Instead, we are *given* spaces that we are "allowed" to occupy, which is neither self-determined nor liberating.

So, what should we do, in order to keep our sovereignty of interpretation? And what really *can* we do? The reality is that we are living in a society that is based on structural racism and still has a long way of decolonization to go before we reach a point where we can really feel safe. I would even say that point is still a utopia. Nonetheless we have to try. We have to fight. And we must carry on, no matter how small or big the steps are, that we take.

So now I would like to share a part of my life where I took some steps which right now influence not only my artistic work but also my political work as well as my everyday life:

Earlier, I was talking about Solidarity and Empowerment. One way of expressing solidarity is by sharing knowledge so that our siblings can benefit from it. The theatre director and curator Julia Wissert did exactly this. I met her last autumn at the Clinch Festival in Hannover – a festival on postcolonial arts, culture and politics – where she gave a lecture and shared her experiences on the question, "How can theatre be decolonised?" She talked about going into and working within the institutions being as valid as deciding against that step. She talked about taking care of oneself and activist burnout and said that there is never a final answer to all the pressing questions we have surrounding these issues. She talked about trying to change things while being aware of the toll that *trying to change things* within white institutions can take on one. What she described as most helpful was practical advice and tools. And that she likes to share them with everyone who would want them. Julia Wissert talked about a clause on racism that she had developed together with the lawyer Sonja Laaser. This clause can be used within the framework of a contractual relationship in order to protect parties from racist comments or assaults by the employer's staff.[5]

Basically, this means that if I, as a performer or director, enter into a contract with, for example, a theatre or any cultural institution, I could include this clause in my contract to "protect" me from possible racist actions by the staff and employees of the theatre, the theatre being the employer. "Protect" means that there would be actions and consequences in place if there were a racist incident.

My colleagues and I approached Julia Wissert, and she agreed to use the clause. Sonja Laaser sent it to us. The clause provides that if there has been any kind of racist action, the affected party can report it to the artistic director, who will have to deal with the situation. Hence, the responsibility for dealing with a racist incident, comment, or violation does not lie solely with the affected party, but there is an official handling in place that has to take care of the situation. One possible example of

---

5   For more information on the clause and its development see: https://www.antirassismuskla usel.de/; last visited July, 1st 2021.

taking care of the situation would be the artistic director in state obligatory work-shops for their staff to learn about racism, power structures and power imbalance and what it means that they are part of a society that is based on structural racism. These workshops would not only help the artistic director and their staff with clos-ing a professional gap within their profession. But it also takes away the focus from the person who had to suffer through the racist incident and puts the obligation to act where it belongs: on the one who committed the racist act.

If the employer or staff fails to fulfil their contractual obligations, the affected party can withdraw and terminate their contract immediately. Of course, this would only happen in a worst-case scenario, as no performer, artist or director really wants to interrupt their artistic work suddenly and would only do so as a last resort to an otherwise terrible situation.

During our ongoing contract negotiations as Technocandy with Theater Ober-hausen, we inserted the clause into the contract. We sent it to the theatre adminis-tration so they could finalize the contract. The administration took quite some time before they sent the contract back for us to sign. By then, we had already started working on our performance at the theatre. To our surprise, the contract, which we needed to sign for us to be legally protected, was missing the anti-racism clause. After some back-and-forth with the administration and seeing that they weren't co-operative, we contacted the artistic director of Theater Oberhausen to introduce the clause into our contract. We explained the clause and its purpose to him, and he agreed to add it to our contract.

Fast-forward to today: the theatre administration refused to include the clause in our contract. Until a week before our premiere, we did not have a contract, and the theatre administration also claimed that the clause had no legal basis. This is untrue, as a lawyer has developed it and has been legally examined. During our negotiations with the artistic director, we clarified that we would be taking action if we still didn't have a contract shortly before our premiere. We decided to bring up the issue in an interview we were giving about our performance in the national newspaper *taz*. We gave the artistic director, on our part, the generous opportunity to read the interview a couple of days before it was published in order for him to be able to give feedback if there was anything he wouldn't want to be printed. He read the article and didn't object to its publication. Nevertheless, since the interview was published, our Per-formance Collective has suffered persistent attacks via media outlets, theatre staff and local newspapers. What we, as a Performance Collective that deals with racism, queer- and trans-issues, have allowed ourselves to do, is unthinkable for a white in-stitution: instead of being thankful that we, as a Performance Collective that usually works in the precarious independent scene, were allowed by a white institution to work in their halls, we were criticizing them. And not only that, but we were criti-cizing them publicly.

The backlash, the shitstorm and the punishment that we, as a group as well as individuals, have endured since are too many to recount here.

What I think is important and what I want to stress and share with you all is that it only shows how important this clause is. The moment we found a tool which would protect us from racist acts from individuals as well as structural racism by a white institution and their administration, this administration immediately pulled out all the stops on their patriarchal and hegemonic power to protect themselves and the dominant order. This can be described as a logical reaction within a system in which it is not *us* who hold the sovereignty of interpretation on what is a racist act but that this sovereignty stays with the dominant power.

Right now, I am talking about an institution, not theatre groups and collectives working within the independent theatre scene. But that doesn't mean the clause can't be applied to the independent scene, either. It is quite important to understand that this scenario could have happened very well in any free theatre group. We have to understand that it is not "the bad institutions" versus the tolerant alternative theatre scene but that structural racism interlaces with any and every part of society, arts and culture. Hence, it is vital that also we, in this space, whereas I understand – most of the people work in free theatre- and performance groups, adapt our given working conditions and circumstances and see how we can responsibly apply this anti-racism-clause to our work, as well as other tools, to deal with racism and other forms of discrimination. Declarations of intent, for example, the „Erklärung der Vielen", don't do anything for us, who are affected by racism daily, as long as they don't go beyond mere lip service and actually have formulated (legally) binding standards and policies.

I would like to end my input with a tweet I read the other day. It's quite cheesy, but I still like it:

← **Tweet**

 **Shower Thoughts**   ···
@TheWeirdWorld

When people talk about traveling to the past, they worry about radically changing the present by doing something small, but barely anyone in the present really thinks that they can radically change the future by doing something small.

1:31 vorm. · 30. Sep. 2018 · Buffer

Thank you for your attention!

Between Sprachlosigkeit and constant screaming: *Some thoughts on working post Heimat*

Johanna-Yasirr(zz)a Kluhs

2019 fand in Mülheim an der Ruhr ein Netzwerktreffen von Post-Heimat statt, das ich als Mitarbeiterin des koproduzierenden Projekts Interkultur Ruhr begleitete. I was invited to give an introduction speech. The following words hook on this speech, attaching some reflections on the meeting that then was still about to happen. Ich habe mich entschieden, ungefähr so zu schreiben, wie wir beim Netzwerktreffen miteinander gesprochen haben. Was hier eine Mischung aus deutsch und englisch ist, wurde beim realen Treffen mindestens um Arabisch erweitert. Vielsprachiges Arbeiten ist real. Warum also nicht auch das Schreiben?

It might have been in 2017 when I heard first about the attempts to found an empowering network of and for theatre ensembles whose work is especially connected to realities of flight and refuge. As a dramaturg of Pumpenhaus in Münster I learned about Hajusom. As a curator of regional Theaterfestival FAVORITEN 2014 in Dortmund, I started to know Ruhrorter. Being physically mostly located and mentally situated in Ruhrgebiet, I started following the work of Mülheim based theater initiative for some years.

Ausgehend von einem sehr klaren Blick auf die existentiellen Benachteiligungen, denen viele Mitbürger*innen mit Flüchtlingsstatus ausgeliefert waren und sind, soll hier im und mit dem Theater ein temporärer Raum der Wahrhaftigkeit geschaffen werden. Ein sehr spezifischer und ernsthafter nicht-dokumentarischer Theateransatz entsteht, der die Beteiligten nicht zur Kapitalisierung der eigenen Erfahrungen treibt, sondern die gemeinsame Arbeit an der ästhetischen Form in den Mittelpunkt des Zusammenseins stellt.

Ruhrorter haben sich 2012 gegründet. Hajusom 1998. And then 2015 and its repercussions came along. Um die vorher zumeist vereinzelt agierenden Ensembles entsteht eine Nachbarschaft. Mit der verstärkten Aufmerksamkeit auf Körper, die Flucht und Migration ausgesetzt sind, beginnen andere freie Gruppen und auch einige staatliche Theater ihre Ensembles zu ergänzen. Being situated in the same challenging conditions as longtime operating initiatives had been for years, the longtime operating initiatives understood the potential of uniting forces. They hooked on the possibility of creating attention for their working situations. Die so zu erkämpfende Sichtbarkeit zielt in drei Richtungen:

Der Gesellschaft

Flucht und Migration werden in Deutschland als tagesaktuelle Ausnahmen erzählt. Zwar wächst das (Selbst-)Bewusstsein vom „Einwanderungsland", gleichzeitig stehen als kanonische Narrative vor allem Erzählungen von (temporärer) Prekarität, Heimatverlust und Re-integration, politischer und humanitärer Krise, etc. zur Verfügung. Es ist schwer, eine Politik der Differenz auf diesen Erzählungen aufzubauen. Ich habe es von Anfang an als Anliegen des – durch teilweise jahrzehntelange Arbeitserfahrungen – weitsichtigen Netzwerks „Post-Heimat" verstanden, 2015 auch hier als Brennglas zu verwenden. Der Heraufbeschwörung der Einzigartigkeit dieser Präsenz von Menschen mit Fluchtgeschichten in Form einer konzentrierten Krisen-Erzählung hält das Netzwerk, auch durch die Titelgebung, eine Erzählung von Historizität entgegen: Richtung Vergangenheit und Zukunft. Damit verbunden ist auch ein Selbstappell an die Strukturen der gesellschaftlichen Bezugnahme selbst.

Der Institutionen

Die Arbeit daran findet in der Arbeit an neuen Theaterformen und -stoffen statt, aber auch daran, Förder-, Präsentations- und Probestrukturen einzurichten, die der realen Komplexität des Theaterschaffens in einer Migrationsgesellschaft entsprechen. The working realities of Post-Heimat groups is so different from the structures of funding bodies and collaborating institutions. Theatre is about present bodies. Im Kontext von Flucht und Migration sind wir permanent damit konfrontiert, dass der anwesende Körper keineswegs selbstverständlich ist. But that it has to be constantly defended in the crossfires of European migration politics. In this specific intersection of theatre and Aufenthaltspolitik, doing theatre means visa and residence operating, networking, lobbying and fundraising. Its members are policy instructors, archivists, friends, consultants, activists, research institutes, sociologists, and urban planners. The production of theatre is anyway not protected from the rules of the outside world, its migration policies, societal conflicts, racist ideologies and stereotypes or unjust distribution of resources – but in the case of the network members of Post-Heimat the environment is cutting right through the middle of what it means to do theatre. The norm(al) of the theatre is excluding the largest part of possible theatre forms and makers. Monolinguality / the dominance of German language, genre borderism, professionalism, and the big 1x1 of German bureaucracy are just some components I want to mention here. Creating a network of groups which are highlighting the problems which are caused through these conditions, die aber gleichzeitig sehr verschiedene Machstatus im Feld haben, multipliziert die politische Potenz. Die Entwicklung einer klaren kulturpolitischen Agenda war mithin auch ein großes Anliegen des Netzwerktreffens in Mülheim.

Der Produzierenden selbst

Die Hauptkommunikationsrichtungen des Netzwerks zielen nach außen. Es schien immer klar, dass das Netzwerk einen Common Ground miteinander auch als Mittel zum Zweck der kraftvollen kulturpolitischen Aktion schaffen muss. In order to achieve a standing for themselves individually, each member has a different strategy. To mention some: Creating sovereign forms of non-documentarist work with mixed groups or: just working with professionally educated people. Working with people who are explicitly not refugees, but people in exile. Strengthening the members of the groups to get them in a professional training and curriculum here. Die eigene Existenz behaupten heißt also immer: Distinktion. E.g. from initiatives which are less professional, successful, probably less "consequent". To overcome these dynamics of concurrence is a self-given challenge of Post-Heimat. Das Ringen um Produktionsethiken im konkreten Theaterschaffen, die kritische Überprüfung der eigenen Narrative und ihrer (unfreiwilligen) Implikationen und der Machtverhältnisse in den eigenen Gruppen oder zwischen ihnen und den auftraggebenden Institutionen, war sicher ein zentrales, wenn auch untergründiges Thema des Mülheimer Treffens. Invitations to a strong self-critique were brought out vigorously by a community of researchers, who were accompanying the meeting. Not being forced to hold on to an always precarious artistic reality of production and self-sustenance, the researchers were providing the freedom and urge to discuss the internal conflicts and questions. Creating change in the outside necessarily has to ground on a change in the own habits and blind spots. But: it's one of the most dangerous activities. As it's destabilizing from within, it depends on a strong frame in order to fulfill itself. Da dieser allerdings nicht gegeben ist, sondern auch erkämpft werden muss, bleibt oftmals nur die Verteidigung als möglicher Aktionsmodus. Oder eben die Arbeit an einem gegenseitigen Halt in einem Netzwerk, das den Konflikt zum Common Ground erklärt und so starke und schützende Strukturen schafft, in denen Fragilität existieren kann.

Willingly or not – Post-Heimat theatre initiatives and ensembles are institutions of critic. „Einfach Theater machen" ist hier immer schon eine politische Kampfansage. Ganz programmatisch wird hier Abstand genommen von der Idee eines scheinbar natürlichen genealogischen Bezugspunkt des Theatermachens – die Initiativen stehen in einer Zukunft, deren Gegenwart erst noch entwickelt werden muss. Und sie machen es selbst.

A reflection

Kenda Hmeidan

I was asked to prepare a keynote for the PostHeimat event "Encountering the Future" 2019, which took place at the Maxim Gorki Theatre. Here, I will share some thoughts from this Keynote. Back then, when I started writing the text and thus reflecting on the productions I participated in during the past couple of years, it only became harder and harder for me to formulate a conclusion and to have clear answers to the questions which accompanied me from the moment I arrived until now. So, this text is not a "how-to guide"; instead, I am writing to share and reflect upon some of my experiences at productions at Gorki Theatre.

I am Kenda Hmeidan. I come from Syria and moved to Berlin in 2016, after finishing my acting studies at the Higher Institute of Drama and Art in Damascus. I joined Gorki as a member of the Exil-Ensemble.

The language is one of the first and foremost challenges I must face as an actress in Germany. I actually have to translate the whole text, word by word, and jump between three languages: Arabic, English and German. By now, I call it "the language obsession." The moment I analyse the words, I start to feel them, and I can immediately start playing with them. It is interesting to notice how every language has its structure, which I must follow. Each language puts me as an actress in a different playground. I notice how my voice has a different pitch and how my face and body move to express myself. There is certainly a difference from the way I act in Arabic.

I remember a friend of mine once told me about a writer who wrote about languages, and this sentence stayed with me. She said: "Every language has her own eyes, and speaking a second language is like having a second soul." Of course, in the beginning, it is unusual. Who is this person talking? I feel it is not really myself. Now I realise it is me, with new tools to describe myself, using new methods to work and acting under new circumstances.

Furthermore, there is the complicated matter of rehearsing in a foreign language. After three years in Germany, I thought I had grasped and understood the language quite well. Nonetheless, discussing plays, expressing my thoughts and improvising – in German, for example – is a complex process.

I must be highly focused and do my best to follow what's happening. Because I have to ask many questions to understand the process, I sometimes feel isolated, especially when I am the only one who doesn't speak German. In some situations, it is not enough to understand the general idea or feel what's happening on stage. One needs to grasp every idea very concretely: Why, when, where, and what is the message underneath all of it?

Sometimes, I miss what I like most about acting in theatre, which is the discussions within the group during rehearsals, when each team member shares an idea or a thought, which opens a new door, developing the content together and collectively working on the material. I miss the kind of discussions that inspire the whole process. During those times, when everyone is sitting around the table speaking in German very fast and coming up with new ideas, I am busy running from one person to the next, trying to figure out what is going on. And the moment I actually get it and can comment on this particular idea, they have already moved on, starting a new discussion about another topic. This gives me the feeling of always being late and forced to run through ideas actually to feel present. At this point, language becomes dull and not very interesting to discover and learn.

Then I participated in the play *Ausser Sich*, directed by Sebastian Nübling (2018), which was like a revelation for me. It is a play after the novel by Sasha Marianna Salzmann, 364 pages, in German. I read six pages from the original book, and then I had to ask for the book in English. I studied it, then went back to the German version and started to prepare for my role in German. I took my time to prepare the play thoroughly in advance. I felt like I owned this language for the first time in Germany. I learned how to make this language mine, how to prepare the text, bend and form it, and not just say it. I could act and feel the text, and I let it pass through me. This feeling is incredible because this had been one of my biggest fears before I came to Germany. I always ask myself: how can I own the text on stage? It is not my goal to phonetically memorise the text, and I don't want this to become the case when working in a foreign language.

Hamletmaschine (dir. by Sebastian Nübling 2018) is also one of my most meaningful experiences at Gorki. The working language was mostly English and Arabic since six people of the cast were native Arabic speakers. So ironically, the director and the assistants sometimes felt isolated. They waited until we finished the discussion, and then we translated for them. *Hamletmaschine* was more like a dissection process of the text and transforming this process to images, movements and embodied experiences. There was a huge see-through curtain splitting the stage into two spaces; on it, the text was written in German and Arabic. So, the matter of language is up to the audience; they choose when to read and in which language. I remember how my confidence as an actress got back to me; I didn't need language to express myself because bodies can tell stories, too. This play is an experiment to build a bridge and reach the audience. Connecting with the audience, thus holding the tension, transmitting a feeling and entering a sort of silent dialogue.

This connection sheds light on a further important aspect. I am an Arabic actress; this implies a politically charged background. While practising art in Syria, I actually never had the chance to voice out my political opinion on stage due to extreme censorship. So, for the first time, I encountered a space of free speech and freedom to express my political and social views. Finally, I am able to understand that my opinion does count, and therefore, I carry a responsibility. So, I need to find my stance to understand the political system I am situated in and the audience I am performing for. Some of the work I did at Gorki isn't about my personal story or my political background, but I notice that many people still read my work through the lens of my background. This means they expect a particular image, a fixed story, but the performance does not always correspond to my personal story or background. So, I ask myself about the content, the group of people I supposedly represent, and the culture I stand for. Do I have a particular responsibility towards my audience and fellow colleagues to break certain stereotypes?

So, I end this reflection with more questions and thoughts.

Do I want to tell my personal story on stage? If the answer is yes, then how and in which form? Actually, in which language?

And if the answer is no, what is the reason? What remains private and why?

While trying to settle in a new country, learn a new language, politically position myself and prove myself as an actress, I wonder what role I play in this society. Am I a professional actress working in a theatre? Does my political background and the war in Syria define me and my work? How can I escape this loop? This narration? To ask it differently and in a larger context: How can I encounter the future?

Colonial Neighbours – on how to boil rice with a pot full of air/on the wickedness of imagination

Lynhan Balatbat-Helbock

Each day, humanity is walking closer to its end.

People did not live a waking hour without pain caused by the imagination of home and its ever-changing borders. Many wars, some fondly forgotten only to be reenacted in different times yet similar spaces, have been waged under the treacherous imagination of what *Heimat* and its extension should look, smell and sound like.

we think, therefore, we are...

we imagine; therefore, others are not...

The PostHeimat project, a network meeting in cooperation with *Maxim Gorki Theatre* and the *Theater an der Ruhr*, was initiated to dedicate space to encounters to question notions of migration, representation, identity and finding forms of alliance within theatre and the arts. SAVVY Contemporary was invited to think along these lines and propose a display format that engages with the conference.

The participatory archive project Colonial Neighbours, which hosts a series of material and immaterial traces, focuses on the stories behind the objects, their entanglement from the donor to the object, and our situatedness in the perpetuating power mechanisms of violence. The archive that Bonaventure Soh Bejeng Ndikung initiated is hosting objects, stories, packaging material and traces that can be found in the cellars, attics, urban space or our memory.

The donated objects that are often marked by racist content and uncanny shapes are haunted by a past that is not yet fully revealed or understood. The collective engagement with the archive purposefully points to the orchestrated gaps within history, society, education and politics regarding the colonial period of Germany and its repercussions.

When SAVVY Contemporary´s archival project Colonial Neighbours was invited to participate in the project, it was important that the collection of objects speaking of and to the colonial history of Germany would not stand alone.

LUCID DREAMING– was conceived as a part of the *FRAGMENT* series, which is composed of interventions in and out of SAVVY Contemporary's long-term collective archive project on German colonial history. In this series, artists, researchers, activists, and cultural producers are invited to engage with the Colonial Neighbours objects, activating the archive's content and critically engaging with its content.

In the sixth edition of the FRAGMENT series, the Berlin-based artist Lizza May David was invited to overshadow some objects with an artwork in which she explores the notion of representation of domestic workers from the Philippines.

In the mixed media work "Looking Inwards" (2008), which was composed of video footage of a domestic worker and archival materials, we experience an intimate portrait of the working and living space of a domestic helper (the artist's aunt) in Hong Kong. Filming within the interior of her employer's household, including the furniture, view from the window and personal belongings, the video visualizes how power relations are interconnected with private space.

Lizza May David´s work display was arranged to converse with objects from the Colonial Neighbours archive directly. One of the objects from the archive, which is a journal called Kolonie und Heimat (1907–1920), was published by the Frauenbund der Deutschen Kolonialgesellschaft (Women's Association of German Colonial Society), which was one of the most influential organizations of the German empire that campaigned for an expansive colonialist policy. The articles written in German show clearly how race and gender constructions were established on different levels and fields of colonial policies: on the example of labour policies, education and moralities, through the discourse of hygiene, purity and health and within the field of ethnology, photography and advertisement.

The Frauenbund promoted the colonial project within the German empire and trained and sent out white German women to the colonies to serve as 'keepers of German manners and morals.

How we imagine and subsequently see, hear and define our opposite is heavily influenced by a long genealogy of hatred. Not only are the remnants of this violent period lingering in our attics or basements, but the very same foul mechanisms that enabled the displacement, the amplification of one's lands through the limitation or dispossession of someone else's that are still in place.

When SAVVY Contemporary's archive project got invited to engage with the Post Heimat ENCOUNTER, it was important to walk back in time, highlighting fragments that support the very same structures that have denied people's right to mobility, land, dignity and life, then as much as now.

The Colonial Neighbours display with these toxic objects and Lizza May David's intimate portrait of an individual claiming space in writing her own story despite the oppressive white narrative that holds one captive was an invitation to reflect on the ongoing colonial entanglements that blur our vision in redefining borders, Heimat, belonging and ultimately how we relate to one another.

This is the main door of the house.
I start here.
This is the shoe cabinet.
And on the other side, there is a chair for you to sit on when you put on your shoes.
This is the dining table,
together with the living room on the other side.
[blank screen]
[blank screen]
There is a terrace in the living room.
I will open the door,
and outside, this is the scenery.
This is the Hongkong Stadion,
the Indian Club,
overlooking the Sea.
This side is already Causeway Bay.
This is the corridor going inside.
From the corridor, on the first door, at the left side, this is the study room.
This is the collection of my boss:
Toy soldiers.
[blank screen]
He likes collecting toy soldiers.
[blank screen]
This is the guest room,
located at the right side of the corridor
[blank screen]
[blank screen]
And this is the children's room.
And this is the master's room.
And this is the master's toilet.
And this is the kitchen.
It's full of cabinets, surrounded by cabinets.
This is the back of the door.
And this is the washroom.
Servant's room. Oh, servant's bathroom, I mean.
We have a back door.
Beside the washroom, there is the servant's room.
It's quite small, but we are happy about this because of our privacy.
They have two servants.
So, we have a double deck.
One can sleep on the top, and the other can sleep on the lower part.

Or deck, I mean.

This is the upper deck with the cabinets, which one servant can be used.

Mali ng English ko [My English is wrong]

And this is the lower deck.

I am occupying this.

And since the room is too small,

we have no cabinet to put our clothes.

So, I think of an idea of how to hang my clothes.

I just put it in plastic and put it outside of the wall.

There is also a cassette here.

And we can play CD.

Sometimes, if we have time to listen to it.

We have no TV.

So we just listen to the music.

We usually finish our job at night, around 10 o'clock.

And it's time for us to go to our room.

Sometimes, we are not sleepy yet, and then we listen to music.

And if it's schooldays, we get up around 5.30.

Because the girls are packing lunch.

Because they are whole day in school.

But if they do not pack their lunch, we are getting up at 6 o'clock.

And when it is weekend, we can get up at 7.30.

Looking Inwards

2008, DVD PAL, 4:3, Single-channel video, color, sound; 1 framed letter and mini-DV cassette

This video shows the apartment in Hongkong, where my aunt Nerry Hernandez has lived and worked as a domestic helper for more than 14 years. She independently filmed this footage without me asking her to do it, in order to fill in missing scenes for the documentary "Two Years More," which I was creating about her. In order to respect the privacy of the employer's family she asked me to cut out scenes with family pictures, which could be seen in the video. My artistic intervention in this case meant to change the "censored" family pictures into a blank screen and show it to a wider audience.

The result is "Looking Inwards", an intimate approach about body and space, ethics of image-making and turning gazes. It provides a glimpse into her life, captured with a mini-DV camera that she specifically arranged for this purpose. The footage was made in the same year (2005), when Youtube.com was just starting to be launched.

Looking Inward © David&Hernandez

Looking Inward © David&Hernandez

IV. Es

Language Between World Theatre and Theatre in Exile: From the impossible collective understanding to the possible collective imagination

A Talk with Azadeh Sharifi

says

Thinking Diversity Anew for Equal Rights in Performing Arts

s

Transnational Theatre Encounters: Reflections on Mediation and Power

A Theatre Practice-based Exercise in Doing and Undoing Diversity: The Open Border Ensemble (2017–2020) Experiment at the Münchner Kammerspiele

and

Ta

Witnessing a New Stage in German Theatre

lk

Das PostHeimat-Netzwerk als Contact Zone

(En)countering the Future

s

Notes on Intersectional-diverse Dramaturgical Approaches

A Conversation with Azadeh Sharifi by Ruba Totah and Jonas Tinius

Ruba: *How do you describe contemporary European theatre from the perspective of inclusion, diversity, and openness? What are the achievements and failures when discussed from perspective of theatre?*

Azadeh: I would like to start from a German perspective and then move on to contemporary European theatre. In Germany, there is the idea that theatre – and all other art institutions – is accessible to everyone. The old cultural policy credo "Kultur für alle" (culture for everyone) goes back to the 1980s, and Hilmar Hoffmann suggests that it's a matter of education and mediation so that different social groups and social classes can enjoy the programme of these institutions. And since most of the German institutions are funded by state and city governments and the funding comes from taxes, all people in Germany fund the state and city theatres, and all should have access. The relatively cheap tickets, at least compared to other European countries, underline this claim that no structural barriers could exclude people. That is far from reality. These institutions are elitist, bourgeois, and exclusive. German theatre has a long history of being embedded in an idea of German nationhood and ethnic and national unity, but also in a feudalistic system where the artistic leader has unlimited power. White cis-men mostly lead German theatres; the programmes and repertoire are still oriented towards a white German middle-class audience with plays that are mostly written by men and directed by men with mostly white cismen as the leading characters. To sum it up, the German theatre is neither diverse nor has any big changes for becoming so in the near future. And I would think the same goes for many other Western European countries.

I would even go further and say that when we, as a society, talk about diversity, it is to cover up the racist and colonial structures that are hidden underneath. Because diversity, at least within neoliberal contexts, always suggests that there is a norm and a core of society and the rest, in terms of class, gender, race, sexuality and ability, are deviations from this norm. And I don't want to undo the amazing work, the fight and the struggle of BIPOCs and other marginalised groups. However, I am becoming more and more hesitant to use this term (diversity) and rather emphasise the white colonial structure of the institution.

German society and its cultural institutions have changed dramatically, at least if we look into how German society looked like after WWII. Still, this moment in time has always been exceptional due to the Holocaust. Since at least 1955, German society has changed through migrant labour workers, refugees (and here I am not talking about the wave of people in the past ten years, but at least the past 40–50 years from Vietnam, Chile, Iran, Sri Lanka and many other regions of the planet), German minorities like Sinto/Sintize, German Jews, and Black Germans and other minoritised groups who have 'resurfaced' in Germany.

What has changed after over 65 years of labour agreements and many different struggles and fights of racialised groups is that the second and following generations of former migrants and non-white Germans are claiming space within German society. They are fed up with the experience of exclusion, discrimination, and the image of Germany as a solely white, Christian nation. The term postmigrant society has been coined from the postmigrant theatre movement precisely for that reason, suggesting that Germany is in a constant transformation and that migration is one of its principal driving forces. But other movements and communities (ADEFRA, ISD, Kanak Attack, etc.) also deeply impacted how change, or at least partial change, was achieved.

Ruba: *This intergenerational aspect of migration is crucial, I agree, also for the concepts we develop to understand change and transformation. How would you consider the relationship between intergenerational experiences of migration, and the development of the concept of postmigrant society?*

Azadeh: I think it is necessary to be very precise regarding the history of art/theatre productions by and with marginalised communities and subjects. I feel that there is a myth or a claim that "migrants" (that is, non-white descendants of former migrants) became artists through postmigrant theatre. While it is true that post-migrant theatre, Ballhaus Naunynstrasse as the theatrical space and artists like Shermin Langhoff and Tuncay Kulaoglu have opened a door for many artists who came afterwards. From 2008 onwards, when Ballhaus Naunynstrasse re-opened, postmigrant was declared a label by artistic director Shermin Langhoff; The idea was that a white German majority could and should no longer claim that racialised and minoritised communities and subjects were "voiceless", they would lack talent, artistic quality or all in all, culture. These, by the way, are statements that have been asserted by politicians, cultural policymakers, and leaders in the artistic field over the years when they justified why racialised and minoritised communities remained under-funded, excluded or simply not even considered. Shermin Langhoff, now one of the most powerful artistic directors in the German theatre, stated that

"Who has the right to say 'That is art'? And 'that is not art'? How art should be or not be. Or what is part of art and what is not part of it. There is a power of labelling that is outside of our reach, a power of interpretation that is (ironically) not completely in our own hands." (Freitext 2013:9; my own translation)

Ruba: *You discussed the term "post-migrant" by proposing it as a movement pushing forward an intervention in the theatre scene. Listening to you brings me to our very own PostHeimat network of which Jonas and I are part as researchers, but which also includes artists, activists, and theatre groups who already have been working or had worked with artists from different backgrounds. Within the network, we are introducing another term, and the post-migrant term is infiltrating it in one way or another, and that is the idea of PostHeimat. The network also builds on the concept of "dehumanisation" developed by Bilgin Ayata. Across our different encounters, we have thus been discussing what is the relation between post-migrant theatre and a PostHeimat vision?*

Azadeh: I think it is interesting to think through concepts that come from cultural (or even community) practice and theoretical or academic discourses. It makes sense to appropriate labels, concepts and even derogatory terms to make them your own or something else. It's a resistance strategy that has been used over and over by marginalised groups and subjects. If Horst Seehofer can create a *Heimatministerium*, why can't those who are excluded from the initial idea re-imagine what this idea of "Heimat" would mean? I myself am highly suspicious of the term. It is always conceptualised with some idea of nationhood, language, ethnicity, belonging in mind. And I would rather stick to a form of strategic essentialism, as with "post-migrant", that stays suspicious and very aware of why there is a need for these identity politics. Maybe it's because I myself am a refugee child who never belonged neither there nor here. How is this place, these people, this nation my Heimat when I should have better died on the way to claim my own story?

Jonas: *The concept of "post-Heimat", as you already alluded to with reference to Seehofer, was a director response at a particular moment in time in German society and politics. More than anything else, we were perhaps interested with the term to problematise precisely these binaries of belonging and not belonging, because as you rightly point out, too many cultural narratives are rooted, quite literally, in the idea of fixed identities.*

Azadeh: I stay alert with certain terms like *Heimat*, which can be repurposed or used deliberately to include new meanings – and we have this discussion around a lot of these terms where there is controversy as to whether the violent, exclusive, or derogatory meaning and history of it can be erased, rewritten or at least given new meanings. Maybe for some communities, this might be possible, but this will never be the case for someone like me who even gets censored for speaking her mother tongue in public. My experience, like many others, doesn't fit into the concept of *Heimat* because I would rather use a Farsi word, which would be so much closer to a feeling of belonging that I have. I am not suggesting that I am in any way fluent in Farsi, nor do I feel connected to Iran or Iranian society. Still, my experience as a person who fled Iran with her family to come to Germany with the feeling of diaspora is multifaceted when it comes to language. Farsi is my secret and beloved mother tongue for private family conversations and very intimate and nostalgic feelings. At the same time, the German language and Germany are always the spaces where I had to find myself, place myself, and alienate myself. I am drawing from my very personal experience to make a bigger point. If we, in the truest sense of the word, want to decolonise our institutions, and I speak about the decolonisation of German academia and German art institutions, because they are deeply rooted in colonial epistemology, we can't operate in the same old terms or insert new meanings to them. Audre Lorde's wise words always and still ring true: We can't dismantle the master's house with the master's tools. And I think, in many ways, we are still trying to fit in, to make the system work for us, while we know that the neoliberal system has already swallowed us.

We might now have more and more BIPOCs in leading artistic positions, and they are doing an amazing job, still fighting and struggling to keep the doors open for others and the next generation while simultaneously being constantly evaluated or criticised by state funding agencies, the media, and a white majority "audience". But if we don't keep a radical position, acknowledging that, for example, we want to be part of the German art institutions or academia, which means making a bigger compromise, to make decolonisation rather a metaphor than radical action, we also become the problem. I think this goes for us, BIPOCs who are "inside" the system, as well as our white allies.

Jonas: *You already alluded to the entanglement of the academic and artistic production of knowledge. How do you conceptualise the relation between the two in terms of the relation between epistemological, aesthetic, and social change across the fields of theatre and academia?*

Azadeh: I think, frankly, that the change in art institutions is a little bit further than the change and discussions in academia. People are still more comfortable talking about racism and colonialism when they concern places far away, for instance on the African continent or in the US, and choose to speak rather about "integration" and "inclusion" of migrants, about "diversity", which in the end still always means the Other, instead of questioning the paradigms of their fields and disciplines. But some changes are inevitable and unstoppable. And the changes are, at least in the university and art colleges, demanded by (BIPOC and white) students. I experience much gratitude from students who tell me that they have hardly had any BIPOC professors or teachers, and that they see it as a big loss. I have been teaching at many different universities in Germany, Austria, and Switzerland, just to name the countries that also concern the PostHeimat network. Many of the students are active and call themselves activists. They are interested in being artists, art scholars, or scholars and work actively towards dismantling the colonial, patriarchal, and neoliberal systems that keep so many of us and them out. The Black Lives Matter movement and regional, local BIPOC anti-racist work inspire them. This is true for students in Bern as well as for UdK students here in Berlin, and I hope that true change is coming.

But in general, German theatre studies are almost unaffected by the development and changes, not really able to react to the demands and also far away from discussions that are currently happening on an international level. Sruti Bala's article on decolonising theatre and performance studies has been one of the main impacts for, at least European, discourses and departments, and international institutions like PSi have pledged towards an antiracist and anticolonial practice not only to show solidarity to the Black Lives Matter Movement, but also to acknowledge and dismantle the complicities of their own positions.

The frustration is very real. Together with other German theatre scholars, who are all German, but not all based in Germany, we have started a (small) network. We are creating a platform for the conversations currently missing from German theatre studies.

Jonas: *One of the biggest issues we dealt with in the PostHeimat network, but which is crucial also beyond our activities, is how institutions sustainably deal with criticality. How do you remain critical, maintain a spirit of doubt and questioning, of calling into question norms and power, without having an initially critical practice or idea become the norm and thereby hegemonical again? We see this in the dissolution of so many of the groups, who simply didn't receive funding anymore, because "migration" was struck off the list for relevant cultural funding policies, and got replaced by the next big thing: digitaliy, AI, which will then be replaced by another one in ten years again.*

Azadeh: I am not surprised. These systems are never made to include "diversity" and implement it, like many other terms before. I am thinking of Sara Ahmed, who once said that commitments to diversity or to diversify are, in fact, "non-performatives" that do not bring about what they name. Can we trust these institutions, even if they are led by someone who comes from a marginalised community? No, we can't. We can't build our careers on diversifying these systems while we actually are complicit in exploiting people and their lives for the entertainment of a (white majority) audience. I don't believe that any of the projects where refugees were put on stage to tell their story to a white audience have made these audiences more "understanding" of the circumstances of the actors. These projects were targeting a white audience because a non-white audience is very familiar with the experience of violence, not belonging, migration, and loss.

The question is, rather, how can we build networks, relationships, and connections that are sustainable, acknowledge the needs of those who are in precarious circumstances, and enable us to create other ways of engagement? I really like how Elisa Liepsch, Nadine Jessen, and Ewelina Benbenek have tried to think about the art institution of solidarity. It is one attempt to think and engage. But then again, I am suspicious if these are possible within the walls of these art institutions.

Ruba: *I do not want to end our conversation with a pessimistic view will pose a question about the positive that we could take forward. What do you see in theatre and academic practice that makes you hopeful?*

Azadeh: I do believe in the power and magic of art, especially theatre and performance! But I remain pessimistic towards the institution itself when it comes to accessibility and decolonization. And it might stem from my experience and my current desire to let go. Letting go of the idea that the processes can be done within these institutions. If we acknowledge that they are deeply rooted in a colonial and imperial tradition, why do we want to change them? Why not burn them down?

In one of my seminars, one of my students, her name is Zelal, called us all out and said „Das Kind ist in den Brunnen gefallen" (the child has fallen in the well), meaning there is nothing to change. And I do understand her more than ever. I think as long as we don't change the rotten system from its core, burn it down, and build something that is truly built for the majority and not an elitist group, we are only putting a bandage over dead flesh.

But who am I to throw the first stone? I fought for so long to be in the system, and I now rely, like other tokens, on holding this space very close because it is clear to me that it will be taken away if I become undesirable. And this is something that has happened to all of us tokens in these institutions.

Jonas: *Whether we want to be optimist or pessimist, we are grappling with these issues. Perhaps the worst that could happen is that we either blindly believe in progress, or give up like a nihilist. We are in neither of the two states and I think that is a good thing. But who knows?*

Azadeh: I agree with you on this point. As I see all these amazing students and some dear colleagues who are willing to do the work within academia and art institutions. They will be holding the people in power accountable. And they are doing it right now. Many current changes would not have been possible without the so-called prior generation, and now I am putting my hope also in the so-called next generation. That is a beacon of hope that I have for Germany and its art institutions (and hopefully also its academic institutions). BIPOC and marginalised communities are no longer willing to be put down. They are fighting, questioning, challenging, and hopefully building something that unsettles the colonial patriarchal, and neoliberal structures.

Transnational Theatre Encounters: Reflections on Mediation and Power

Ruba Totah

In the past ten years, Syrian migrants' life stories have played on European stages, urging an anthropological query on migrant artists' transnational cultural experiences. In 2016, I started a research journey to understand how migrating artists from Syria formulated their cultural experiences in Europe. I based the query on the relationship between transnationalism and culture, which heightens issues of cultural freedom and is directly connected to the Arab uprisings. Before and after settling in Europe, migrating performing arts communities from Syria and other Arab countries ventured to stand against hegemonies on freedoms by emphasising discussions around nationalism and interculturalism. My anthropological research[1] delved into these discussions, connecting artists' subjectivities and free will with means of nationalising, de-nationalizing, and de-colonizing the national and transnational spaces they inhabit. The research explores how imperialism and its subsequent global systems, authoritative regimes, and solidarity spaces have furnished discussions on nationalism and influenced the development of artists' mobility and subjectivity. It provides that artists' transnational cultural experiences comprise homemaking trajectories and relational aesthetics (Totah 2020a, b), which became cases of interculturalism that hamper migrant artists' holistic subjectivity representations on stage and limit their investigation beyond their subject towards their free will (Totah 2021b).

At the beginning of my research journey, I felt that I was in a time machine travelling virtually through Palestine, Germany, and Syria in various historical moments during the thirties, forties and the last decade. These 'travels' revived various conceptions of nationalism that people held in these places, and they aided my analysis and understanding of the performance of transmigrants in Europe today. Encountering communities of various backgrounds challenged the assumptions and preconceptions that I brought to the research as an ethnographer and revealed a challenging connection with Western forms of anthropology. By constantly contemplating

---

1   This paper is partially drawn from my doctoral dissertation *Cultural Transnationalism and the Arab Uprising: Migrating Artists from Syria to Europe.*

and rethinking my conceptions, I aimed to define what Smith and Guarnizo (1998) provide as transnationalism from below while closely considering artists' specific historical contexts. Thus, I combined reflexivity and immersion approaches to lead a multi-site and non-Western-oriented bottom-up study of transnationalism. This method broke binaries and hegemonic conceptions when exploring transnational concepts beyond a general and unchallenged Western-oriented application of diversity and inclusion.

This article demonstrates how my position as an anthropologist affected the conclusions I stated above about artists' free will and their subjective development on European stages. The article provides counter-narratives from a non-Western perspective by demonstrating the value of biographicity and apprenticeship as ethnographic approaches and their relevance to specific moments during the Open Border Ensemble (OBE). It considers aspects of an anthropologist's positionality in the intercultural space of transnational theatre practice and reconsiders the margins of liminalities in this space.

My ethnographic research relies on formulations I concluded while spending time in Europe – primarily in Germany – since 2016. As a result of modernism, Western anthropology often focuses on realising the 'other' in its aesthetics and explanations. To the contrary, I aimed to understand smaller local narratives that may appear relevant to postmodernism from a non-European perspective. In this way, the artists' and author's narratives may be transformed into an activity in which politics, aesthetics, history, and interpretation converge. My research thus became an attempt at what Said called, 'continuing, protracted, and sustained adversarial resistance to the discipline and the praxis of anthropology (as representative of "outside" power) itself' (Said: 299). The grounded approach relatively broke the 'relationship of force between the outside Western ethnographer-observer and a primitive, or at least different but certainly weaker and less developed, non-Western society' (296). As such, I make conclusions on nationalism and subjectivity – where exile, gender, resilience, and homemaking are the main tools for breaking the dominant anthropological perspective. This analysis has challenged the definition of 'diversity' in spheres dominated by European theatre makers' perspectives by including non-European ones, and it contributes to expanding the discussion beyond the canonisation of the diversity approach in Europe. It provides an existential understanding of migration experiences in the creation of art by posing questions of mediality and translation.

Methodological Positionality and the Transcultural Space

The research was conducted during an apprenticeship within the performing arts sector in Germany and beyond[2] as the main site of empirical questioning and methodology. Data collection was completed using a variety of methods: biographical interviews, discussions during multiple meetings and the Post-Heimat meetings and encounters, and participant observations in two creative processes at the Münchner Kammerspiele and Schauspiel Hannover theatre organisations. At Münchner Kammerspiele, I observed the aesthetics of the theatrical productions of the OBE while the team prepared a trilingual theatre piece. However, my role evolved naturally into a practice approach, where I combined observations with support to the team, becoming an interpreter and an 'advisor on dramaturgy', as the team members called me several times. Thus, the experience developed into an apprenticeship approach, which suited the empirical methods by enriching my understanding of interculturalism and transnational theatre concepts. The ensemble also benefited from my dramaturgical and communicative support. Overall, it was a rewarding learning experience for all members of the group who participated in this transnational theatre experience.

The four-month apprenticeship included daily contact with artists from January to May 2018[3]. We spoke about the performance, coping with the weather, living conditions in the new country of Germany, sharing food, and attending other performances. During the first rehearsals, I regularly attended to observe the project team. Initially, I silently sat to the side, only observing, taking notes, and helping with some translations and interpreting. I was present daily with my notebook, and I clarified my note-taking purpose. As I answered questions about my notes, speaking the artists' languages helped me forge unintentional bonds between us, which made the discussion about my role clearer. On the third day of rehearsal, I was asked to shift my role to an interpreter (Arabic-English-Arabic) due to the actual interpreter's incompetence in (German-Arabic-German). My silent, note-taking observer role thus shifted into an active interpreter and cultural mediator role of daily one-on-one meetings, group improvisations, and translation of some texts. I wrote my reflections and notes during breaks or after the rehearsal sessions. I intended to do the interpreting only until another interpreter was found. However, the director indicated that the project team felt a need for the socio-political facilitation that I did, so I was asked to continue with the interpretation task. The artists had become

---

2   The research scope included Germany, France, the Netherlands, Sweden, Italy, and Austria.

3   The artists were theatre actors and amateur dancers. The four-month apprenticeship, from January to May 2018, included daily contact with artists from Syria, Palestine and Germany who were chosen for their talent to participate in the OBE, whereas I arranged with the Münchner Kammerspiele to study the creative processes of the OBE.

accustomed to my interpretation style and were comfortable speaking freely with me. Some artists expressed that my presence gave them a sense of home, primarily through the culture-specific jokes and songs we shared. I was later asked to join the team on stage as a translator, but I expressed that it would not be possible.

Later, two weeks before the premiere, the team invented a 'wooden machine' for translation as a solution to the problem of translation in a trilingual performance. The wooden machine replaced me during the rehearsals, and I returned to being an observer. Three days before the premiere, the director decided to 'activate' my role, and I was again asked to give input on improvisations and texts in the final rehearsals. I helped finalise the Arabic versions of the texts, provided translations, and did some dramaturgical content advisory.

For the benefit of research material analysis, my apprenticeship at the Münchner Kammerspiele contributed to an in-depth understanding of the moments I observed. It also enabled rechecking of analysed moments and interviews as I continuously revisited my reflections and field notes to check the reasonability of my analysis. I also reflected upon questions concerning my participation in the artists' group and my position as their representative in the research discipline. Being aware of my sociocultural background, my anthropological representation relates to Said's description: 'bear[ing] as much on the representer's world as on who or what is represented' (2013: 303). My anthropological lens is thus dispersed throughout the totality of imperial history, modern conditions, and the postmodern gaze, all accumulating to form an understanding of the artists' and my transnational experiences. In the following section, I demonstrate aspects of reflexive ethnographic anthropology in studying various realities defused within the transnational performing arts experience at hand.

Interpreter as a Mediator Between Realities

During the apprenticeship, a reflexive reality emerged from my shifting role between an observer and a participant (interpreter). As an interpreter, I engaged fully during the rehearsals to the extent that I was once told, 'You are almost acting while interpreting, [you] danced as I did while interpreting, and you even sang it.' My immersion is un-unbiased by my cultural, linguistic, and political background – but contemplating my immersion enabled me to reflect on multiple possible realities of the intercultural space.

One reality emerged from my active interpreter role, where I mediated the relationships and understandings between the artists and the production team. The topics of improvisation were impacted by the interventions I was asked to provide, thus demonstrating a different reality than when my role was only to observe. Additionally, my role as an interpreter led to a different reality than that provided through the silent but unignored central position of the 'wooden' translation machine that replaced me on stage. Despite the many distortions that any translation process could cause in a theatre performance, all members agreed that translation/interpretation was central to this performance and any other transnational work environment. Hence, immersion in the practice of interpreting enabled a reflexive reality and established closer contact with the improvised material. It engaged me, the researcher, with the emotional state of the artist being interpreted and promoted a trusting relationship with the team that facilitated observation and later interviews. Interpretation turned the research method into an apprenticeship by providing a mutual learning experience.

However, my inability to be a human interpreter present on stage challenged the dramaturg and the artistic choices that were made. Rehearsals about memories and personal stories shifted once the silent wooden machine's unavoidable central position replaced the translator on stage. The machine was physically and symbolically huge enough to drive improvisations around it, allowing for stories centred around the wooden machine's story. In a way, the wooden machine conquered the space on stage and created a new reality by obliging the artistic team to find a way to adapt to its physical and symbolic presence as the metaphorical elephant in the room. Although the artists did not discuss the machine's usefulness, they all engaged in finding ways to improvise around its presence. Their memories about machines and German machines' reputations were brought to the improvisation process. Here, I realised how my absence as an interpreter-mediator infused the shift from intersubjective connections among the artists and production team concerned with subjectivity development in the intercultural space to post-migrant-led intersubjective connections that constitute artists' representations on stage. The shift had moved the intercultural self-exploring medium to an intercultural self-exploring medium led by the context's demands. These demands of context, which aimed to create a space of beyondness (the post-migrant space reality), left behind an essential component of the self as unexplored – the one being explored in the process before the machine appeared. To avoid the machine's centrality and create mediation between the Arab-speaking artists and the audience without relying fully on the machine, the director led the improvisation process towards having the German actor play the role of interpreter for the audience, recreating the context dominion into a White-Western dominion. The result was thus a dominated intercultural space.

Within this dominated intercultural experience, theatre as a collaborative space enabled mediality to thrive. The interpreter's role as a cultural mediator between the German and non-German participants – whether it was the German artist or me – was crucial in creating a bridge between ideas, inviting similar grounds where thinking and ideas could emerge, and enabling artists to focus on other aesthetics connected to style, improvised moments, and content. Additionally, many aspects of the improvisations in the intercultural space focused on artists interpreting – through different styles of their choice – what their colleagues produced in the dramatic moment. These interpretations may have been for reasons of solidarity, mockery, or playfulness in the improvisational mode. The whole performance became a space of mediality of artists' various ideas and memories, communicated to each other and the audience. In some cases, the artists preferred not to interpret, mediate, or use mediation – rather, they improvised beyond what their colleagues and the translation produced. These improvisations beyond the system of rehearsals required further translation and cultural explanations. However, these mediality processes could not transcend Western dominance of the intercultural space.

Observer as a Mediator of Intercultural Spaces

Three physical spaces in the creative process contributed to my ethnography's anthropological understanding through reflexivity and immersion. These were the general rehearsal location, the smoking room, and the ice-breaking game corner. The rehearsal and performance locations were outside the theatre premises, in the city's suburbs. The choice of the location, which the theatre administration made, was intentional. Almost all members of the artistic team complained – to me, first, but then to the theatre administration– about its remoteness and the inability to create intercultural spaces with the other ensemble members of the theatre institution. Despite artists' complaints, however, the answer was always that nothing was to be done.

The second location, the ice-breaking game corner, was created within this rehearsal location. This was a space where the artistic team played a 'game' in which one of the performers proposed encouraging daily exercise before the rehearsal began. (The performer who proposed this later left the project because of dissatisfaction with the production's approach to solidarity.) The game used a ball and four connected squares drawn on the floor to form one larger square. Four artists or team members could play at a time. Each stood in one of the squares and passed the ball with one hand to the person in the next square without the ball touching the ground twice or touching the body. The game, independent of language, built a solid communicative channel between the artists and revealed challenges among them. Fuelled by the need to exercise before each rehearsal, the regularly played game enhanced individual communication and helped solve some uneasy moments. The game became an intercultural issue solution and an energetic vein in the highly unliked and cold rehearsal location. The game's continuation after the performer's departure brought to my mind, and likely to others as well, the reasons for his leave. The game was based on complementary efforts and players' competence, whereas the play was based on mediality.

The third location was also part of the rehearsal space: the smoking room. In addition to the artistic team's official meeting table, this alternative space revealed unofficial tensions that emerged during the creative process. Artists usually moved to the smoking room to smoke a cigarette. However, I observed that the Arabic speakers and German speakers often chose to use the smoking room at different times. These group splits were spontaneous at times and intentional at others to discuss dissatisfaction issues. The smoking room eased the language shifting at the smoking room (mostly spoken Arabic) and at the meeting table (mostly spoken German). Whenever the split happened, it appeared to be a mechanism to handle or take a break from intercultural disparities.

Additionally, a new layer of explanation of the smoking room emerged when a female Arabic-speaking artist joined the team and used the room to smoke a cigarette. As tensions with the female artist heightened on a professional, character basis, the male participants lessened their visits to the room when she was around. They visibly shifted their smoking to the men's changing room. As an Arabic-speaking team member, I was once invited to a private talk with the female participant in the smoking room. She confided that she found communicating with the male performers difficult and was thinking about leaving. Haunted by preconceptions about gender relations, I played a supporting role, encouraging her to continue until the end, despite the various pressures. I was also invited to the men's changing room to discuss the male artists' dissatisfaction with the director's strategy, the female artist, and translation issues with the dramaturg. I played a listening role there and encouraged them to speak their minds. These dynamics taking place in and in relation to the smoking room revealed that several canonisations and categorisations played a role in the intercultural experience, even within an environment of solidarity. Several discussions with the German-speaking group members revealed other tensions and perceptions of the state of the group. However, these were never brought to the official table or to the smoking room.

In summary, the interpreter and observer roles I played during my immersion and apprenticeship at the theatre project contributed to shaping the research outcome and formulating my strategies for analysing the experiences of migrant artists. The transcultural, intercultural, and cultural issues of the three physical spaces and the relational space between them illuminated that a post-migrant space comprises components of analysis beyond the mere experience of living together. A post-migrant space concerns the history of artists' subjective experiences and my experiences in the field of performing arts. Moreover, in a post-migrant intercultural context, translation becomes a salient component to directing, manipulating, and leading mechanisms of managing differences between individuals.

To better understand individuals' own perspectives of their experiences, biographical interviews shed light on the artists' feelings and experiences. The following sections demonstrate the findings of this research's ethnography and biographical interviews in relation to the transnational cultural experiences of the artists.

Making Biographicity of Artists

Biographical interviews formed one of my primary data collection methods. I conducted semi-structured interviews with 23 artists over two years (2017–2019). Each interview revolved around one question: 'Every one of us has a story. What is your story?' To answer this, artists extensively narrated personal life stories and focused on their stories of engagement in art and theatre. Through follow-up questions to encourage openness to share stories, I informed the artists about previous research related to the Palestinian and Arab performing arts scene from the late twentieth century until now. Sharing my own perspective infused further sharing of stories and incidents related to common knowledge of Arab performing arts. It also helped artists reflect and connect their current stories with past moments and build on conclusions throughout the interview. The interviews were mainly conducted in Arabic and took place at artists' workspaces, theatres, and cafés, which are public spaces where the surrounding majority spoke a language other than Arabic. Language furthered harmony in the interview, even if the shared stories would not change if the surrounding people understood the language. This created an unintentional connection between me and the artist during the meetings.

Biographies collected in this manner have been described by Rosenthal (1997) as narrated life stories where artists demonstrate the meaning of experiences and include the temporal order of the life story in the present time of narrating or presenting it. The biographies included stories, reflections, conclusions, moments of hesitation, and momentous realisations, which led to the research's investigation of complex multi-scalar social fields (Totah 2020a) and aided in the construction of migrant artists' biographies. Their self-development through narrating their life stories constituted their biographicity (Totah 2021a), which is the process reflecting their ability to shape and reshape their story about their transnational experiences. The context of their biographicity construction in such an interview setting demonstrates the common spatial and historical grounds that the interview established, combining the artist's experience with the anthropologist's. It could be described as a space of reconnecting or personification (through myself) of the confrontation with home. Artists' self-development journeys comprised my presence with theirs, interweaving with shared concerns about the social structure that made our meeting possible. For example, the concepts of dictatorship and censorship were familiar to us both, creating a connection that was used to clarify difficult points during the interview.

Within artists' biographicity, the narration brought both the anthropologist and artist into a common level of liminality. It established a shared liminal space that continuously referred to the artwork as a social event. Both the artists and the anthropologist contributed to establishing the liminal space with the spectator. Both referred to the past with its connection with the present in its interpretation. The liminal space established the relational space of theatre as a social event, which includes an aspect of the past and the present, referred to as biographical narrations' 'problematic sites of contemporaneity' (Totah 2021 b). As such, the liminal space of the transnational theatre experience challenged an understanding of the migration experience as simply the process of travel. Rather, it is holistically constructed by relying on the overall artistic and social experiences of artists as humans in a migration context.

Transnational Theatre Research: Biographicity and Apprenticeship

My methodological positionality brings into discussion the extended explanations by Bourriaud (2002) and Wannous (1996) on how relational aesthetics is a modernist form of art relations, participation, and exchange that advocates social change. By calling the artwork a 'social interstice' (5), Bourriaud (2002) proposed that relational aesthetics seeks to expand the understanding of art by inviting human relations around it, including its production and its reception, instead of limiting it to independent and private symbolic spaces (5). In contrast to society's increasing functionality against finding relational spaces under global contingencies, artwork can create such a relational space. Art involves intersubjective encounters resulting from themes of togetherness. Politically, this art form situates relational aesthetics around it in the liminal space between aesthetics and politics, and it rejects the aesthetic autonomy that distinguishes pure and political art. Thus, art as a political form transforms relational aesthetics into a process that resists art commodification by the cultural industry. It utilises artists' biographicity – in the case of Arab artists in Europe – as a tool for resisting. This art simultaneously turns the anthropologist into a political agent against pre-set research design.

Specifically, the transnational cultural experience of migrant artists becomes relational through their intercultural experiences, which comprise their intersubjective encounters around boundaries and physical borders, as well as their connections with their home country. It also includes my perceptions as an accompanying researcher. The dialogue that the artwork creates throughout what Bourriaud explains as the 'being-together' experience (8) produces negotiations and confrontations around both the self and the environment, which form the artistic practice's quintessence. In this case, the anthropologist shares the responsibility that artists hold towards others in this dialogue, which is their representation of the artwork's desired world and its meaning.

In the same sense, Wannous 1996 viewed theatre as a 'social event' in which bonds between an actor and the audience lead to the theatrical phenomenon. He considered that theatre production creates a fertile collective feed. The production does not merely collect individual efforts but also creates a rich dialogue and collaborative creation that gradually reveals the group's identity. In the case of the OBE, as the relational dynamics of the performing artists' transnational experiences constituted the social interstice or the social event, the anthropologist joined the collective force. Inducing understanding of the interaction around artists' legal, cultural, and social status occurred through their homemaking trajectories and biopolitical performativity, resulting from in-depth discussions of past, present, and liminal spaces (Totah 2021b). These interactions and discussions contributed to their onstage biographic representations and meanings. By recreating this social interstice throughout their migration, the artists aimed to reclaim their free will. The anthropologist, in this case, contributed to the biographicity of artists but was not able to contribute to their free will. Such a state of contribution is also worth further exploration if the anthropologist is from a Western background, which I am not. This means that the transnational dynamics of togetherness in a relational aesthetic space, in the here and now, are constantly confronted by the social fields' powers, where they take place and do not achieve utopia.

On the other hand, when artwork introduces confrontation, Bishop describes this as 'antagonistic relational aesthetics', which reveals new perceptions of subjectivity revolving around 'the presence of what is not me renders my identity precarious and vulnerable, and the threat that what the other represents transforms my sense of self into something questionable' (66). Antagonistic aesthetics calls for questioning the quality of the relationships in the transnational theatre space and the democratic meaning behind the dialogue it allows by revealing tensions, exploitations, subversions, and works against quality. The migrant performing artists' relational dynamics comprise aspects of Bishop's antagonism. They are situated in an intercultural, transnational context, where multiple levels combine to create the being-together experience. As they emerged from the multiple realities explained earlier, the relational dynamics that artists experienced in the transnational social field are antagonistic on many levels, including their relationships with peer artists, the director, and the audiences. As a mediator for reflexivity and a liminal companion, the anthropologist contributed to confrontations by enhancing artists' agency in the intercultural space. Artists' dynamics in the creative process consisted of intercultural strategies and encounters. However, post-migrant solidarity dominions explained earlier stood against the capability of the creative process to excel with the antagonistic relational aesthetic spaces that may transcend artists' subjects towards their freedom. As such, understanding the antagonistic aesthetics of a social event must intersect with a political understanding of power dynamics and the transnational social field of artists' experiences to better target intercultural relationships between artists.

This paper demonstrated how my position as an anthropologist affected my analysis and conclusions about artists' free will and their subjectivity development on European stages. By focusing on demonstrating biographicity and apprenticeship as ethnographic approaches, as well as their relevance to specific moments during the OBE, this paper introduced the multiplicity of roles the anthropologists assumed in conducting transnational theatre research. In conclusion, in an attempt to challenge Western hegemony, an anthropologist becomes a political agent against pre-set research design. In an intercultural space, the anthropologist shares artists' responsibility towards others and simultaneously contributes to reality-making. An anthropologist may contribute to the biographicity of artists but is not able to contribute to their free will because transnational relational dynamics of togetherness in a relational aesthetic space are constantly confronted by the social fields' powers and dominions.

References

Bishop, Claire. "Antagonism and Relational Aesthetics." *October* 110 (2004): 51–79. doi:10.1162/0162287042379810.

Bourriaud, Nicolas. *Relational Aesthetics*. Paris: Les Presses Du Réel, 2002.

Rosenthal, G. National identity or multicultural autobiography? Theoretical concepts of biographical constitution grounded in case reconstructions. *The narrative study of lives*, 1997, 5, pp 21–39.

Said, E. W. *Reflections on exile: and other literary and cultural essays*. Granta Books. 2013.

Smith, Michael Peter, and Luis Eduardo Guarnizo, eds. *Transnationalism from below*. Vol. 6. Transaction Publishers, 1998.

Totah, Ruba. "Negotiating 'Home' Borders: Creative Processes Hosting Syrian and Palestinian Syrian Artists in Europe." *European Journal of Theatre and Performance*, vol. 1, no. 2, 2020, pp. 424–461.

Totah, Ruba. "Negotiating 'Home:' Syrian and Palestinian Syrian Artists in Borderlands." *Civil Society Review*, 2020, 22–45. https://doi.org/10.28943/csr.004.009. Accessed 2 Dec. 2020

Totah Ruba. "Transnational Subjectivities of Arab Artists in Europe." *Critical Stages/ Scènes Critiques*. June 15, 2021. Accessed July 06, 2021. https://www.critical-stages.org/23/transnational-subjectivities-of-arab-artists-in-europe/.

Totah, Ruba. Cultural Transnationalism and The Arab Uprisings: Migrant Artists from Syria in Europe. PhD diss., Johannes Gutenberg University Mainz, 2021. Mainz: University of Mainz, 2021. 1–168.

Totah, Ruba. "No Room for Bare Life on Stage: Biopolitics of Syrian Migrant Artists Performativity." *Borders in Perspective. The Biopolitics of Borders in Time of Crisis*, edited by Astrid M. Fellner, Eva Nossem, and Tetyana Ostapchuk, vol. 7., 2022, forthcoming.

Wannous, S. *All works*. Damascus: Alahali Publishing, 1996.

A theatre practice-based exercise in doing and undoing diversity: The Open Border Ensemble (2017-2020) experiment at the Münchner Kammerspiele

Krystel Khoury

Introduction

My reflection on post-Heimat and theatre is undoubtedly linked to my three years of working experience at *The Münchner Kammerspiele* – Munich's city theatre – for and in the *Open Border Ensemble* project. In February 2017, I was invited to think through this project and be in charge of this ensemble, an initiative that I would consider an endeavour of diversity. The initial project involved three performers from Syria who were invited to work at the theatre. My work involved setting up and overseeing the entire ensemble season program through daily interactions with the theatre director and later liaising regularly with it and the *OBE* performers. It is there that I encountered the term post-heimat for the first time. And it seems hard for me to dissociate it from the very specific German political context and cultural history, which my relatively short experience in Germany made me only partially grasp.

My nomadic professional experience across geographies – Lebanon, Egypt, Jordan, France, Germany, Greece, and Belgium – encompasses participation and immersion in projects initiated by encounters between artists from different backgrounds. While actively engaged in those projects, I consider them as live laboratories and fields of research. The narrative and analytical thoughts for this contribution follow this approach. As someone with a background in anthropology, examining the intercultural dynamics that occur during artistic and creative processes and the mechanisms that are put at stake for its emergence are some of the focuses of my research interests. The research hereby is based on a methodology ranging from ethnographic material to personal reflection, including participant observation, personal notes, online and in-print communication by the theatre, first-hand experience of situations, and informal conversations. I also acknowledge my direct implication in specific artistic decision-making processes related to the project and the limited room for manoeuvre when it came to some. If being a researcher in parallel or connection to my position within the *OBE* presents a methodological challenge in terms of the spectrum of implication variating from familiarity to distinction with the object/subject of research – more so in the context of intercultural encounters, it is with what it gives as having "been taking in" – *pris dedans* as has shown Favret-Saada (1977), having been implicated and involved that I hope this writing can be perceptive.

I would like then to mention, following a feminist epistemological tenet (Haraway 1988), that this reflection is a situated one incorporating my own structural location and professional genealogy. It is as a non-German speaker, yet trilingual, a non-white female, yet holding at that time a certain privileged position as the *Künstlerische Leitung* that I wish to contribute to the discussion around the post-heimat topic. I find it important to voice out from where I am writing, notably because I have participated in shaping this project. Also, I want to emphasize my reflexive exercise that pertains to the question of who can speak for whom in cultural encounters where power dynamics are inherent to the process itself. I am, therefore, in this paper speaking up as a 'halfy' (Abu-Lughod 1991), someone whose cultural identity is mixed by virtue of migration and education, from an in-between position, where belonging is more a matter of longing simply to be.

If as stated[1] the term *post-heimat* "stands for a heterogeneous process" and "a mode of thinking and enacting" the relation of individuals to society "with diversity as value"; I wish to shift the reader's gaze on diversity as a more-than-a-value by focusing on the empirical practice of 'doing diversity' borrowing the expression to Sarah Ahmed and Ellen Sawn (2006) and how undoable sometimes it can be, taking a German institutional theatre context as a case study, from the perspective of the 'in-between worker' that I was. More specifically, I chose to investigate this process through the different ways the mother-tongue language of the OBE members (Arabic) was used on stage and in theatre productions. Drawing from the different works of Sarah Ahmed, I conclude with a reflexive approach to diversity of labour to generate knowledge and learnings for further discussions on the complexity of what such a practice entails for future envisioning in the field of post-heimat theatre.

Doing diversity: a challenging practice

The Open Border Ensemble project was run by the Münchner Kammerspiele for three years, from 2017 to 2020. This project was to contribute to the politics of diversity that the newly appointed artistic team under Matthias Lilienthal's direction started instigating, amongst others, upon their arrival two seasons earlier. An arrival coincides in 2015 with the reopening of the Austrian-German borders

---

1   In *Problematizing PostHeimat*, a statement drafted by the research group of the PostHeimat network during and after Encounter #04 at the Maxim Gorki Theater in March 2020.

for newcomers to reach the city of Munich. It was an artistic as well as a political decision to bring back – not to say to bring in – within German institutional theatre conversations about working conditions of refugee artists, otherness, inequalities, privileges, lack of representation and misrepresentation of non-white and non-German theatre protagonists. These debates did not come all at once; they were instilled progressively by the audience development team led by Anne Schulz. Unlike what Himan Banerjee (in Ahmed, 2012) observes regarding diversity policy (in educational institutions), it was not meant in this artistic institution for "accommodating conflicting heterogeneity" but rather for stirring them[2]. Diversity in this context was part of the policy expressed by the theatre that wanted "to dare to experiment, even radically, rather than endlessly repeating recipes of success"[3]. The team was genuinely concerned about how to start activating concrete inclusivity. Punctual events such as the Open Border Congress and festival organized in 2016 and more regular ones such as the Welcome Café came as manifests of this interest. Including three performers from Syria forming the Open Border Ensemble in the theatre program, 17/18 was a step further (Totah and Khoury, 2018). In this climate, the Münchner Kammerspiele also hosted the first post-Heimat encounter co-organized in April 2018 with Mülheim-based Ruhrorter, an art and theatre collective.

On an artistic level, the idea of the *Open Border Ensemble* was conceived to acknowledge the presence and participation of newly hosted non-German artists in the theatre and as an aesthetically progressive opportunity for the German theatre scene, particularly in Munich. It sought to contribute to a transnational theatre, allowing different narratives from cultural and socio-political contexts to emerge, be shared and negotiated in the German institutional theatre setting. It aimed to forge a new experiential, collaborative path by resisting borders and artistic isolation and to invite the artists to experiment with another professional theatre experience than the one they had or were having at that time in their country.

At this point, it seems crucial to situate the Münchner Kammerpiele aspirations during Lilienthal's leadership: a prominent German theatre institution willingly foregrounding international collaborations, a theatre house open to and commissioning German and non-western European theatre makers[4], a city theatre operating within a shifting global political context that was deviating towards more nationalism and isolationism. In fact, those years witnessed the rise of radicalized fascist right-wing ideologies not only in Europe but in other parts of the world

---

2   We have received a letter from a member of the Friends Committee of the Kammerspiele addressed to the theatre direction contesting the idea of the *OBE* project.

3   Letter to the audience by Matthias Lilienthal, Theater program Season 2017/2018.

4   To name a few: Rabih Mroué, Amir Reza Koohhestani, Toshiki Okada, Lola Arias, Anestis Azas and Prodromos Tsinikoris.

while the Trumpian era was triumphing. A series of positive actions were organised in resonance or following a butterfly effect. Amongst those, workshops addressed exclusively to "people of colour". Workshops and talks on and against racism were held in parallel to theatre productions that were tackling it[5]. It will not be an understatement then to say that the theatre was opening spaces to counteract those drifts using its own tools, even if this was met at times by resistance from within the theatre itself, what Ahmed (2009) would highlight as the "paradox" of diversity work, or outside of it[6]. Indeed, overcoming the constraints of an institutional anchored habitus is a long process that requires strenuous efforts.

It was quickly understood that for any transformation to happen within the theatre, the leading direction should be willing to engage concomitantly in a transformational process on a structural level too. The attempt here was like Fowler's (2020) notes regarding the Münchner Kammerspiele 'to enable new border crossings, tackling themes of diversity, mobility and migration not only in the artistic repertoire but also in the theatre's personnel'. With months passing, the theatre work towards diversity was shaping following a more inclusive and intersectional understanding. The KammerQueers[7] initiative against normative uniformity in the theatre was provided space and time, in other words, visibility and resources – even if limited. Working conditions of female workers and abusive behaviour were given space to be outspoken. Workshops aiming at activating codes of conduct and policies against sexual harassment in the theatre working spaces to which all the theatre employees were called were taking place. A 'strike' by some of the theatre woman workers was held on March 8, 2019, as an act to more acknowledgement of their labour. Theatre productions addressing climate catastrophe, whether through the youth march movements or in a more apocalyptic way, were set and many other actions were taken. The theatre was searching thoroughly for ways to give up some of its conventional institutional rationale. Yet, not to 'accompany' but to be actively part of a rather spontaneous grass-rooted, growing Western global movement of awareness and revendications towards more social justice.

It is within this ongoing entangled constellation and multi-layered ecology that the team[8] behind the Open Border Ensemble had to continuously move. It had to

---

5   Anta Helena Recke Mittelreich – the Black copy 2017, *Die Kränkungen der Menschheit 2020*, by Anta and in January 2020 *Race Me* by Myriam Ibrahim.

6   Discussions with director Myriam Ibrahim during the production period of *Race Me*.

7   *KAMMERQUEERS*, a queer association linked to the Kammerspiele, was formed and involved in the discussions of how art institutions should facilitate their questioning. As noted in the program of 2019/2020: "Kammerqueers, a collective of Queer people from the Kammerspiele: we are anti-racist, anti-cissexist, definitely queer, and trying to navigate and change the institution that is the Kammerspiele" trying to navigate and change the institution.

8   The team dedicated to the Open border Ensemble was constituted by two employees: one full-time *OBE* worker (myself) along a part-time production manager with the support of

find ways to navigate troubled waters, and keeping up with glocal considerations. It had to constantly reconsider the Open Border Ensemble's position, its function and what it simultaneously represented for the Syrian diasporic artist's community as well as for the artistic community in Syria – to which the artists from the OBE still belonged and were connected, what it represented moreover for the diasporic Arab artist's community. It also reflected on what role has the Open Border Ensemble beyond those communities in relation to policies and mechanisms of diversity, mobility, and migration within a German institutional theatre system.

From the theatre perspective, diversity in this specific case – inviting Syrian performers, which means artists who will be *seen* on stage and as regular theatre employees – was embodied. As a sub-entity to the theatre ensemble during its first season, this made it possible for the *OBE* to be hyper-visible and exposed in a white institution. If it could be argued that such an endeavour contributed to the whiteness of the institution being concealed, the existence of the *OBE* was, on the other hand, confronting the institution to its whiteness and confirming it. As Ahmed (2012) puts it:

> "(…) diversity matters not as a description of such spaces (of what they are, or what they have), but as a sign of what they are not. (…) In other words, if the appeal of diversity is that it conceals inequalities, then we can expose such inequalities by exploring the terms of its appeal."

As said, the theatre director did not want to 'repeat recipes' but rather to challenge through its ensembles' performers what those latter might represent or not in the mind of their audience. However, this matter carried a delicate equation lying in equating the diversity of individual theatre experiences with the diversity of national backgrounds. Doing diversity was part of the institution's agenda. However, this vision was not necessarily the priority for the subjects involved in its process. Even if the *OBE* productions of 2017 did include other performers from the theatre ensemble in their cast, still, conversations amongst the *OBE* performers about how they would be or were represented on stage by the theatre directors brought up a feeling of wariness linked to fears of being tokenized as the 'Syrians saved from war'.

Behind the scenes: working with the unknown

On the other hand, critics such as why not have directly included the performers in the ensemble of the Münchner Kammerspiele were formulated. The ideal scenario in

---

Anne Schulz from *Kammer4you*. The production managers of the Open Border Ensemble were consecutively: Susanne Ernst, Julia Zehl and, Charlotte Hesse.

the long term would have been to gradually 'dissolve' the *OBE* as a separate entity or radically and symbolically enlarge it to include all the theatre performers. However, looking at the conditions and logistical complexities of the reality on the ground that the theatre had to deal with made this an unreachable utopia. One of those complexities was the overall financial planning of the project: the first financial support ran for only eight months, after which applying for another funding was needed but not guaranteed. This conditional co-funding and limited duration enabled only vaporous possibilities of how it can be further shaped. The unknown in terms of financial sustainability had an impact on the existence of the *OBE* itself, putting it on shaky feet and achieving its long-term aims. After the second financial support was granted for the 18/19 season, the project artistically shifted in its core. The performers became part of the cast of the programmed theatre productions for the season and were even offered spaces to create their work.

While the performers were waiting for their visas and preparing to cross the borders from Damascus to Beirut to reach Munich, the team first had to gather the material conditions – mainly appropriate accommodation, which is hardly found in a city like Munich. Indeed, the artists were not 'guest artists' coming for one production, 'refugees', or 'migrants' since the initial contract was eight months and going back to their country was theoretically possible. Thus, the status of the *OBE* performers challenged existing habitual categories in a stimulating way. It created an unprecedented situation within the theatre system and, as such, could only be dealt with through inventing ways along the way.

The work also comprised administrative appointments, logistics regarding arrival and stay, internal and external communication about the project, a cultural program for the performers outside the rehearsals and in connection to cultural organisations in the city, optional language courses, etc. Additionally, in September 2017, when the theatre season opened, the pre-production of the first *OBE* theatre play had to start. Production schedules were fixed. Since it was conceived to happen in multiple open spaces on the outskirts of Munich, the production process was more complicated than a production taking place *in* the theatre. For instance, constructing a set that could fit in a van had to be negotiated depending on law restrictions. Scouting for locations, permits and approvals needed to be requested from different city services. Quickly enough, it appeared that more human and financial resources were needed but could not be provided. A gap between the symbolic commitment to diversity and the experience of the ones involved started to be felt. Besides, the performers were still waiting for their visas, and no one knew when they would arrive or if they would arrive. For the theatre director, whose working process was based on storytelling and content material derived from the main participants in the project, this meant growing tension as the rehearsals were regularly postponed until the arrival of the performers. For a theatre structure such as the Münchner Kammerspiele, where the routine of accurate scheduling and "thinking ahead" prevails – especially on the technical, planning and communication levels, this main unknown was un-settling. However, at that point in the existence of the OBE, we had started to be acquainted with the logic of waiting and working on the short term. We were em-bracing this unknown as a main constitutive factor of the project.

When the performers finally arrived after a long journey in February 2018, Mu-nich was snowy and grey. The "welcoming" dinner, which the theatre had imagined and organized for them, was cancelled as they were too tired. The clock was ticking, and the next step was to delve into the rehearsals of the first production[9] – with-out having the time to become familiar with the theatre structure or the city. The rehearsal space available was in a location far from the main theatre. Although this was due to technicalities, the distance from the main theatre created a disturbing, irreversible feeling of unintended exclusion.

Diversity work: the invisible labour of the "outsider within"

Despite all the preparations, this unpredictable false start marked the performers and the working dynamics at stake, which needed to be constantly adjusted, adding a challenge to the process and its functioning. Indeed, the conversations often in-cluded bipolar positioning, with unequal power dynamics at play between the the-atre as an entity, the actors or the employers and the employees, or the different theatre working methods in Syria and Germany.

This labour required resilience and the ability to listen, understand, explain, re-formulate, communicate, and mediate. It would only be productive at that stage if the performers could express themselves using the language in which they are the most comfortable– their native language – Arabic and if it could be communicated to the theatre artistic team and reflected upon together. I was the person who flu-ently spoke English – the chosen working language for this international context- as well as Arabic which I related to as a mother tongue. I was also the person fully ap-pointed to serve this project by the institution. It was, therefore, expected that I take this responsibility. Needless to point out here that more than speaking the perform-ers' language, it was about embodying a knowledge of the context the conversations generated.

This ongoing diversity work was highly demanding emotionally and intellectu-ally. It required to be mindful of not reinscribing ethnocentric thinking and, by ex-tension, white and non-white power hierarchies. It was constant, and since it was

---

9   For an analytical perspective on the creative process of this production, you can read: Totah R, Khoury K. Theater against Borders: 'Miunikh–Damaskus'—A Case Study in Solidarity. *Arts.* 2018; 7(4):90.

ungraspable, it was often unremarkable or unseen and, as such, undervalued, although at the core of the project. It consisted of bridging, even though those bridges could not be identified by naming the category to which the work belonged.

Both the institution and the performers were speaking to each other through my position. This often gave it an ambiguous status in terms of belonging to the project as *an outsider within* (Hunter 2006). A positioning that was also blurred by my adapting capacity to shift from coordinator to dramaturge, to production manager, to artistic director for this project. Indeed, my labour was trans-passing due to the borderless nature of the project. The fact that it covered undefined or very broadly defined tasks surely made the labour exciting but extremely exhausting and frustrating in the long run. A fragment from my notebook dating from the beginning of the project in 2017 insightfully reads:

"We should make the best out of it, they said. Who are 'we'? me as representing the institution, me as my own person, me as a cultural manager, me seen as a person from Lebanon? Who are 'we' addressing ourselves to?"

'Who is the 'we' addressing?': on speech language

The Münchner Kammerspiele, with its peculiar position in modern German theatre history, is well-known for being a leading German-speaking theatre. By adopting a politics of internationalization and inviting non-western European theatre makers to work with its performers, the problems of the theatrical speech language were brought on stage. As one of the many significant components of the semiotics of theatre (Fischer-Lichte 1992), the speech-language affects the processes of meaning-making and reception. Hence, for the main stage of the theatre – *Kammer 1*, permanent technical equipment was installed for surtitles. All productions playing on this stage had German or English surtitling, depending on the theatre production's primary language. This had an impact on the type of audience coming to the theatre. A new non-German speaking audience could finally discover German theatre plays, while regular audiences were given the opportunity to get familiar with non-German speaking plays. Furthermore, with the *OBE*, a presentation text of the project in Arabic was included in the 17/18 season program, along with a presentation of the Welcome Café in Arabic and Farsi. Trivial gestures in other multilingual contexts were significant transformational ones for the Münchner Kammerspiele, calling for a renewed audience to contribute to a more transnational theatre experience.

In addition to the question of what is being said and to whom it is addressed to, the question of who is speaking and what this "who" represents on stage had to be openly addressed with the arrival of the Syrian performers (Totah and Khoury 2018). It meant negotiating the interplay of internal and external pressures arising from the organizational and economic frameworks of the institution (Garde 2021).

Also, including non-German speaking performers in the theatre institution meant demanding theatre-makers to encounter other theatre practices and understandings and confronting them with a language they do not understand. When dealing with diversity, it is an additional layer of complexity to the creative process, narratives and aesthetics. From the German theatre perspective, beyond embodied diversity, the presence of an 'unknown' language was a trigger to disrupt familiar sounds, including the one seen as the stranger. As Garde (2021) points out, this was meant to challenge theatremakers and audiences "to engage with the everyday realities of societies in transformation". The non-understandable language by a German audience became one of the signs through which diversity could manifest itself. For three years, the *OBE* performers participated collectively or individually in more than ten[10] theatre productions – four of which I was thoroughly involved in artistically. More than highlighting the simple manifestation or absence of the 'unknown language' on stage, I wish in the following to examine the different usages of the Arabic language on stage by recalling some of the productions that included performers from the *OBE* to uncover the plurality of mechanisms that needed to be invented for doing diversity.

First Season

In fact, the first season of the *OBE* was quite exceptional in terms of experimenting with the Arabic language on stage. Discussions about language and work conditions with the two female directors, German Jessica Glause and Argentinian Lola Arias came before the rehearsals. Inviting a person who could translate from Arabic to English or to German[11] to join each process was agreed upon. The interpreter played a key role. It quickly became the mediator figure next to the dramaturge within the asymmetrical relations between the director and the performers shifting binaries into triangular dynamics (Khoury 2016). However, both directors saw that if this would facilitate the process, the issue of language was more than a mere detail within the context of the *OBE* project. Working with a documentary approach

---

10   The theatre productions included: 'Miunikh-Damaskus: Stories of One City' by Jessica Glause, 'What They Want to Hear' by Lola Arias, 'Dionysos Stadt' by Christopher Rüping, 'MacBeth' by Emir Reza Koohestani, 'The Life of Vernon Subutex' by Stephan Pucher, 'Melancolia' by Felix Rothenhäusler, 'For the Last Time' by Kinan Hmeidan, 'iREHAB' by Majd Feddah, 'Im Dickicht Der Städt' by Christopher Rüping, 'Kränkungen der Menschheit' by Anta Helena Recke, 'Passing – It's so easy, was schwer zu machen ist' by Renée Pollesch, 'MAL' by Marlene Freitas.

11   We could not find an Arabic-German interpreter for the duration of the creative process of Glause production and invited researcher Ruba Totah to join the process and translate from Arabic to English.

that emphasizes the lived experience of the performers had to be dealt with artistically. Their approach included creating a theatrical text based on first-hand narratives from the cast. This gave the director space to explore and reflect upon a sensical use of the language.

In the case of 'Miunikh-Damaskus: Stories of One City', we have already examined in a previous article (Totah and Khoury, 2018) how this matter was addressed by the director from the start of the creative process as a challenge to be surpassed. The participant observer reported:

> '"How do we manage language together?", "How to avoid misunderstandings?", "How to initiate a space to know each other?", "This will be important for our work, especially since there are three languages," "The most difficult thing is the language now," punctuated the director's introductory speech on the first day of rehearsals.'

We demonstrated how translation operated as a creative strategy in paving the way towards a third common space. As a matter of fact, this was translated on stage through different mechanisms: one was to make the German performer repeat the content of the Arabic text spoken by the performers in German as a slightly desynchronized dubbing. To avoid redundancy, this required the performer to have high acting skills. The other was to include in the scenography a 'translation machine' in the form of an old school fixed sharpener where instead of the pen, a paper roll would unfold with the transcription of the translated text activated with a handle by the performers. Both ideas had an aesthetical playful resonance with the content of the speech – one performer was working in dubbing before joining the *Münchner Kammerspiele*, and the sharpener was mentioned during rehearsals by another performer.

In Lola Arias' 'What They Want to Hear', the relationship between the languages of the speech became one of the main concepts the play revolves around dramaturgically. This politically engaged theatre play was mainly based on the re-enactment of an asylum seeker's fateful interview to get refugee status in Germany. This interview engaged the asylum seeker, who was a Syrian archaeologist, an interpreter, and an employee from the *BAMF* as the main characters. The text was written throughout the rehearsals in the theatre as opposed to for the theatre. The process was an incredible exercise in multilingualism. It was developed using the three main characters' spoken languages – Arabic and German as well as English as the communication language all the team spoke – none of which was the director's native language. The team included a trilingual interpreter who worked on translating parts of the text and later as a *souffleuse*. The final version was written in three columns for each language. During the rehearsals, dialoguing around which language to use was often debated before making the final decisions. 'Who is the play addressed to' came often. Arias heard how the performers wanted to relate to their respective language and found a mechanism to embrace it. To stay faithful to the reality of the situation, the asylum seeker was narrating his story in Arabic, the employee was asking her questions in German, and the interpreter was shifting from one to the other with all that this action held: reinterpretation, cultural presumption, misunderstanding, etc. The scenography set was composed of a ground floor, the *BAMF* office, and an upper floor where the narrative actions of the story were taking place. One of the three languages was used depending on who the performers were representing. Comments by the main protagonist were inserted in some scenes. Those were said in English and addressed to the audience. One comment by a technician from Afghanistan was said in his native language. The surtitles of the interview were projected on the floor, separating the upper part from the lower part like an information banner. The rest appeared on the middle top of the stage. The overall process was intense on many levels, with the team often getting lost in translation. Regardless, Lola Arias did succeed in a *tour de force* in creating and directing a theatre production where the core speech was in a language that she could not understand the subtilties of, a play where a German-speaking, Arabic-speaking or English-speaking audience could all comprehend the story.

The ten-hour-long performance 'Dionysos Stadt' by Christopher Rüping included one of the *OBE* performers. Throughout the performance, he only spoke in Arabic and English. There was dramaturgical research on the characters he played in regard to how he would be represented. In the first chapter of the play – which included four – he was given the role of Zeus. The God of Gods condemns Prometheus for illegally bringing people fire, a symbol of light, enlightenment, and self-empowerment. In 'Dionysos Stadt' Zeus comes up from hell and asks Prometheus why – *leish:* "One day people will use it to build the bomb." Bombs against themselves and against the gods. People will use it to make war. The reference here is direct when uttered by a performer from Syria. Rüping's production reflected clearly on the language speech on stage with care towards German and non-German audiences. The English-German translation was sometimes part of the scenography staging itself. In the third chapter based on improvisation, the audience was given an English document to follow the plot on stage. This is without forgetting the humour where, for instance, one of the performers starts speaking in English and, before shifting to German, recommends the audience to kindly ask the Bavarian neighbour for translation if needed. The presence of a non-German performer in the cast had proven to have included an awareness of the complexity of the use of different languages in theatre throughout the process and that ended up included organically in the production itself without a feeling of 'forcing' such an inclusion but rather working with it meaningfully as one of the many components of the theatre making. For this play too, the choice of the translator-facilitator was determinant in how he became part of the team and the relationship he developed with the performer as well as the team. Also, it should be noted that the German versions of some of the Antique

Greek plays had to be found in their Arabic translation, which was not available in Europe. We could luckily find one last copy in a Beirut library that travelled with us to Munich.

Second Season

This experience paved the way for the second season, where no production tailored for the *OBE* was programmed. Instead, the performers were acting in theatre-programmed performances. This was the case in 'MacBeth', 'Vernon Subutex', and 'Melancholia'. Each of these experiences presented its peculiar challenges. At this stage, it is important to note that some of the performers were starting to get familiar with the German language as they were following courses. For 'MacBeth', both *OBE* performers were given lines in Arabic as well as in German for their secondary roles – which did not put them in a very comfortable position. The experience of 'Vernon Subutex' was different. It was agreed upon that the performer would speak in German. He was provided with a pronunciation coach to practice his accent. This was a productive training that informed the performer. However, in the end, since he did not have the capacity still to master German yet, he learned his text by heart and spoke it in a fair, good German but without understanding its inherent structure. Whoever knew this detail, was amazed by the effort. Whoever did not could not even hear an unfamiliar accent. A seamless integration into the dominant language was activated for the sake of the play. Indeed, the performer had to *act* the language. As for 'Melancholia', adapted from the movie, the *OBE* performer acted in English while the rest of the team was performing in German. This came as a dramaturgical choice knowing also that the original movie script was written in English.

Aside from that, the theatre enabled the small-scale productions of two individual works by *OBE* performers: 'iREHAB' by Majd Feddah in collaboration with Denis Metaxas and 'For the last time' by Kinan Hmeidan with Rabelle Ramez and Rita Hajjar (video). 'iREHAB' was played only for one night. It expressed, using psychedelic surrealistic esthetics, the turmoils of the performer-director and his theatre experience in Munich. The text was in English but mostly projected. In this theatrical essay, Feddah spoke back to the politics of the theatre instead of speaking on it. Such a 'speaking back' involved a refusal to play a 'good' actor or represent what the theatre system expected of him. It embraced literally and metaphorically the stranger and its strangeness while looking to disturb the audience of any familiarity that would make them understand the inside world of the performer-actor. The title itself, including the notion of rehabilitation, presumed the alienated condition of the protagonist but also the prejudice against him as an Arab[12]. On the other hand, 'For the Last Time', a video performance based on Jean-Luc Lagarce's text 'Juste la fin du monde', introduced a reflection on the meaning or feeling of non-belonging to a specific place, nomadism and therefore, the possibilities of starting anew. The unending cycle of constructing and deconstructing was illustrated concretely by the performer building a real wall that he would destroy at the end of each performance. In the video projection, we heard his voice reading the text in German. Indeed, the performer wanted to address this work to a German-speaking audience. Not yet feeling comfortable speaking the language, working on and recording the text in the spoken language of the 'new place' came as an effort of wanting to be understood at least by the local audience.

Third and Last Season

After going through all these linguistic experiences and questionings, the third season, which happened to be the last, witnessed radical experimentation. Doing diversity seemed to have its limits somehow. In 'Passing – It's so easy, was schwer zu machen ist' that elaborates on what is to be authentic and what is to be a "passing through", director René Pollesch chose not to translate his play to English and not to have surtitles. As a result, the play – knowing the central role text has in Pollesch esthetics – was inaccessible to non-German speakers and the text of the *OBE* performers ungraspable by the German audience. Preserving local languages as opposed to English seemed to represent a kind of political gesture that mattered more than what was being said. Following a similar thread in terms of shifting away from translation, inviting one of the *OBE* performers to join the team of choreographer Marlene Freitas Montero's 'Mal – Embriaguez Divina' questioned what could then be a theatrical experience outside of spoken words. Where to locate diversity in the meta-language of the body?

Conclusion

After contextualizing the process and the complex dynamics at stake within the *Open Border Ensemble* project, I briefly tried to identify how the notion of diversity on stage was brought on stage by the theatre makers who had to engage with the *Open Border Ensemble*, considering language as one of the visible signs of diversity. Looking chronologically as an outsider audience at how the non-German language was used in the different productions of the *Open Border Ensemble*, one could conclude that the

---

12   In Arabic, the title would read إرهاب which means terrorism.

theatrical process followed an evolution line: from a laboratory of doing diversity through challenging monolingualism, to a process of 'integration' where bilingualism was experimented, to an acculturation process where the hosting German language took over the hosted language or made sure it is heard but without encountering it. However, such an analytical approach dismisses the specificities of each project and the accumulated knowledge by whoever is taking part in and shaping this diversity work, making it sound easy and simplifying what is an extremely ambivalent process.

What certainly remains in question is how to activate a more holistic, intersectional and non-managerialist diversity work on the ground? In which way should we consider rethinking the conditions, resources and tools of diversity work outside of its labelling and marketing? How, then, to continue doing diversity beyond assigning it to a diversity agent within a theatre structure[13]? Indeed, if the existence of such a position brings forward issues of inequalities and injustice and more awareness towards the ways cultural and arts institutions are doing things, it still is problematic. As Ahmed argues (2012), other bodies are discharged from doing the work by making some bodies responsible for diversity. Consequently, those diversity bodies are stuck in reproducing a circle of privileges they are trying to break out from, while being the ones generating valuable knowledge of institutions and trying to transform them.

For as long as diversity is associated with the need to 'include' the others in a broader ecosystem defined by the hosting culture and not redefined together with the host, where the hosting/hosted relationship is willing to rearticulate its terms, and as long as the others are identified as such by what makes them different (in appearance and language etc.) from whoever belongs to the dominant culture, dealing with diversity ironically would necessitate maintaining the racialization of those others as 'bodies out of place' (Ahmed, 2000; Puwar, 2004). Redefining thus diversity requires moving away from the "stranger fetishization" (Ahmed 2000), whether as the origin of danger or the origin of celebrating differences, to comprehend how the stranger is not anybody but a socially constructed body. More broadly, in a vision that seeks to reflect on what a post-heimat theatre in Germany could be, it seems to me essential to keep on challenging the understanding of how to do diversity work, and to what extent it is doable and to when.

---

13   The *Post-Heimat Network* started to delve into the discussion of cultural diversity way before the creation of the diversity agent position for German cultural institutions. In fact, it witnessed its emergence. This position was specifically created and financed by the *KSB* within its *360° program* (2018–2023) to guide the diversity-oriented process of change at their respective cultural institution in Germany. For more, read Ozlem Canyürek, *Cultural Diversity in motion*, transcript Verlag, 2022.

Bibliography

Abu-Lughod, Lila. 1991. 'Writing Against Culture', in Richard Fox (ed.) *Recapturing Anthropology: Working in the Present*, Santa Fe, NM: School of American Research Press, pp. 137–162.

Ahmed, Sara. 2000. *Strange encounters: embodied others in post-coloniality*. London: Routledge.

Ahmed, Sara. 2009. *Embodying diversity: problems and paradoxes for Black feminists*. Race Ethnicity and Education, 12:1, 41–52.

Ahmed, Sara. 2012. *On Being Included: Racism and Diversity in Institutional Life*. Durham, NC: Duke University Press.

Ahmed Sara. 2017. *Living a feminist life*. Durham, NC:Duke University Press.

Ahmed Sara and Swan Elaine, 'Doing Diversity' in *Policy Futures in Education*, Volume 4, Number 2, 2006.

Favret-Saada Jeanne.1977. *Les Mots, la mort, les sorts. La sorcellerie dans le Bocage*. Paris, Gallimard, NRF.

Fischer-Lichte, Erika. 1992. *The Semiotics of Theatre*, translated by Jeremy Gaines and Doris L Jones, Bloomington and Indianapolis: Indiana University Press.

Fowler, Benjamin 'Dangerous Border Crossings: Nicolas Stemann's Merchant in Munich' in *The merchant of Venice The state of a play*, eds. M. Lindsay Kaplan, Bloomsbury, 2020.

Garde, Ulke, 'Negotiating Unfamiliar Languages and Accents in Contemporary Theatre', in *Theatre and Internationalization, Perspectives from Australia, Germany, and Beyond*, eds U. Garde, John, R. Severn, Routledge, 2020.

Goldmann A.J. 2018. 'In Conservative Munich, a Theater Turns Radical and Defends Refugees', *New York Times*, July 13, 2018: https://www.nytimes.com/2018/07/13/theater/muenchner-kammerspiele-matthias-lilienthal-refugees.html

Haraway, Donna. 1998. Situated Knowledges: The Science Question in Feminism and the Privilege of Partial Perspective' in *Feminist Studies* Volume 14, issue 3: 575–99.

Hunter, Shona, 'Working for Equality and Diversity in Adult and Community Learning: Leadership, Representation and Racialised 'Outsiders Within', in *Policy Futures in Education* Volume 4, issue 2: 114 – 127, 2006.

Kaplan Daniels, Arlene. 1987. *Social Problems* Volume 34, Number 5: 403–415.

Khoury K, Wierre-Gore G. 2017. « Détourner les asymétries : étude de cas à partir d'un processus de création chorégraphique ». In *Revue Traverse* : 123–137.

Puwar, Nirmal. 2004. *Space Invaders: Race, Gender and* Bodies Out *of* Place, Oxford and New York: Berg.

Totah R, Khoury K. 2018. "Theater against Borders: 'Miunikh–Damaskus'—A Case Study in Solidarity". In *Arts*. 7(4): 90.

Thinking Diversity Anew for Equal Rights in Performing Arts

Özlem Canyürek

Abstract In this article, I discuss the inclusion-oriented understanding of immigration-generated diversity by German cultural policymakers. I argue that a change in mindset in cultural policy is imperative for developing and advocating for a new non-discriminatory pluralistic discourse for the performing arts scene where an *Umleitkultur* (detour culture), proposed by the PostHeimat Network, can flourish. I explore a diversity vision following the idea of *Umleitkultur*, which offers a new form of engagement with "difference".

First, I examine the prerequisites of a diversity discourse in which Whiteness, Christianity, masculinity, heterosexuality, and able-bodiedness are not seen as the norm of society. In this context, I introduce the concept of *thinking and acting interculturally* as a cognitive tool for a cultural policy that strives to pluralise the performing arts field. Then, I propose a set of criteria for thinking and acting interculturally, envisioned as a means of a semantic shift in cultural policymaking towards recognising and validating multiple othernesses. Lastly, I claim that cultural policy's task is to generate framework conditions that foster bottom-up processes, aiming at an accessible performing arts scene for the entire artistic workforce.

Diversity is Not an Instrument of Inclusion

Since the early 2000s, the promotion of cultural diversity has been one of the main objectives of cultural policies of the *Bundesländer* (federal states) and municipalities in Germany. The federal government also supports diversity-centred projects through additional incentive programmes from various funding bodies. However, promoting diversity through canonised arts is often seen as the ultimate remedy for all societal issues. A glance at the funding structure and the concepts promoted through various funding programmes reveals the obvious. Although Germany is characterised by social diversity, diversity has mainly been associated with labour migration from the 1950s onwards. In cultural-political terms, diversity and migration are firmly linked with one another, and cultural diversity is introduced as part of an inclusive framework to integrate "culturally distant" immigrants[1]. Hence, diversity is seen as a point of destination that will be reached on the condition of these "particular immigrants" integrating into the imaginary homogenous German culture (Canyürek 2019: 404).

The ethnicity-focused cultural-political discourse on diversity singles out "migrant others" (Mecheril 2003) and lately refugees[2] as the addressee of policy measures. In parallel to this approach, cultural policies have been introducing countless diversity funding schemes at all three levels of government under the motto of "promoting diversity" through concepts such as interculturality and transculturality. The funding institutions often evaluate inter-and transcultural projects as good examples of integrating migrant others and refugees into society and emphasise the contribution of these projects to social cohesion and dialogue between different cultures (Canyürek 2021). In some cases, even project owners do not agree with the labelling of their work as integration-based participatory projects, and they underline that they produce artistic work together with migrantised and refugee artists.[3] Moreover, as stressed by theatre scholar Azadeh Sharifi, "policy bodies and cultural institutions treat interculturality as if it is synonymous with socio-culture[4] practice, and for them, intercultural art per se does not meet the quality standards of 'German high culture'" (2011: 242).

This intense focus on cultural integration designates migrant others and refugees as the sole agencies of intercultural and transcultural encounters, those

---

1   I use the phrase "immigrant" to refer to its use in cultural policy, aware of the fact that it is not a neutral term since it designates a distance between people of German and non-German descent.

2   I employ terms such as "refugees" and "people seeking refuge" based on their usage by cultural-political actors and performing arts institutions and initiatives, aware of the fact that they are not synonymous. I seeks to, on the one hand, draw attention to the different applications of the term "refugee" in cultural policy and theatre practice; on the other hand, I aim to underline the difficulty of conceptualising a legislative term without disparaging people to their legal status or contributing to the construction of a collective "refugee identity".

3   As part of my doctoral study, I examined three independent theatre initiatives, namely boat people projekt, Hajusom, and Ruhrorter, and conducted interviews with the representatives of these three theatres. All the interviewees stated that it was expected of them to use a certain vocabulary (e.g., participation, inclusion, integration, diversity) in the funding applications, and their works are still often seen part of socio-culture and cultural education fields, and usually supported by the funding programmes of the actors of these fields. Although boat people projekt, Hajusom, and Ruhrorter were nominated for various inclusion/integration awards many times and won some of them, they regard themselves as political theatres, engaged with the social realities of Germany and their localities.

4   Socio-culture emerged as a concept in German cultural policy to prompt efforts towards the democratisation of culture from the early 1970s onwards, opposing the elitist character of the arts and promising culture for all.

assumed to have a "migrant and refugee identity", and disregards the other parties of artistic interaction. The position of the White majority society remains external to cultural diversity. As Sarah Ahmed states, "'we" emerges as the one who has to live with it [cultural diversity]' (2000: 95). The process of change is only ascribed to migrant others. This mindset reduces from the very beginning the probability of a dialogical encounter in which all sides are subject to transformation.

Kulturnation and *Heimat* under Construction

The emancipation of the notion of diversity from the inclusion/integration frame is ultimately linked to renouncing two ideologically overloaded cultural-political concepts, namely *Heimat* (home) and *Kulturnation* (culture nation). Culture has always been at the heart of Germany's self-definition (van der Will and Burns 2015). The idea of a culture-defined nation, *Kulturnation*, —in different forms— signifies cultural unity and is still strongly influential in cultural policymaking (Bloomfield 2003; van der Will and Burns 2015; Wesner 2010). This unity refers to the unification of Germany and does not involve the cultural capital of the nation after the labour migration of the 1950s. On the other hand, *Heimat* anticipates an idea of an exclusive home, enclosed in a rigid national frame that defines the boundaries of belonging. As Shermin Langhoff puts it, '*Heimat* is, and always was, "fatherland" and is thus inseparably linked with the patriarchy as a concept' (2020: 477). I argue that there is a firm bond between the concepts of *Heimat* and *Kulturnation*. They still reflect a conservative conception of a historically rooted White masculine national identity and space. Even though *Heimat* and *Kulturnation* have taken on new forms and gained (arguably) less controversial meanings, they cannot escape from the *Leitkultur* (leading/guiding culture) discussions since both terms define top-down culture in a concealed manner.

The idea of an equality-oriented diversity discourse requires a new understanding of inclusive culture in an intercultural society where national and cultural spaces are not defined by the hegemony of the White, Christian, male, heterosexual, and able-bodied. Intercultural society refers to 'a community that is never final, always, infinitely, in process, a community without fixed borders, which, furthermore, has a singular "membership" that constantly puts assigned roles or, indeed, the idea of membership as such, in question' (McDonald 2011: 378). This spontaneous process appoints various forms of otherness as the subject of transformation.

It is a sine qua non for cultural policies at all levels of government to support discussions, developments, and structures that contribute to the pluralisation of knowledge production and dissemination in the performing arts scene. In this context, PostHeimat offers a refreshing perspective on reconsidering the meanings of cultural identity and home. PostHeimat 'signals a pluralistic re-appropriation of *Heimat*' (PostHeimat 2020: 1) that pursues a novel interpretation of nation and recognises the multiplicity of being. I envision this alternative interpretation of *Heimat* as a counter-concept that disowns the way of thinking that separates human beings into various compartments and assigns them the role of representatives of certain ethnic groups. Conversely, PostHeimat provides the opportunity to acknowledge identity as a dynamic entity. It seeks to reflect the image of a society, understood as being under construction, in which the idea of culture is always in the making, in constant process. To this end, I read the notion of *Umleitkultur* by the PostHeimat Network as an invigorating suggestion to challenge the national narrative and the static and monolithic perception of "the culture", since the concept entails the pursuit of 'a non-normative culture accepting detours, rather than straight roads' (PostHeimat 2020: 1).

In the following subsection, I explore the potentiality of a concept that corresponds with a dynamic and fluid diversity narrative that confronts the present rigid and restricted boundaries of "Germanness" in line with the notion of *Umleitkultur*. With this endeavour, I aim to seek out a concept for a non-hierarchical performing arts scene in which heterogeneity of thoughts, experiences, knowledge, aesthetics, and world views can be articulated, appreciated, and circulated as normality.

Going Beyond Dialogue: Thinking and Acting Interculturally[5]

Diversity is inseparable from the identity dimension of culture. Typically, cultural policies recognise community/group identities and produce plans and measures accordingly to enhance the participation of diverse community cultures in the arts. The objectives and funding criteria of many public funding programmes promoting diversity reveal that the individuality of identity is often overlooked. Artists are referred to as people with a "post-migrant perspective" and lately "exile perspective", representing cultural diversity. Further, the limits of their "playground" are strictly defined, confined to migration and displacement as if they cannot hold multiple artistic perspectives and positions.

Linguist Peter McDonald (2011) suggests using the adverbial form of interculturalism, *thinking interculturally*, as an alternative conceptualisation to multiculturalism, varieties of cosmopolitanism, and interculturalism. He claims that the adverbial form 'identifies the intercultural as a diverse, risky and lived process' (2011: 372). McDonald argues that cultures are never separated and distinct but always exist interculturally:

---

5   This and the following subsection, "Indicators of Interculturality in Performing Arts", were derived from my doctoral thesis *Cultural Diversity in Motion: Rethinking Cultural Policy and Performing Arts in an Intercultural Society* (Bielefeld: transcript Verlag, 2022).

The merits of a formulation like 'thinking interculturally' lie firstly in the fact that it avoids the bounded logic of the prefix 'multi-', giving priority to this movement across cultural borders of various kinds. It still, of course, assumes that such borders exist and, therefore, that culture (...) plays a powerful role in the world, contributing to many individual and group self-understanding. What the adverbial formulation underscores grammatically is that these borders are porous and labile. (...) Since all cultures, including dominant ones, are less coherent and more mixed than we like to believe, or that the political pressures of a particular moment might require us to believe, the intercultural as an ongoing, open-ended process is all-pervasive. (2011: 372–373)

Moreover, the adverbial formulation is instrumental in comprehending the changing demographic structure of contemporary Germany as well as the individual dimension of identity; it also makes room for a new understanding of an intercultural community, which is envisaged in constant progress and transition. This understanding emphasises that 'singular beings with their plural identities [are] confronted by underlying structural forces around them, and these forces may put their singularity at risk' (McDonald 2011: 381). People, with their multiple identities, are the subjects of interaction. Being in an encounter with one another opens the process of a living dialogue that includes both agreement and conflict between dynamic identities (Ahmed 2000; Cantle 2012; Wood et al. 2006).

In this paper, identity is understood as multiple (Hall 2000) and intersectional (Crenshaw 1989). Following the above-mentioned line of thought, I examine the adequacy of the concept of thinking and acting interculturally for a pluralistic diversity vision by approaching it beyond the perspective of dialogue between different cultural communities.

Based on the proposal by McDonald (2011), the new conceptualisation, thinking and acting interculturally, is a heuristic attempt at reconsidering the meaning of cultural diversity outside the prescribed frames that operate as promoting versions of a static, insulated, and impermeable "us" within a nation-state, not allowing multiple othernesses to occur. Thinking and acting interculturally, on the other hand, signifies a conceptual tool, a frame of mind, which should be manifested in the strategies, actions, and organisational structures of performing arts institutions and initiatives. It seeks to offer a reflective outlook on dealing with processes of othering and the underlying power dynamics.

Thinking and acting interculturally by no means suggests cultural hybridity. It describes a curious, relentless learning process that allows co-creating versions of culture in constant motion, and it includes ambiguity, conflict, negotiation, and transition. In this understanding, marginalised positions are not determined as "the other" since the idea recognises the meeting of multiple fabrications of otherness, inspired by the conceptualisation of Fiona Sze (2004: 127). Thinking and acting interculturally enables transformative encounters for all members of society.

Indicators of Interculturality in Performing Arts

I examined three independent theatre initiatives, namely boat people projekt, Hajusom, and Ruhrorter for the concept formation. These theatres comprise the *casing*[6], which is part of a case study research analysis presented in my doctoral thesis. Through the casing, I sought to link the theoretical proposition to the empirical basis (Ragin and Becker 1992) in order to reify the conceptualisation. The evaluation of the casing provided different elements of thinking and acting interculturally. Moreover, in this query, the academic and practice-based knowledge exchange of the PostHeimat Network enabled determining various attributes of the concept of thinking and acting interculturally.

The following interlinked aspects are identified as the essential features of thinking and acting interculturally. By no means is the list of criteria complete; it is instead envisioned as a stepping-stone for a semantic shift in diversity discourse, a contribution to the efforts towards recognising cultural diversity beyond a management model that employs cultural differences for organisational efficiency (Faist 2009). The criteria are considered analytical parameters for a change in mindset for the White-dominated German performing arts field. Hence, they are formulated as indexes of an interculturally organised theatre practice. For this reason, the features of thinking and acting interculturally listed below signify a cognitive tool for the performing arts scene rather than a cultural policy measure. One should bear in mind that learning to deal with difference and ambiguity does not alter the existing structural inequalities (Nising and Mörsch 2018: 142). Cultural policy should tackle institutionalised inequalities, discrimination, and racism through an explicit cultural policy vision, careful planning, and implementation strategies for the pluralistic transformation of the theatrical sphere.

The following criteria refer to the interconnected ways of engaging with various axes of difference, the social and political construction of otherness, and the power disparity between partners in artistic exchange:

---

6   I use the alternative phrase "casing" instead of case, following the suggestion of Ragin and Becker, 'as a research tactic (…) to resolve difficult issues in linking ideas and evidence' (1992: 217). As a cultural policy researcher, my interests were decisive in delimiting the boundaries of the cases. The casing was stimulated by concept formation and it involved 'not selection on a random basis or the basis of typicality, but on the basis of theoretical interests in cases' (Ragin and Becker, 1992: 222). Thus, constructing the theoretical framework of the conceptualisation and collecting the matching empirical evidence to exercise the relevance of the conceptual proposition is more precisely denominated as casing.

Motivation: Critically examining one's conduct and motives for 'making diversity a goal' (Ahmed 2012). The foremost question is whether the commitment to diversity is related to the fact that 'it is obviously (now) "the right thing to do"' (Vertovec 2012: 306). People that hold privileged positions should interrogate the credibility and authenticity of their motivations (Süngün 2016: 151), especially within White artistic practices and institutions. In this regard, motivation is a decisive signal for determining whether engagement with diversity is understood as an artistic interaction between different realms of experiences and knowledge.

Process orientation: Recognising process as an open-ended and continuous learning practice, not limited to various phases of artistic production. Process orientation fundamentally denotes the processes of encounter and exchange, which involve ambivalence, conflict, and contingency. It refers to all forms of deliberation and communication between institutions/initiatives and professional and amateur artists with observable exclusions and different overlapping identities. It also refers to the relationship with the audience. At the level of reception, it means to perceive the process as a way of conveying a diverse array of views, expressions, knowledge, and experiences using performance. These creative processes turn theatre into a space for the mobilisation of juxtapositional othernesses without neutralising it.

The ethical dimension of dialogue: Being occupied with the question of how to develop an ethical approach without perpetuating the existing frames that treat some people as "the other". First and foremost, ethical communication refers to a mindset that 'resists thematising others as "the other"' (Ahmed 2000: 144). The ethical premise in this context primarily entails disowning the narrow perception of the human condition. Creating a heterogeneous space includes acknowledging human beings as multiple othernesses with various perspectives, orientations, and affiliations.

On a related second level, the ethics of communication calls for abandoning superior positions that carry the traces of colonial continuities. In this interaction, the White German majority society is internalised as normative, the one that dominates, and "the other" is assigned as subordinate. Terms of communication, on the contrary, require seeing the performative space through a non-insular lens that recognises intercultural society as the norm.

Conditions of emancipation: The frame of empowerment starts with questioning the basis of intent and the terms of autonomy. Given the scale of profoundly and historically rooted power dynamics, the liberation of the artistic expressions of "the other" often rests upon the perception and accompanying implications of the dominant positions. Thus, a critical engagement with empowerment recognises 'the hegemonic discourses that reproduce them [hegemonic positionalities], such as whiteness, heteronormativity, patriarchy, Eurocentrism, etc.' (Steyn 2015: 382). In turn, such an understanding entails 'a self-reflexive critique that questions the ways of "giving a voice" to the systematically silenced' (Cañas 2017a: para. 3). The claim of commitment to diversity further raises questions about the sites of emancipation: What is the basis of emancipation? Who is in the position to set the boundaries of empowerment, and what are their intentions? What are the limits of outside intervention? It should also be taken into account that the aspiration to empower marginalised groups and artists for a fairer representation could unintentionally reproduce clichés; "hence, there is a risk that the representations of "the other" imprison the subjects in stereotypical images strengthening the ideology of *"the national-self* and *the immigrant-other"'* (Benjamin 2013: 23). This suggests that the recognition of marginalised people as autonomous subjects and equal partners in determining the conditions of empowerment and negotiating power is vital for the establishment of non-hegemonic forms of interaction.

Standing in solidarity: Challenging the unequal distribution of power and opposing various forms of exploitation of excluded performing arts professionals, seeing artistic solidarity and cooperation as a form of resistance, confronting those binary lines between "us" and "the other". Theatre as a space of resistance also means a reflection of an artistic practice that seeks to transgress the historically constructed privileged positions. Hence, it is essential to acknowledge solidarity as a counter strategy for the self-empowerment of marginalised people in their struggle against exclusion. It follows that what lies at the foundation of constructive cooperation is whether it is mutually beneficial. Building fair cooperation, based on trust and consensus, entails a continuous exploration of its conditions, structures, and processes; from the onset, there is an agreement on cooperation itself as an experiment (Hampel 2015). However, one should not dismiss the possibility of cooperation being challenged by conflicting expectations and needs.

Networking: Given the exclusionary structure of the German performing arts scene, networking is one of the modes of solidarity practiced through artistic exchange to overcome structural barriers and share know-how and resources. The synergy between performing arts institutions and initiatives, artists, and researchers could be considered a form of cultural activism in which the arts, politics, and activism blend (Verson 2007), as well as a mode of cultural resistance (Duncombe 2002) envisioning the concept of democracy through collective action which contributes to the development of participatory approaches (della Porta and Diani 2006). In this regard, it is also a modality of a bottom-up, alternative policy prospect that explores the possibilities of new equality-based political-artistic imaginaries in the theatrical space.

Aesthetical frame: Aesthetics refers to a mode of negotiation of the self through knowledge exchange. This negotiation process is understood more as an act on a political and ethical level than the aesthetics of performance. It is characterised by the motivation to deal with existing inequities in artistic exchange and concerned with the ways of production of theatrical knowledge outside the Western canon. It searches for trajectories that explore exchange beyond the hybrid, universal, or cosmopolitan appropriation of culture proposed and practised by the same Western theatre vision. As articulated by Bharucha, "the 'universal minimum' that can be said to initiate any intercultural exchange is extremely fragile, based more on intuition and good faith than on any real cognisance of the Other" (1999: 15). In this context, the answers to the following crucial questions serve as measures of a genuine inter-action: What does the aesthetical frame aim to convey? Who determines it? What are the conditions of that particular aesthetics? How and for whom is it designed?

Narration of a multiplicity of experiences: Various forms of narrativisation of experiences foster the development of new theatrical expressions. The Western appropriation of the "cultures of the other" tends to fabricate reductive cultural narratives around diversity, migration, and displacement. These narratives hinder the authentic articulation of artistic expressions by the racialised and marginalised artists and performing arts professionals coming into contact with the majority society.

In the German context, considering particularly the current overexcitement around engaging in "refugee work" and doing migration-oriented "diversity/inter-cultural/transcultural projects", even the most well-intentioned approaches often generate victim narratives. These perspectives confine migrant others and refugees to a frame that forces them to perform victimhood and stereotypical roles assigned to them. Alison Jeffers describes this attitude, which unveils itself in the emerging canon of refugee theatre in the UK, as 'the need for the "right" kind of refugee story in which complexities are smoothed out to create a simple linear narrative of individual crisis and flight' (2012: 46). This perception does not serve the aim of perceiving "the other" as creative, skilled, knowledgeable, or autonomous beings. On the contrary, as Cañas aptly points out, "this perpetuates a dynamic in which those remain a passive, self-apologetic voice in the national place rather than a galvanising force, utilising social commentary, and involved in acts of political engagement" (2017b: 69). Hence, a range of multiple narrations of experiences would facilitate the exploration, validation, and circulation of different types of stories in which racialised and marginalised voices are not (re)imaged by the Western theatre canon and reduced to simplistic fictitious characters.

Multilingualism: Monolingualism is recognised as one of the indexes of German drama theatre. This is related to the historically rooted establishment of theatre as a medium for representing the national interest of the Bürgertums (bourgeoisie) (Israel 2011: 61). On that account, the German language is still associated with the ideals of the nation-state which prevail in the theatrical canon, although its educated middle-class audience has been shrinking (Mandel 2013). This aspect also reveals whose needs and expectations the programming is designed for. In addition, "multilingualism is used by the majority of theatres at most as a conscious stylistic device in individual, content-wise appropriate productions, if, for example, communication problems on a linguistic level are thematised" (Holthaus 2011: 154). Considering the transnational configuration of the world, showing disinterest for linguistic diversity is no longer a possibility. As dramaturge Björn Bicker states, "it is inevitable that immigrant artists will change the formal language of German theatre practice; hence, it will not be possible to maintain the primacy of the pure German (stage) language for long" (2009: 30).

Recognising the interaction between languages is an integral part of multiperspectivity and the reality of an intercultural society. If theatre is understood as the self-reflection of society, then it should be conceived as a space that communicates with various characteristics of this society, including its language. The linguistic aspect refers not only to the modes of communication between theatre, actors, and audiences as a feature of performative strategies but also a connection between the memories of citizens and the histories of societies; the history of the past, present, and future in the making.

Being self-critical and self-reflexive: Having the willingness to develop self-reflexivity and a critical mode of self-understanding to confront the established boundaries and the deconstructive absolutisation of differences in interactions in the theatrical space. For reflexivity to be transformative for all parties involved, the question of 'how we can at the same time do justice to the other's otherness (and [their] (...) own situatedness) as well as to ours' (de Schutter 2004: 51) should be embodied as a vital principle. Following this logic, self-reflexivity reopens a potentiality for thinking critically about deficit-oriented imaginaries of difference ascribed to "the other". One's self-understanding depends primarily on the question of whether the differences are entrenched in essentialist partitions attributed to "the other" within the structure of an artistic medium but also in one's mind.

Solidarity, Collective Thinking, Engendering Collective Memory

Two years of participant observation based on process-tracing demonstrated that although boat people projekt, Hajusom, and Ruhrorter have different strategies and artistic formats, they commonly acknowledge every human experience as equally valuable, and understand diversity as a dynamic learning process that involves critical self-reflection and the continuous transformation of perspectives and artistic methodologies to connect with the contemporary German society. However, in its limited scope, this article cannot exhaustively introduce the approaches and working methods of these theatre initiatives. Instead, I briefly focus on three aspects that signify the foundation of the conceptualisation of thinking and acting interculturally.

Founded in 2009, boat people projekt defines itself as a political theatre committed to socio-political matters. In their first years, the theatre collective had made mostly plays with refugee youth, focusing on their arrival and living conditions in Germany. The name "boat people projekt" originates from the group's first production, *Lampedusa*, and is associated with the reality of refugees trying to arrive in Europe by crossing the Mediterranean Sea. In the following years, the artistic perspective of the collective changed tremendously through collaboration and networking with excluded artists. Recently, the theatre has been in the pursuit of a new name:

> Over the course of time, we have become conscious of the fact that through our name, we label the people we work with. As we ideally want to prevent this, our name is currently under discussion. Due to the growth in awareness and knowledge of the group's work, a radical change is difficult. As yet, this question has not been resolved. (boat people projekt 2021)

Starting from 2015, standing in solidarity with these artists has gained importance for boat people projekt. The theatre collective started co-producing with displaced and racialised theatre-makers. In 2016, Nina de la Chevallerie, director and co-founder, initiated a research project with Rzgar Khalil, funded by the *Homebase – Theatre for the Coming Society* programme of the Performing Arts Fund, to identify the structural problems displaced theatre professionals face regarding access to the theatre scene in Lower Saxony. Towards the end of 2017, boat people projekt, together with the State Association of Independent Theatres of Lower Saxony (Landesverband Freier Theater Niedersachsen) and the Federal Academy for Cultural Education Wolfenbüttel (Bundesakademie für Kulturelle Bildung Wolfenbüttel) organised a meeting titled "New Connections" to network with professional artists seeking refuge in Germany. The engagement with research projects was subsequently followed by the aspiration to share the working space of boat people projekt with racialised directors and artistic teams.

Hajusom identifies itself as a transnational ensemble determined by collective thinking. Since 1999, the theatre initiative has been working with young performers of various cultural backgrounds. A non-hierarchal artistic exchange between team members is one of the vital components of the creative processes of transcultural performances. This exchange, however, is not seen as the assemblage of "foreign cultures" or the reflection of cultural hybridity. On the contrary, it is perceived as a process that enables individuals to incorporate their visions, images, world views, articulations, and artistic responses in the collective idea of Hajusom. To avoid reducing refugees within the confines of identity, the initiative is concerned with exploring new storytelling formats that display actors as beyond refuge-beings. Correspondingly, the collective opposes pre-defined Eurocentric/Western projections and labels placed on the artistic profession, theatre education, and training. They consider these prescribed categories to be barriers to the acknowledgment and enunciation of diverse forms of knowledge.

For Hajusom, the central objective is the continual circulation of heterogeneity of knowledge and its transnational performative methodology. Hence, they adopted the concept of "each one teaches one" to deal with the hierarchical relationality between various positions in the organisational structure, such as the one between the co-founding White artistic directors and other team members. The concept of "each one teaches one" relates to facilitating the self-expression of the younger team members. In this context, empowerment is understood as searching for ways to build channels for multi-vocal conversations. Hajusom established two artistic platforms, namely *Lab* and *Transfer*, as part of its implementation strategies of knowledge production and artistic methodology dissemination. Experienced members are part of the artistic management; they give training and workshops to newcomers. Hajusom recognises them as the protagonists and transmitters of the transnational way of thinking and the working strategy of the theatre collective.

Since its establishment in 2012, Ruhrorter has been working with young refugees. The theatre initiative describes themselves as a refugee theatre. They emphasise that "refugee" is a legal status, not an identity, recognising it as an ethical responsibility to decisively underline the difference between legal status and the complex nature of identity. This choice is also interrelated with contributing to the efforts towards removing the barrier between "us" and "the stranger", bringing "the stranger" from the position of "object" to the position of "subject".

The aesthetical framework of Ruhrorter relies mainly on non-discursive forms of expression created during long rehearsal processes. This approach was adopted from the artistic format of the Theater an der Ruhr that delineates a 'specific theatre methodology which premises upon discipline and the cultivation of the self that foregrounds the aesthetics of a reflexive theatre' (Tinius 2015: 185; Tinius 2023). The focus is placed on the establishment of self-consciousness rather than the theatrical product per se. Hence, process orientation is deemed essential for supporting performers in their mental preparation for learning how to form conscious body movements, develop improvisational impulses, and gradually shape their expressions.

This specific mindset is also a strategy to connect the narratives of otherness, marginalisation, and abandonment by intertwining the history of the postindustrial Ruhr Valley with the experiences of displacement. The theatre employs various artistic strategies to renounce the mentality of "presenting other cultures" to the audience. One of the methods Ruhrorter uses to avoid subjectivities within ethnic boundaries is to create communication between refugees, residents, and the neglected past of the former industrial spaces. The core idea is to make theatre not in a conventional theatre setup but in a space with its own story, such as a former asylum seekers' accommodation centre, former women's prison, vacant commercial property, etc. The minimalistic aesthetics, combined with mental preparation and presence, is employed to make the stigmatisation and isolation of refugees and long-forgotten places visible and to negotiate the history of the future.

A Call for an Accessible Performing Arts Scene

Discussions on diversity cannot be disassociated from systematic exclusion, discrimination, and racism in the German performing arts scene. All cultural policy actions, implementation strategies, and funding schemes aimed at promoting diversity must primarily deal with the imbalanced power structure that generates inequalities. One way of reducing the access barriers for the marginalised and excluded artistic workforce is to continually support a diversity discourse that enables the establishing and thriving of an *Umleitkultur*.

Various independent performing arts initiatives and networks actively advocate equal rights and an inclusive theatrical landscape. However, they operate under severe financial constraints, subsidised almost solely through project-based funding. One of the tasks of cultural policy should be to support these non-institutionalised structures that manifest the dynamism of diversity. These have a considerable potential to nurture normalising cultural differences and contribute to the development of a fairness-based discourse on cultural diversity.

Investing in flexible and exploratory structures for the diversification of knowledge, including production, dissemination, and reception, is part of generating the framework conditions for the creation and cultivation of a new pluralistic diversity discourse for a non-hierarchical performing arts scene. To develop an accessible performing arts field for all, cultural policy should provide long-term funding to promote learning laboratories and bottom-up modalities that relentlessly search for new ways of understanding the needs and expectations of an intercultural society.

References

Ahmed, Sara. 2000. *Strange encounters: Embodied others in post-coloniality*. New York: Routledge.

Ahmed, Sara. 2012. *On being included: Racism and diversity in institutional life*. Durham, NC: Duke University Press.

Benjamin, Saija. 2013. "Towards interculturalism through meaningful identities: An overview of the first 4 conferences." In *Interculturalism, meaning and identity*, edited by Daniel Boswell, Roger O'Shea, and Efrat Tzadik, 1–24. Oxford: Inter-Disciplinary Press.

Bharucha, Rustom. 1999. "Interculturalism and its discriminations: Shifting the agendas of the national, the multicultural and the global." *Third Text* 13 (46): 3–23.

Bicker, Björn. 2009. „Theater Als Parallelgesellschaft? Über Das Verhältnis von Theater Und Migration." In *No integration?! Kulturwissenschaftliche Beiträge zur Integrationsdebatte in Europa*, edited by Sabine Hess, Jana Binder, and Johannes Moser, 27–34. Bielefeld: transcript Verlag.

Bloomfield, Jude. 2003. "'Made in Berlin': Multicultural conceptual confusion and intercultural reality." *International Journal of Cultural Policy* 9 (2): 167–183.

boat people projekt. 2021. "boat people projekt." Accessed June 10, 2021. https://www.boatpeopleprojekt.de/boat-people-projekt/

Cantle, Ted. 2012. *Interculturalism: The new era of cohesion and diversity*. London: Palgrave Macmillan.

Canyürek, Özlem. 2019. "Cultural diversity in theatre: Immigration and German cultural policy." In *Forschungsfeld Kulturpolitik – eine Kartierung von Theorie und Praxis: Festschrift für Wolfgang Schneider*, edited by Daniel Gad, Katharina M. Schröck, and Aron Weigl, 399–406. Hildesheim: Universitätsverlag Hildesheim; Hildesheim: Georg Olms Verlag AG.

Canyürek, Özlem. 2021. "Promoting cultural diversity in the German theatre landscape." In *Performing arts between politics and policies: Implications and challenges*, edited by Ana Letunić and Jovana Karaulić, 38–50. Belgrade: Faculty of Dramatic Arts; Zagreb: Academy of Dramatic Art.

Cañas, Tania. 2017a. "Diversity is a White word." *ArtsHub*, January 9, 2017. https://www.artshub.com.au/education/news-article/opinions-and-analysis/professional-development/tania-canas/diversity-is-a-white-word-252910

Cañas, Tania. 2017b. "Three angry Australians: A reflexive approach." In *Performing exile: Foreign bodies*, edited by Judith Rudakoff, 59–74. Bristol: Intellect. https://doi.org/10.2307/j.ctv9hj90p.7

Crenshaw, Kimberlé. 1989. "Demarginalizing the intersection of race and sex: A Black feminist critique of antidiscrimination doctrine, feminist theory and antiracist politics." *University of Chicago Legal Forum* 1989 (1): 139–167. https://chicagounbound.uchicago.edu/uclf/vol1989/iss1/8

de Schutter, Helder. 2004. "Gadamer and interculturalism: Ethnocentrism or authenticity." In *Interculturalism: Exploring critical issues*, edited by Diane Powell and Fiona Sze, 51–57. Oxford: Inter-Disciplinary Press.

della Porta, Donatella, and Mario Diani. 2006. *Social movement: An introduction*. 2nd ed. Oxford: Blackwell Publishing.

Duncombe, Stephen, ed. 2002. *Cultural resistance reader*. London: Verso.

Faist, Thomas. 2009. "Diversity – A new mode of incorporation?" *Ethnic and Racial Studies* 32 (1): 171–190.

Hall, Stuart. 2000. "Who needs identity?" In *Identity: A reader*, edited by Paul du Gay, Jessica Evans, and Peter Redman, 15–30. London: Sage Publications.

Hampel, Annika. 2015. *Fair Cooperation: Partnerschaftliche Zusammenarbeit in der Auswärtigen Kulturpolitik*. Wiesbaden: Springer VS.

Holthaus, Christina. 2011. „'Jeder macht das mal auf seine Art und Weise': Ansätze und Herausforderungen einer interkulturellen Spielplangestaltung." In *Theater und Migration: Herausforderungen für Kulturpolitik und Theaterpraxis*, edited by Wolfgang Schneider, 147–158. Bielefeld: transcript Verlag.

Israel, Annett. 2011. "Kulturelle Identitäten als dramatisches Ereignis: Beobachtungen aus dem Kinder- und Jugendtheater." In *Theater und Migration: Herausforderungen für Kulturpolitik und Theaterpraxis*, edited by Wolfgang Schneider, 47–64. Bielefeld: transcript Verlag.

Jeffers, Alison. 2012. *Refugees, theatre and crisis*. London: Palgrave Macmillan UK.

Langhoff, Shermin. 2020. "Taking history personally: Knowing that neither memories are already memory, nor stories already history." *European Journal of Theatre and Performance* 2: 464–487.

Mandel, Birgit. 2013. *Interkulturelles Audience Development: Zukunftsstrategien für öffentlich geförderte Kultureinrichtungen*. Bielefeld: transcript.

McDonald, Peter D. 2011. "Thinking interculturally: Amartya Sen's lovers revisited." *Interventions: International Journal of Postcolonial Studies* 13 (3): 367–85.

Mecheril, Paul. 2003. *Prekäre Verhältnisse: Über natio-ethno-kulturelle (Mehrfach-)Zugehörigkeit*. Münster: Waxmann Verlag.

Nising, Lena Prabha, and Carmen Mörsch. 2018. „Statt 'Transkulturalität' und 'Diversität': Diskriminierungskritik und Bekämpfung von Strukturellem Rassismus." In *Jahrbuch Für Kulturpolitik 2017/18, Band 16, Thema: Welt. Kultur. Politik. Kulturpolitik in Zeiten der Globalisierung*, edited by Ulrike Blumenreich, Sabine Dengel, Wolfgang Hippe, Norbert Sievers, and Institut für Kulturpolitik der KuPoGe, 139–150. Bielefeld: transcript Verlag.

PostHeimat. 2020. *Problematising PostHeimat*, April 11, 2020. https://www.postheim at.com/research-en/

Ragin, Charles C., and Howard S. Becker, eds. 1992. *What is a case? Exploring the foundations of social inquiry*. Cambridge: Cambridge University Press.

Sharifi, Azadeh. 2011. *Theater für Alle? Partizipation von Postmigranten am Beispiel der Bühnen der Stadt Köln*. Frankfurt am Main: Peter Lang.

Steyn, Melissa. 2015. "Critical diversity literacy: Essentials for the twenty-first century." In *Routledge international handbook of diversity studies*, edited by Steven Vertovec, 379–389. New York: Routledge.

Süngün, Ülkü. 2016. „Solidarität und Dissens: Ülkü Süngün im Interview mit Caroline Gritschke." In *Geflüchtete Und Kulturelle Bildung: Formate und Konzepte für ein neues Praxisfeld*, edited by Caroline Gritschke and Maren Ziese, 149–154. Bielefeld: transcript Verlag.

Sze, Fiona Siang Yun. 2004. "How interculturalism performs: Performativity, performability and theatricality of interculturalism." In *Interculturalism: Exploring critical issues*, edited by Diane Powell and Fiona Sze, 127–134. Oxford: Inter-Disciplinary Press.

Tinius, J. 2015. "Ethical self-cultivation as the politics of engaged theatre. How theatre engages refugee politics". In: A. Flynn and J. Tinius, eds. *Anthropology, theatre, and development: The transformative potential of performance*. London: Palgrave, p. 171- 202.

Tinius, Jonas. 2023. *State of the Arts. An Ethnography of German Theatre and Migration*. Cambridge: Cambridge University Press.

van der Will, Wilfried, and Rob Burns. 2015. "Germany as *Kulturnation*: Identity in diversity?" In *Routledge handbook of German politics & culture*, edited by Sarah Colvin, 198–217. New York: Routledge.

Verson, Jennifer. 2007. "Why we need cultural activism?" In *Do it yourself: A handbook for changing the world*, edited by The Trapese Collective, 171–186. London: Pluto Press.

Vertovec, Steven. 2012. "'Diversity' and the social imaginary." *European Journal of Sociology* 53 (3): 287–312.

Wesner, Simone. 2010. "Cultural fingerprints – The legacy of cultural values in the current cultural policy agenda in Germany." *International Journal of Cultural Policy* 16 (4): 433–448.

Wood, Phil, Charles Landry, and Jude. 2006. *Cultural diversity in Britain: A toolkit for cross-cultural co-operation*. York: Joseph Rowntree Foundation.

(EN)COUNTERING THE FUTURE:
Notes on intersectional-diverse dramaturgical approaches

Christopher-Fares Köhler

"So that is how to create a single story, show a people as one thing, as only one thing, over and over again, and that is what they become." – Chimamanda Ngozi Adichie[1]

Looking Back / Moving Forward

For more than 12 years there has been a shift of discussion about diversity and representation on and behind the German theater stages. These discussions are closely connected to certain social-political events, but first, I think it is necessary to agree on the following: there is no *one* perspective of diversity, but there is – in my opinion – certainly *one dominant* idea (and perspective) that has prevailed for a long time in thinking of diversity in public discussions when it comes to theatre and the arts in Germany.

As I write this text, 1,5 years of the coronavirus pandemic have put German theatre institutions on a halt. Slowly, vaguely, things started to open up again. This "halt" opened a wider space of discussions about theatre institutions, power and misuse, racism and oppression, and talks about identities and representation(s). The call for structural reform of state and municipal institutions dominated the German cultural press, blogs, and comment sections. But these topics are not new; they are just being made visible and shed light on what has been hidden for far too long. I believe that we are in a state of in-between. German theatre is in a state of in-between. In the following pages, I would like to discuss and define tools for intersectional and diverse dramaturgy, as one cannot be thought of without the other. Various writers and dramaturges have written articles stating and defending a certain status quo. In their texts, they get personal, compare theatre rehearsals to war situations, and

---

1   Chimamanda Ngozi Adichie. 2024. "The Danger of a Single Story." Ted.com. TED Talks. 2024. h ttps://www.ted.com/talks/chimamanda_ngozi_adichie_the_danger_of_a_single_story/tr.

gaslight actors who choose to speak up. They completely ignore the fact that the "accusers" had to endanger their working places and careers, arguing that 'it isn't more than personal hurt' and diminishing them by going to the very personal level themselves. They bully them into an argument without understanding or acknowledging the structures of power that are in place, or worse, just calling them bad actors and ending the discussion.

So where to go from here? Retreat? Remain silent? I would like to emphasize the perspective of being *in-between* and put it into relation with the terms of intersectionality and diversity. Maybe the 'mess we're in' could be considered an 'in-between' moment for the development of dramaturgy that opens spaces up. Dramaturgies move away from the single-story, the static discourse that holds us back.

From Postmigrant Theater to an Intersectional-Diverse Theater

Since 2008, the term Postmigrant Theater (Postmigrantisches Theatre) has been a milestone and turning point of theatre discourse in Germany. Performers took the stage, presented their bodies and stories, countered and played with stereotypes, and proclaimed that they were more than their backgrounds, ethnicities, and associated stereotypes. Matthias Warstat describes the Postmigrant Theatre as a process in which post-migrants of the second and third generation now present a 'patchwork', a plurality of identities, that go past the concept of "Heimat" and "Belonging",[2] distinguishing themselves from the first generation of their parents, who mainly came as "Gastarbeiter*innen" in the 1960s and 1970s to Germany. Warstat also emphasizes that the idea and concept of bringing migration onto the stage is not a new one. Amateur groups and performers outside the state and municipal theatre system have been working within their communities for years before coining the term. Adding the "post" proclaimed: We move beyond those identities of nations and belonging.[3]

But exactly therein lies a paradox, which Warstat also points out. Once I place myself in this frame, I appear. I emphasize myself as that which I am not, which I do not want to be reduced to. Postmigrant Theatre was an important process at a time in which theatres, ensembles, teams, narratives, and texts in municipal and state theatres were predominantly male, white, cis, heterosexual, mostly academic, and seemingly unquestioned. Then came the Arab Spring, and in Lebanon, Yemen, and Syria, protests turned into uprisings, coups, and civil wars.

---

2   Warstat. Matthias. Postmigrantisches Theater? Das Theater und die Situation von Flüchtlingen auf dem Weg nach Europa in: *Vorstellung Europa/Performing Europe*. 2017. Theater der Zeit.

3   „Sie signalisiert eine Bewegung der Ablösung von den migrantischen Herkunftsmilieus und den mit diesen verbundenen Identitätszuschreibungen." – *Vorstellung Europa/Performing Europe*. 2017. Theater der Zeit. (p.29)

For German society and in the German theatre context, the Syrian Civil War marked a turning point. Syrian migration to Europe, to Germany, has been changing the discourse in society and the theatre world. The Syrian migration also pushed further the question of what diversity is, especially that it was and still is predominantly connected to the idea of backgrounds.

The loop of narration

Since 2015, we – and by this "we" I refer specifically to the German theatre context – have seen a significant increase of plays, performances, and productions that dealt with the topics of war, refuge, and trauma regarding the Middle East. What started as projects initiated by white German artists dealing with the problems of the Middle East, shifted more and more towards Arabic artists, mostly Syrian theatre-makers, who now live and work in Germany and form different collectives and ensembles that transformed the German theatre landscape. Examples of this are the Exil Ensemble at Gorki Theater in Berlin, the Open Border Ensemble at Münchner Kammerspiele, or the Collective Ma'louba in Mülheim an der Ruhr. Once again, we are at a point of artists and individuals who are first-generation migrants, who have either come here through refuge or – and this is much less talked about – came here by choice.

I would like to propose a thesis: the discourses that emerged since 2014 mirror the problems that German theatres have when it comes to the diversity discourse and the process of "becoming more diverse". To quote Judith Butler:

'I am seeking to draw attention to the epistemological problem raised by this issue of framing: the frames through which we apprehend or, indeed, fail to apprehend the lives of others as lost or injured (…) They are themselves operations of power.'[4]

But what are these operations of power? How can we determine them? There is an operating power of 'framing'. Let us exchange the word framing with the word 'narrating'. So: There is an operating power of the narrative. What we choose to tell, what we choose to leave out, makes the story. Or to paraphrase Chimamanda Ngozi Adichie: the retelling of one single story sets the discourse off to a dangerous field. What is told about a person or groups of people, what is forced as narrative upon one, makes the story.

It gives power to some, while others are doomed to the role of the victim, the villain, or – even worse – are erased completely.

---

4   Butler, Judith. *Frames of War – When ist Life Grievable?* London; New York, Verso, 2009, p. 1.

Who is included in a story is important, but how the stories are told and what part of the stories we are willing to tell is crucial! Looking at the contemporary German theatre and the themes of war, migration, exile, and refuge, two main narratives and styles of storytelling can be observed:

a) **Telling the Story:** Performers and non-actors speak about their experiences on stage, sometimes even connecting it to a parable or mythological story.
b) **Refusing to tell the Story:** Projects that deal with the issues of misrepresentation and unwillingness to play the role of a certain stereotype or one identity. The story is used as a counterargument: I am not this, I choose not to be this, I do not wish to be associated with this. I negate this story.

These two forms lead us into a process, into a "loop of narration". We are stuck in the loop of the narrative. We are forced into the story of oppression and victimisation, bouncing back and forth between telling the story and refusing to tell it. But we somehow can't escape it. Since we are either having to explain or defend against having to tell it.

When discussing the themes of the 'Arabic immigrant', the starting point of the narrative is the story of refuge, crisis, and war. Even when we move away in time and space towards new stories, mostly in German theatre, we somehow manage to return to the loop's starting point of trauma, refuge, and crisis. It is important to point out: people's stories and experiences should not be denied or swept under the carpet of silence. Neither should these experiences be negated. In this argument, the question is rather how are the stories told, and is this the only story that is being told? But what about the past? The parts of identity that happened before the loop?

Or as Chimamanda Ngozi Adichie says:

'Power is the ability not just to tell the story of another person, but to make it the definitive story of that person. The Palestinian poet Mourid Barghouti writes that if you want to dispossess a people, the simplest way to do it is to tell their story and to start with, "secondly." Start the story with the arrows of the Native Americans, and not with the arrival of the British, and you have an entirely different story. Start the story with the failure of the African state, and not with the colonial creation of the African state, and you have an entirely different story.'[5]

---

5   Chimamanda Ngozi Adichie. 2024. "The Danger of a Single Story." Ted.com. TED Talks. 2024. https://www.ted.com/talks/chimamanda_ngozi_adichie_the_danger_of_a_single_story/tr.

Intersectional-Diversity or: avoiding the single-story axis

In 1989 Kimberlé Crenshaw coined the term intersectionality, which can be found in her text *Demarginalizing the Intersection of Race and Sex: A Black Feminist Critique of Antidiscrimination Doctrine, Feminist Theory, and Antiracist Politics*. Her approach is:

> I will center Black women in this analysis in order to contrast the multidimensionality of Black women's experience with the single-axis analysis that distorts these experiences. Not only will this juxtaposition reveal how Black women are theoretically erased, it will also illustrate how this framework imports its own theoretical limitations that undermine efforts to broaden feminist and antiracist analyses. With Black women as the starting point, it becomes more apparent how dominant conceptions of discrimination condition us to think about subordination as disadvantage occurring along a single categorical axis.[6]

This "tool" of intersectional – diversity and power structures gives us the possibility to understand the plurality of concepts, identities, and forces which form political, social identities. The concept of intersectionality helps us to reveal the powers in place that often lead to the erasing of stories, identities, and people. Furthermore, it helps to broaden the discourse of diversity and the way it can be shown in the theater and arts, because as already mentioned: in the German theater we still approach diversity mainly through the axis of background.

Open(ing) the space(s)

Theatre institutions need to reconsider the way they open their spaces for artists and thinkers to appear within them. This may sound simple, but it is something that still does not happen very often yet. Rather than "talking about", or "speaking for", Theatres/ Institutions/Organizations should open the space, so that artists, groups and communities can talk for themselves and allow works to happen, to create artistic spaces that go beyond the reason of making people visible and are done solely for the purpose of being "more diverse".

Oftentimes certain themes, ideas, or topics are set up by the institutions, whereas the artists are being asked to follow. They are being commissioned and therefore expected to fulfill a specific task, instead of being invited for open exchange, rather than consciously communicating ideas and artistic thoughts in an

---

6   Crenshaw, Kimberlé. 1989. "Demarginalizing the Intersection of Race and Sex: A Black Feminist Critique of Antidiscrimination Doctrine, Feminist Theory and Antiracist Politics." *University of Chicago Legal Forum* 1989 (1): 139–67. https://chicagounbound.uchicago.edu/cgi/viewcontent.cgi?article=1052&context=uclf.

open exchange. Oftentimes this leads to frustrations on all sides: artists feeling silenced and mistreated. Institutions are left disappointed because they expected something "completely different".

Opening the spaces for a variety of perspectives allows theater-makers as well as institutions to avoid situations of 'talking about'. It certainly helps with the process of retreating from these "loop(s) of narration(s)" and reaching complexities. These tracks need to be set, so that things can move forward, towards an approach that doesn't only claim diversity but actually works towards a genuine intersectional-diverse approach.

For the moment, it creates two extremely important things to move forward with. First, the development of consciousness for discourses about power relations in artistic works and institutions. Second, multiple perspectives could lead to forms of "radical plurality"[7] of stories, identities, representations, and power on and off the theater and performance stages. These radical pluralities of stories, ideas, and thoughts create spaces that intersect. They shine a light on privilege, on power, and connect, rather than divide. Finding forms of solidarity is a tool that we need for the future to an intersectional – diverse approach, to work with forms of radical pluralities that move away from identifications towards an approach that is conscious towards the power structures and forms of privilege and works towards complexity of stories.

Encountering

When opening a space, we encounter possibilities for the future and create spaces of exchange. When we begin to encounter within a space it is important to acknowledge the power factors that reside within individuals, groups, and institutions in these spaces. We are not equal, since the power dynamics are different for each, and every, one. Making these structures visible, acknowledging them, can be very empowering. It also shows what possibilities and privileges reside within these encounters.

Encountering pluralities and intersections can help us track new forms of solidarity in artistic exchanges. But it also means to ask the question: What is needed in this space of exchange? What stories do we want to tell? How can we tell them? Which (hi)story does my story continue, and which one does it negate? Asking these questions slowly bypasses the well-known structure of fixed ideas, perspectives, and theatre forms, texts, and performances. Spaces and ideas that might never have occurred can be generated due to fixed structures and the so-called 'canon'.

---

7   I refer here to the phrase radikale Vielfalt (Radical Diversity), that can be found here: Czollek, Max. 2020. *Gegenwartsbewältigung*. Carl Hanser Verlag. p.154-155

Encountering is not an easy process; it requires time, active listening, engagement, and a form of trust and preparation. Institutions and individuals need to do their homework, too: It is not a workshop wherein individuals, artists and diversity agents educate colleagues on the ideas of diversity, but a shared responsibility to work within their structures to create the right conditions that will allow spaces to grow.

This also means requisitioning one's perspectives and thinking about forms of communication within departments and the people working therein. And shifts towards sharing knowledge, stories, and thoughts that never were heard before, make visible what has been invisible far too long, and create a future; a new form of canon and repertoire of texts, and aesthetics. This also means going into a process, a form of working that I would like to describe in the next section.

(En)-Countering

Besides the process of encountering, I would like to propose a parallel process of countering: an active avoidance of the single stories that dominate the present, as well as going back in history and countering the past for the present and future.

By presenting stories, individuals, and ideas that have been silenced and untold for the sake of a single story. Repetition forms canon and commemorations, which leads to what is known as "Culture" or "The Canon". Countering is an active process; it begins by opening the spaces and continues with learning how to let new ideas and new people in, making them visible. Countering allows these stories to be told from different perspectives to form a new "Canon of Pluralities". We can also overcome the constant idea of having to play certain dramatic texts and forms repeatedly. And focus on the relevance of the contemporary. This will also give access to a more diverse audience that will connect to the subjects, artists and aesthetics on the theatre stages. It will enable a different form of 'seeing', illuminating what has been there all along. It will allow multilingual, inclusive projects that open the spaces even further. Countering changes the past, not because it denies it, but because it looks back differently. It shows the tracks that have been there all along, that have been disguised and made invisible for the sake of another telling. This can also be an empowering process, laying the track for the present and future. Countering is not a refusal to tell stories or work together. Rather, it is the resistance to repeatedly telling, working, and repeatedly thinking through the same perspectives and ideas. When encountering, we meet and then look for different perspectives that may help to counter what has been there as that what has been told. It can also be a requisitioning of one's perspectives. And it is highly present. Countering means asking what is needed for us to work right here, right now, and move forward. What have I not seen? What could be told here differently?

Emerging Strategies

The previous ideas and notes are still in progress and certainly not finished. Rather, they are emerging points that will hopefully continue to grow. Many ideas were created within spaces around colleagues, texts, artists, activists, discussions, encounters, and networks that grew and developed in recent years. In the middle of 2021, after many months of living in constant alarm, fear, anger, the unknown, and being apart, things seem to be "opening up again" – but what does that mean for institutions like the theatre? Going back to what we know? Go back to business as usual? Where will these discussions take us? I remember when I started working in theatre. I wanted to be part of it because I believed it would be a place where I could find exchange, allies and artistic expression that would resonate with my feelings of being in between. But instead, I felt constantly under pressure, often misunderstood, often "being the problem", and constantly needed to prove myself. I felt the forces of competition and hierarchy and the idea of having to supposedly fit in. I tried to deny my Arab background, tried to be as "German as possible", and emphasised my German background as much as possible to feel accepted and worthy of working within the system. Then I realised that all these supposed "survival strategies" were holding me down; my potential and energy were forced to be kept low. They are strategies that hold us in place and distance us from paths of change and solidarity. Growing up in-between is not a lack but a potential; being multilingual is seeing the world through different perspectives over and over again. Or, as Adrienne Maree Brown writes:

> 'One Major emerging lesson: We have to create futures in which everyone doesn't have to be the same kind of person. That's the problem with most utopias for me: they are presented as mono value, a new greener more local monoculture where everyone gardens and plays the lute and no one travels... And I don't want to go there! Compelling futures have to have more justice: yes; and right relationships to planet, yes; but also must allow for our growth and innovation. I want an interdependence of lots of kinds of people with lots of belief systems, and continued evolution.' [8]

I am hopeful ...

---

8   Brown, Adrienne Maree. 2017. *Emergent Strategy*. AK Press. (Brown 2017, 57)

Language between world theatre and theatre in exile[1]: From the impossible collective understanding to the possible collective imagination

Rana Yazaji

Theatre in Exile proposes a multilayered practice and theory space that engages with a complex system of thematic approaches, topics, and theoretical frameworks: migration, immigration, connectivity, and equality. Integration and diversity. Language, multilingualism, and identity. Structural racism, inclusivity and openness. Diaspora narratives and homeland. Collective imagination and individuality. Borders, barriers and cultural codes. Transnationality and intersectionality. Power structures and cultural margins. Politics and systems. Ethnicity, race, neoliberalism and postcolonialism. And THEATRE. A significant question in theatre in exile, which intensively comprises multilayered and interconnected themes, is language. Talking about language is a way to approach many connected debates, this essay provides methodological reflections we developed as a result of engaging with migrant theatre production in the period before 2022. Some of these reflections have evolved since then, but are principally valid now. It will try to capitulate on three of them: power structures and politics, audiences and spectators, and aesthetics and theatre genres. We will investigate the "One Language. Translation on Stage" project and explore the different approaches to dealing with multilingualism on stage and in the audience, such as visual alternatives to the spoken language and surtitling and translation as a dramaturgy and scenography practice.

One Language is a project launched by Nawras, a non-profit organisation founded in Berlin in 2017. It aims to create a series of collaborative artist-inclusive theatre laboratories to research what approaches could be meaningful to alternate classical translation methods on stage and suggest innovative attempts to better communicate between the artist and the audience. This paper will demonstrate artistic and translation practices as creative examples of dealing with language in theatre. For

---

1   Although it is arguable, theatre-makers in exile is the term we chose to use in this essay. Not only artists but many others have different ways of self-identification. The term is not aimed at any political or social labeling but to identify a state of people who live in another country as a result of political or economic reasons.

this purpose, different scenes from different performances will be highlighted, as well as an interview with Sandra Hetzl, a literary translator from Arabic to German who has been working in theatre translation since 2013.

Influence of context change on the artistic practice

It is challenging to understand the adaptation of artistic practice following the shift in its creation and reception contexts. It is challenging as it differs significantly from one artist to another. It depends on the trajectory this artist has taken to arrive in the new country (context). Moreover, it depends on the artist's practice before this shift occurred and the artist's perception of their identity and career. Specifically, in the case of Syrian theatre-makers who have lived in Germany since around 2015, there is a layer of complexity in attempting to understand the shift in their practice. The complexity results from the possible ephemeral nature of the actual trial, as the arrival to a new context occurred less than ten years ago. Thus, the dynamic is foreseen to change the artistic practice and choices. Relationships with the audience greatly influence the artistic choices of artists in exile. Which story in which language and theatre genre? What emotional and cognitive connection should spectators live with the play, and how? What does the representation of an "Arabic theatre" mean, and to which audience exactly? Could the relation between an artistic production of an artist in exile and a German audience be safe from the "othering"? Is there a third fairer position of artists in exile other than Invisibility or Hyper-visibility?

Invisibility is when a particular group/individual is disempowered and/or un-acknowledge and/or ignored and/or dehumanised for their 'differences'. There are typical double standards when treated and/or mentioned and/or spoken to or about. This could be happening on an individual or a systematic level.

Hyper-visibility is when an individual is being recognised for their otherness or deviance from the "norm". Hyper-visibility could lead to exclusion, social isolation, feeling of being used and/or being treated as a token, performance pressures and stress. Moreover, hypervisibility increases the concern that one will confirm certain negative stereotypes about one's group, which pushes people to act differently. (H. Settles & Buchanan & Dotson. 2018).

Among all the challenges raised, language and translation are central in the creation and reception manners. Rasha Abbas (a Syrian author who moved to Berlin in 2014) said she had written differently since she began to write with translation in mind. She knew how her translator worked, so she had used a language that would be easier to translate" (Dubois, Simon 2016). In his show, "Under a Low Sky" (2019), Wael Ali chose to collaborate with Sherif Andoura, an actor from a Belgian mother and a Syrian father. Andora was born and lived in Europe, and he played the leading role in the play alongside actress Nanda Muhammad, a Syrian actress residing in

Egypt. From the beginning, Ali mixed Arabic and French to write his text. The text is a round trip between the past and the present, a documentary theatre performance based on a flowing narrative and fragmented text that combines a personal record of the loss of the past and politics between two countries: France and Syria (Al-Charif, Bissane. 2021).

Further, Mudar Alhaggi, A Syrian playwright who moved to Berlin in 2015, says, "I can never imagine myself writing my plays in any language other than Arabic. Also, I cannot imagine the Syrian audience in Syria watching my last play, the Return of Danton." In "Reine Formsache", the play that joined Mudar Alhaggi and Wael Ali, the question of language is put forward on stage from the first scene: Die Geschichte (the story). Two actors sit and narrate how they arrived at this moment (here: Paris and now), when they left Syria, where to, and when they came to France, why they are playing in this closed room, and what problems they are discovering through playing. They also "inform" the audience about their physical characteristics. With his blue eyes and grey hair, he is unsuitable for the role of villain or terrorist or Mediterranean guy. Language is a question, they say. They keep playing in Arabic and talk about his incapability of playing in French. Still, just after they say so, they play the role of a theatre director in French, trying to convince a producer to invest in its production. They also narrate the story of the play they wrote in their closed room; what if she returns to Syria and at the border, she'd be grilled by some quite peculiar officer? Through this "story-telling", the actress narrates a particular Arabic genre of text called Dihliz. When she finishes, she confirms that Dihliz could not be translated, although a surtitling in German did not stop. The actress still explains the traditional use of Dihliz, taking spectators from the actual to another time where we can start our story. She says Dihliz is about the words' rhythm, sound and music.

Translation between communication and meaning-construction

Tobias Viet, Schaubühne's artistic executive producer, said: "Sometimes on the street, you hear more English or French than German, and these are people we think would be interested in our work". The assumption of a non-German audience has led the theatre to include two to three productions subtitled in English and two to three in French every month. According to Viet, the proposition of non-Germans in the audience has doubled to approximately 30 per cent on such nights (Brady-Brown, Annabel. 2012). Another reason for subtitling is introducing international guest performances to a German audience; Old Hebbel Theatre has done that since the mid-1990s. It is also a practice that we expect in international theatre festivals and encounters as a part of their mission to introduce international theatre to a local audience. Regarding Arabic theatre produced in Germany, the assumption that subtitling is needed to introduce international theatre to a German audience deserves further examination. World theatre means travelling as a theatre or being a guest, crossing cultural borders to show something new and unusual to another world playfully. But world theatre is also present more and more within a city, be it in the Theater du Soleil in Paris, in the Gorki Theater in Berlin or the Theater an der Ruhr in Mülheim, wherever people from different cultures come to find new access to theatre (Griesel, Yvonne. 2014).

The perception of language as a medium for communication leads to understanding the spoken language on stage and translated written language on-screen on the linguistic and aesthetic levels. This approach allows us to look carefully at how good the translation is, technical matters such as synchronisation between the spoken and written word, and transferability of the original text's poetic feeling, all this summing up to question the experience the audience lived watching the performance. However, the perception of language as a medium to transmit emotional meaning and cultural context takes the question into a totally different debate concentrated around the artist's identity behind and on stage. In this sense, if you see language as the process of meaning-constructions, the politics of translation take on a massive life of its own. (Spivak, 2009).

Theatre-makers in exile are not theatre guests or touring artists. They are part of the city and the theatre scene where they live and practice. Artists in exile have moved from the middle to the margins of the cultural system in their countries of origin by leaving them to join a margin (s) in their new countries that do not yet influence creatively or politically. However, the change of prevailing systems and discourse is not the result of linear processes. The cultural margins can eventually play an influential role.

Simon Dubois argues in his essay "Renegotiating Artistic Identity in Exile: The Making of a Syrian Creative Landscape in Berlin" that we should look at exile not so much as a physical matter of moving from one place to another and/ or as a particular social and psychological condition, but instead as part of the Syrian artistic system reconfigured outside the country's borders. By choosing Beirut and Berlin as their residence places, the Syrian arts professionals had also chosen two culturally dynamic cities which were very open to international influences. Is it then fair to assume that this renegotiated identity of a sector restructuring itself outside the country's borders is highly influenced by limitations of translation and the constant need to "be explained" to an unknown audience? This position influences translation decisions and artistic choices centred around the constant questioning of the artist's ability to extract a particular meaning from the creative practice as a whole.

Thus, theatre-makers in exile live a different relation to translation than other theatre-makers who play internationally. Artists in exile have this audience in mind through the creative process and are looking at their theatre practice through the lenses of an unknown language, aesthetics, and audience. It also means that contrary to the reason behind translating theatre to allow local or international audience access to a local or international theatre, translation in the case of artists in exile is "the only" possible political decision giving theatre-makers access to the audience but also a system of creation, production and touring.

Power and Politics

Reflection on translation in theatre is not limited to the artistic practice as such. Translation as an act is a response to a need. This need is partly the result and the source of power relations. The translation is in itself a political decision and action. Making certain plays or texts accessible to a particular audience is a decision taken on a policy base, be it the theatre's policy or a city or a state. Languages divide people into those who can speak directly to others and those who need a mediator/translator to transmit the meaning. The first laboratory of the *One Language* Project focused on exploring how language reflects and expresses these power structures. This reflection process waved from language in everyday life to the sense of othering and colonialism that hides in our language due to "acknowledging" or "censoring" terms and expressions. Participants tried to reflect on why language is political and how the shift in power relations could be tested through theatre. Language is political because it can include or exclude; it defines or determines what is deemed as usual and what is "othered"; it also controls what you know and what you don't have access to. Adopting an official language or language in a country or a cultural policy determines "normal" communication, and without precarious critical thinking, it can mean the marginalisation of cultures and peoples and a way to understand history.

Ayşe Gülsüm Özel, scenography and stage designer, and one of the three facilitators of the project wrote and proposed a case study around the Nuremberg Trials (1945–1946)[2], analysing it as the official birth date of simultaneous interpretation, which was invented as early as 1926. The Nürnberger Prozesse was a series of military tribunals the Allied forces held after World War II under international law and the laws of war. The trials were most notable for the prosecution of prominent members of the political, military, judicial, and economic leadership of Nazi Germany. The three major wartime powers, the United Kingdom, the United States, and the Soviet Union, besides France, which was also awarded a place on the tribunal, agreed on punishment for war crimes during World War II. The trials employed four official languages: English, French, German and Russian. Despite the extensive trial

---

2   The case study was written based on several resources: https://de.wikipedia.org/wiki/ N%C3%BCrnberger_Prozesse, https://en.wikipedia.org/wiki/Subsequent_Nuremberg_trial s, https://www.nationalww2museum.org/war/articles/translating-and-interpreting-nurem berg-trials, https://museums.nuernberg.de/memorium-nuremberg-trials/the-legacy-of-nu remberg/birth-of-international-criminal-law/

and error, without the interpretation system, the "six million words" trials would not have been possible and, in turn, revolutionised the way multilingual issues were addressed in tribunals and conferences.

According to the National World War II Museum of New Orleans, "Translation is performed on written works, taking a text in one language and rendering it in another. Translation usually allows for edits and time for consideration and reference. Interpretation is performed on the spoken word, and although there are different types of interpretation, it is often performed extemporaneously without time to consult sources or incorporate edits." It was feared that consecutive interpretation would slow down the proceedings significantly. This led to introducing an entirely new technique, extempore simultaneous interpretation. This interpretation technique requires the interpreter to listen to a speaker in a source (or passive) language and simultaneously translate that speech into another language in real time through headsets and microphones. Interpreters were split into four sections, one for each official language, with three interpreters per section working from the other three languages into the fourth. For instance, the English booth consisted of three interpreters, one working from German, one from French, and one from Russian into English. Defendants who spoke none of the four official languages received consecutive court interpreters.

Many of the participants were former translators, army personnel, and linguists; some were experienced consecutive interpreters, others were ordinary individuals and even recent secondary school graduates who led international lives in multilingual environments. They were chosen based on their broad sense of culture, encyclopedic knowledge, inquisitiveness, and naturally calm disposition. Technically during the process, a yellow lamp signalled, "Speak slower," and a red one was used to request the speaker to repeat the last sentence. Thus, to a certain extent, not only judges and lawyers determined, as generally in trials, the speed of the process, but also the simultaneous interpreters. The defendants reacted differently to the interpretation. Some tried to use flawed interpretations in plea bargaining. Many of the defendants spoke English and other languages, but they used the delay caused by interpretation to gather thoughts, gain time, and perhaps slow proceedings. Furthermore, many thought that the better the interpretation, the better their chances of surviving.

Translation and Understanding

The One Language Project participants presented a scene in two languages through a practical exercise called the 'missing dialogues' led by Ziad Adwan, researcher, theatre director, and one of the project's facilitators. The scene is taken from the play HomeWork, written by Adwan. One character spoke English, which was the lingua franca of the group, and the other character spoke Arabic, a familiar language for only one part of the participants. The scene presented a woman alone in a hotel talking on the phone with someone who was in the front in a fighting zone because she wanted to eat something sweet and was looking for the jam. Other artistic elements that were present in the scene included sound effects done by one participant, two mimers who "translated" the two characters, and a participant who drew the scenery. It was as if the director had dismantled the scene into separate artistic components: language, movement, and sound. The audience had to recompose the elements to make sense of the scene.

During the closing discussion, the group concluded that non-Arabic-speaking spectators could construct and understand the scene's meaning. The only incomprehensible component that hindered building a relationship with the scene was the word "jam". The Arabic-speaking character was looking for jam. While the spectators understood that she was looking for something, and most of them understood that she was looking for food, no one in the audience could understand that she was looking for jam. The two remaining questions here are: Is it necessary to understand the word "jam" to get the scene's meaning? And can the translation screen only light up the word jam?

Here, we encounter the concept of the "pleasure of finding other ways to understand", but we also should answer many questions through the artistic process: could every story, plot, or character speak or be spoken in another language? Who understands what? And how? Do we all understand the same thing? Is it possible to create (mis)understanding? And is it at all necessary to understand or to be understood? Is it possible to educate the audience to accept and enjoy not understanding? Again, what about text-based theatre? How can we share and enjoy the limit of spoken language?

In text-based theatre, when the text itself is in the centre of the play, or when the artistic choice is to transmit the text as it is, the only solution is to keep it as it is, thus using a surtitle. The question remains: did the screen on stage become so established that it is disturbing to play with it and transform it from being a tool to transmit a text, or can theatre-makers still be free to deal with it as an element of the scene? Can we consider surtitle in theatre as another medium to transmit the text so that it is cued like the other 'languages of theatre' (lighting, sound, costume . . . etc.)?

Translation as a practice

Between 2013 and 2021, Sandra Hetzl has translated twenty-five Syrian, Lebanese and Palestinian plays, except for one Egyptian text written in standard Arabic [Fusha]. These dialects are the most familiar to her. The twenty-five texts were translated for public plays or scenic readings, but none were published; as Hetzl states, Publishing theatre in Germany is, unfortunately, rare. Commissioning is always done either by the writers themselves or through festivals or theatre institutions. Although Hetzl was only sometimes commissioned to do the three steps leading to the projected surtitling on stage, those rare cases led to a clear understanding of how beneficial it is for the text and the relation to the audience if the three steps go through one person's hand. The first is translating a stage version. This means simply translating the text regardless of the sentences' lengths or other surtitling considerations. So, as a stage version, it will also include the scenic instructions. The second step is to create the surtitling version that needs a lot of work, including abbreviating, focusing on fitting all dialogues in a two-line format, sometimes using specific software. It is better when the same person does this abbreviation because they will be more capable of emphasising each sentence in a way that fits the overall language of the play; they will also know better what to take away from the text to make it shorter. Hetzl has done this step for approximately half of the texts she translated.

The third step is to be present at two to three rehearsals. Until this moment in the process, the translator does not meet the theatre company, and they don't know the text's staging; their work is limited to dealing with the text. By participating in rehearsals, the translator tests their work; they can understand the rhythm and emotions. They observe when a sentence is set very quickly or slowly. Sometimes, it also helps to understand situational jokes better. "When I translate any text, be it a theatre play, prose or poetry, I always collect my questions, work on the text and communicate with the writer. Most of the time, I happen to understand much more when this option exists.". "In the times where I had the chance to be present in all three steps, I took it very seriously. Conversely, by the commissioners, translation is often seen as a marginal asset; it is mostly omitted, and translators aren't credited, even though they do very sensitive and creative work on one of the core materials of a piece: The text. As a translator, Hetzl sees her work as crucial to the play and deals with it in that way. "When I translate a play, I read the whole play out loud several times with myself; Sometimes I also do lots of research, and then when it comes to running surtitles during a performance, I feel like I'm something between a DJ and a literary translator. Yet in so many cases, the translator of the piece is not mentioned, neither in the brochure nor in any communication outlet, while light designers, makeup artists, and technicians are".

There are essential differences between translating a text for a printed publication and translating a text that ends in the surtitles on stage. One significant difference is related to the nature of the text. Theatre texts are based on dialogues; still, it is worth mentioning that these dialogues in contemporary Arab theatre are primarily written in a dialect, not standard Arabic. Hetzl has translated only very few plays from the Arab Region written in Fusha.

"In a way, I find it's a much 'easier' task to translate from colloquial Arabic, compared to translating from Fusha. When translating from colloquial Arabic, I don't
need to do all the bridging work I have to do when translating from Fusha. German literary texts subtly jump from colloquial and auditive registers to more written ones, as in German, you can easily write in a colloquial without it becoming
slang, dialect, or a deviation from correct German. In Arabic, given the diglossia of
the Arabic language(s), meaning the fact that there are always at least two varia-
tions of Arabic used (a regional dialect / colloquial form of Arabic and as a written
language Modern Standard Arabic) which are primarily isolated from each other.
When I transfer a text from Fusha, to get a vivid literary result, I have to add layers
of colloquial registers to the German text that weren't necessarily inherent in the
more sterile Fusha original. In contrast, when I translate from colloquial Arabic,
the situatedness is directly present in the original text. Another significant and
unfortunate difference is that when I translate a piece of prose or poetry for publication, it goes through profound external copy editing through a third person
before it goes back to me. I can decide on which suggestions of the copy editor I
want to adopt. This process is something that the text benefits hugely from. In
theatre, there is no time or space for such a process. All translations are done for
these one or three nights to flash by in the shining surtitles and then disappear
forever. Yet, from my side, I put so as much work into it as if the translation would
be meant for eternity."

After 2015, many plays were produced by theatre-makers and writers based in Germany and Europe. That was not the case before 2015. In terms of themes and content,
we could describe a tendency for mainly Syrian writers based in Germany to work on
a new self-referentiality, where the theatre company and the rehearsals become the
play's topic. It is something to be further studied and reflected on, but it could result
from a feeling of disconnection with the surroundings held by the artists, of being
thrown back on oneself. In the written text, as Spivak argues, "the translator's task is
to surrender herself to the linguistic rhetoricity of the original text. (...) ignoring this
task is the loss of the literarity and textuality and sensuality of the writing" (Spivak,
Gayatri Chakravorty. 2009). In theatre, this doesn't differ; it just has a whole world
taking place on stage, not a text, but bodies, objects, words, movements, gestures,
anger and joy, sounds, smells, breathing, and much more. The spoken word is one
of what the spectators receive and interpret.

Receiving the theatrical performance is a complex process in which every artistic decision affects the architecture of the theatre space, the psychological state, and
the spectator's expectations. The European audience who decides to go to a theatre
performance by a writer or director from another culture accepts exposure to that
culture. The spectators can base their decision on curiosity, political discourse in the
media, stereotypes about the culture from which the artist comes, knowledge, and
critical ability to deal with the dominant culture. In all these cases, the goal is the

artistic experience that they will live receiving the artistic proposition. This artistic experience is related to and affected by the artist's own artistic experience during and before the production process and their ability to freely find their language and be aware of all levels of relationship with an audience who does not speak their language.

Bibliography

Dubois, Simon. 2016. "Renegotiating artistic identity in exile: the making of a Syrian creative landscape in Berlin". in Blaute, Eva and Blau, Antonia (eds) *An artist who happens to be from Syria*, Goethe-Institut, pp. 19–39.

Mehrez, Hiba. 2019. "Surtitling in Syrian Theatrical Performances Presented in Berlin: A Discussion of Essence and Consequences". Cultural Priorities in Syria Series, Ettijahat. Independent Culture: https://www.ettijahat.org/page/951?_la ng=1#_ftn1

Brady-Brown, Annabel. 2012. "A sur-thing". Exberliner: https://www.exberliner.co m/whats-on/stage/a-sur-thing/

الشريف، بيسان. 2021. التجربة المسرحية السورية الناشئة في أوروبا. حكاية ما انحكت : https://s yriauntold.com/writer/%D8%A8%D9%8A%D8%B3%D8%A7%D9%86-%D8%A7% D9%84%D8%B4%D8%B1%D9%8A%D9%81/

Tuhiwai Smith, Linda. 2012. *Decolonizing Methodologies. Research and Indigenous Peoples*. Second edition. London: Zed Books.

Giesel, Yvonne. 2014. *Welttheater Verstehen. Übertitelung, Übersetzen, Dolmetschen und neue Wege*. Berlin: Alexander Verlag.

Chakravorty Spivak, Gayatri. 2008. *Outside in the Teaching Machine*. Routledge.

Das Post-Heimat-Netzwerk als Contact Zone

Nora Haakh

MAJD: You understand me? MAJA: Ja, I think I do. MAJD: How come? No one understands me back in Syria. I don't even understand myself... (aus: 'Miunikh Damaskus')

„Wie nähern wir uns dem Ziel, in pluralen Gesellschaften gleichberechtigt zusammenzuleben?" formuliert die Soziologin Naika Foroutan eine der drängendsten Fragen unserer Zeit (Foroutan 2019, S.55). Die Frage nach der Gestaltung von Räumen, in denen Multiperspektivität, Mehrsprachigkeit und die Vielfältigkeit von Geschichte(n) nicht nivelliert, sondern als Bereicherung geschätzt werden, wird immer dringlicher. Obwohl sich Deutschland schon lange 'in Transit' (Göktürk, 2011) befindet, wurden die Anforderungen, die eine vielfältige Gesellschaft an alle Beteiligten stellt, in diesem 'widerspenstigen Einwanderungsland' (Flam 2007, S.7) von vielen Institutionen und Angehörigen der Mehrheitsgesellschaft dennoch ausgeblendet. Zugleich werden Räume, deren Multiperspektivität und Vielsprachigkeit sich nicht länger von der Hand weisen lässt, zunehmend zur alltäglich gelebten, breit geteilten Erfahrung.

Dabei geht das Navigieren ins solchen *Contact Zones*, wie die Linguistin Mary Louise Pratt solche Räume nennt, mit vielen Herausforderungen einher. Wenn Menschen mit ganz unterschiedlichen Geschichten und ihrer unumgänglichen Eingebundenheit in asymmetrische Machtstrukturen einer (post-)kolonialen und intersektionalen Gegenwart zusammenkommen, erfordert das von allen Beteiligten neue Kompetenzen. Ein besonderes Potenzial sieht Pratt dafür in künstlerischen Mitteln:

"We are looking for the (...) arts of the contact zone. These will include, we are sure, exercises in storytelling and in identifying with the ideas, interests, histories, and attitudes of others; experiments in transculturation and collaborative work and in the arts of critique, parody, and comparison (including unseemly comparisons between elite and vernacular cultural forms), the redemption of the oral; ways for people to engage with suppressed aspects of history (including their own histories), ways to move into and out of rhetorics of authenticity; ground rules for communication across lines of difference and hierarchy that go beyond politeness but maintain mutual respect (...). (Pratt, 1991, S.40).

Wie gestalten wir mehrsprachige, multiperspektivische Räume der Kollaboration? Die Herausforderungen auf der Suche nach den 'Künsten der *Contact Zone*' stand im Mittelpunkt des Post-Heimat-Netzwerkes. Geteilte Grundlage war die gemeinsame Theaterarbeit von im deutschsprachigen Kulturbetrieb bereits etablierten und internationalen, insbesondere aus Syrien exilierten, Bühnenkünstler_innen.

Durch die mehrmals im Jahr terminierten Netzwerk- und Austauschtreffen sollte ermöglicht werden, sich über Dynamiken und Herausforderungen auszutauschen und sich dabei zu vernetzen, anstatt sich als Einzelkämpfer_innen in parallelen Suchbewegungen mit ähnlichen Fragen herumzuschlagen. Zu diesen Encounters wurden neben Künstler_innen, Dramaturg_innen, Kulturmanager_innen auch mehrere Forschende zur Begleitung eingeladen. Eine Förderung der Kulturstiftung des Bundes gewährleistete bezahlte Reisen und Unterkünfte zu den Treffen, die abwechselnd von den teilnehmenden Projekten ausgerichtet und mit einem künstlerischen Programm mit Arbeiten vor Ort ergänzt wurden.

Wie können wir in einem Kulturbetrieb navigieren, der oft weiterhin von den Machstrukturen durchzogen ist, die er zu kritisieren sucht (Kulaoğlu 2011, S. 401, Schmidt, 2019)? Die künstlerische Suche wurde als Zusammenarbeit innerhalb bereits bestehender inhaltlich-ästhetischer Schwerpunktsetzungen und Arbeitsstrukturen realisiert. Dabei wurden in den Projekten unterschiedliche Strategien gefunden, die Zusammenarbeit in diversen Konstellation kooperativ oder kollaborativ zu gestalten. Auch das Post-Heimat-Netzwerk selbst zeigte sich so als Contact Zone, in der Prozesse abliefen, die exemplarisch für gesamtgesellschaftliche Dynamiken dieses zeithistorischen Moments sind. In den entstandenen künstlerischen Arbeiten wurden diese teilweise zugespitzt reflektiert und sichtbar gemacht.

Im Folgenden möchte ich einige bemerkenswerte Strategien und Dynamiken betrachten, die im Prozess auftauchten und in den Inszenierungen 'Die Probe', 'Your Love is Fire', 'The Situation' und 'Miunikh Damaskus' auf der Bühne als Teil von Stück und Inszenierung thematisiert wurden. Anhand dieser ausgewählten Fallbeispiele sollen einige der Risiken und Wunder (Pratt, 1991) beschrieben werden, die sich beim Navigieren in der *Contact Zone* auf der Suche nach multiperspektivischem, vielsprachigem Theater zu Anfang des 21. Jahrhunderts zeig(t)en.

Den Hintergrund des vorliegenden Textes bilden meine früheren, aus meiner eigenen praktischen Arbeit am Theater genährten, kulturwissenschaftlichen Untersuchungen zu identitätspolitischen Strategien im Kontext des frühen postmigrantischen Theaters und der deutschen Islamdebatte (Haakh, 2015, 2021) und zu Prozessen von Übertragung, Übersetzung und Transfer aus dem arabischen- in den deutschsprachigen Raum im Theater des 20. und 21. Jahrhunderts (Haakh, 2019). Darauf aufbauend beinhaltet der vorliegende Beitrag eine Kontextualisierung des zeithistorischen Moments und der Rezeptionsdynamiken, in denen das Post-Heimat-Netzwerk entstehen konnte. Als Konzepte, die ich zum Verständnis der Dynamiken auch der Suche nach den 'Arts of the *Contact Zone*' (Pratt, 1991) hilfreich finde, erläutere ich insbesondere das 'Theater des Orientalismus' (Said, 1978), in dem eine ungleiche Zuteilung von Spielräumen und Rollen lange normalisiert worden ist, das Motiv des 'Cultural Brokering' (Mandel, 2008), des 'unsichtbaren Rucksacks' unreflektierter Privilegien (McIntosh, 1989) und ein transformatives Verständnis von 'Kollaboration' (Terkessidis, 2015).

Theater als Mikrokosmos und Orientalismus als Theater

„Die Kunst ist jene gesellschaftliche Betätigung, in der sich die Gesellschaft, stellvertretend durch die Künstler und ihr Publikum, vorführt, wie prekär ihre Identitäten und Formen sind und wie diese dennoch und zuweilen erst deswegen gesichert werden können." (Bäcker, 2005, S9).

Die Betrachtung von Theater ist für das Verständnis komplexer, gesamtgesellschaftlicher Prozesse besonders aufschlussreich. Denn das Theater funktioniert als Mikrokosmos für gesamtgesellschaftliche Dynamiken und Erfahrungen, in dem sich Auseinandersetzungen, die in vielen anderen gesellschaftlichen Bereichen auch geführt werden, wie unter dem Brennglas zeigen können. Als 'eine der radikalsten Formen der Erprobung des Sozialen' (Bäcker, 2005, S.9) kann das Theater als Schaufenster Geschichten und Perspektiven vom Rande in den Mittelpunkt stellen, als Spiegel auf die eigene Positionierung in einer komplexen Gesellschaft und die eigene Partizipation an intersektionalen Machtstrukturen zurückwerfen, oder als Labor neue Spielregeln erproben (Haakh, 2021).

Der Kunstraum ist dabei gerade durch seine Ambivalenz besonders aufschlussreich. Einerseits ist er aufgeladen mit der der Bühne eigenen Intensität adrenalingeschwängerten Dringlichkeit und oft hoher persönlicher Betroffenheit. Andererseits ist bleibt er dennoch weitestgehend frei von Konsequenzen im Alltagsleben jenseits der Bühne. Zugleich stellt der Kunstraum aber selbst einen Alltagsraum dar, der Arbeits- und Lebensbedingungen geriert, von denen die Beteiligten unterschiedlich existentiell betroffen sind. Denn das Theater partizipiert selbst in den Dynamiken, die es zu kritisieren sucht:

„Theater ist natürlich kein luftleerer Raum und spiegelt als Mikrokosmos die sozialen Verhältnisse wider. Die gesellschaftlichen Ausschlussmechanismen funktionieren im Kunstbetrieb genauso. Zugleich ist Theater als Kunst-Ort ein widersprüchlicher Raum. Denn zum einen werden bestehende gesellschaftliche Strukturen reproduziert, zum anderen aber entstehen Räume, die diese Strukturen zu überwinden versuchen, zumindest sie in Frage stellen. " (Kulaoğlu, 2011, S.401).

Die kritische Analyse jener diskursiven Strategien, mit denen in westlichen Diskursen ein imaginierter 'Orient' konstruiert wurde und wird, geht maßgeblich auf den Literaturwissenschaftler und Mitbegründer der postkolonialen Kritik Edward Said und seine Studie *Orientalismus* (1978) zurück. Um die Funktionsweise dieser diskursiven Strukturen zu erläutern, griff er auch auf die Metapher des Theaters zurück:

"The idea of representation is a theatrical one: the Orient is the stage on which the whole East is confined. On this stage will appear figures whose role it is to represent the larger whole from which they emanate. The Orient then seems to be not an unlimited extension beyond the familiar European world, but rather a closed field, a theatrical stage affixed to Europe." (Said, 2003 [1978], S.63).

Mit Hilfe dieses 'Theaters des Orientalismus' führe sich der sogenannte Westen sein selbst konstruiertes Bild des 'Anderen' vor:

"What it is trying to do (...) is at one and the same time to characterize the Orient as alien and to incorporate it schematically on a theatrical stage whose audience, manager, and actors are for Europe, and only for Europe. Hence the vacillation between the familiar and the alien [...]." (Said, 2003, S.63).

Durch Wiederholung und die Verwendung vereinfachender und spektakulärer Marker würden solche Konstruktionen in einem kulturellen Repertoire festgeschrieben, das sogar in der Auseinandersetzung mit dem 'Anderen' in Selbstbezüglichkeit verharre:

"Underlying all units of Orientalist discourse – by which I mean simply the vocabulary employed whenever the Orient is spoken or written about – is a set of representative figures, or tropes. These figures are to the actual Orient (...) as stylized costumes are to characters in a play (...)." (Said, 2003, S.71)

(Wie) Reproduziert sich das 'Theater des Orientalismus' weiterhin und (wie) wird es in Frage gestellt?

Plötzliche Willkommenskultur und die Abwesenheit zeitgenössischer arabischer Dramatik im deutschsprachigen Theater

„Wollen wir an diesen Produktionen der herrlichsten Geister teilnehmen, so müssen wir uns orientalisieren, der Orient wird nicht zu uns herüberkommen [...]" war Johann Wolfgang von Goethe überzeugt (vgl. Göckede, 2006, S.185). Er schrieb dies auf dem Höhepunkt seiner (ebenso begeisterten wie großzügig über Quellenverweise hinwegsehenden) Auseinandersetzung mit arabischer und persischer Dichtung, als Kind seiner Zeit. *Strange Encounters* (Ahmed, 2000) jenseits des eigenen Horizonts waren lange als nicht alltägliche Erfahrung verhältnismäßig wenigen Weltenwandler_innen vorbehalten.

Das sieht heute anders aus.

Von „Der Orient wird nicht zu uns herüberkommen..." zu „Wir schaffen das!". Was als eine von den zivilgesellschaftlichen Protesten (dem sogenannten 'Arabischen Frühling') in den Nachbarstaaten inspirierte Welle kreativer Interventionen im öffentlichen Raum begann, mit Graffiti, Demonstrationen und zahlreichen Aktionen, in denen Aktivismus und Performancekunst ineinander verschwammen, wurde mit der gewaltsamen Repression des beginnenden Aufstands im März 2011 durch das Assad-Regime zum Beginn eines blutigen Konflikts, der bis heute andauert.

Die syrische Theaterszene war zu diesem Zeitpunkt aktiv, gut ausgebildet, und zunehmend international präsent. Für die Ausbildung am Konservatorium in Damaskus bewarben sich Studieninteressierte aus der ganzen arabischsprachigen Welt. Die Nachwirkungen der sozialistischen Bruderlandschaft zeigten sich in der Vernetzung mit russischen Schauspielschulen. Das Theater wurde von staatlicher Seite subventioniert, aber auch kontrolliert. Der Drang nach der Ausweitung von Spielräumen motivierte die Suche nach neuen Räumen und Formen für die Darstellenden Künste (vgl. weiterführend Yasiri, 2014, Ziter, 2015).

Einige der der hoch produktiven syrischen Theaterszene entstammende *Artactivists* wie Mohammad Al-Attar, Ziad Adwan oder Mey Seifan wirkten 2011 bereits mit internationaler Präsenz. Für die meisten Menschen in Deutschland dauerte es aber noch vier Jahre, bis das Geschehen in Syrien nicht mehr über verpixelte Youtube-Videos vermittelt, sondern durch tausende menschliche Erfahrungsträger_innen verkörpert mitten in Europa ankam – im Sommer 2015, der zum Zeitpunkt des Verfassens dieses Artikels je nach politischem Interesse als Sommer der 'Flüchtlingskrise' oder aber der 'Willkommenskultur' in Erinnerung gehalten wird. Angesichts der ungewohnt großen Zahl der zur gleichen Zeit Ankommenden wurde eklatant sichtbar, wie mangelhaft nach Jahren juristischer und finanzieller Einschränkungen des universellen Rechts auf Asyl die dafür bestehende Infrastruktur auf die Bedürfnisse eines Einwanderungslands zugeschnitten war. Zivilgesellschaftliche Akteur_innen sprangen ein – auch die Theater.

So wurde ab Sommer 2015 in und um die Theater in einem nie da gewesenen Ausmaß mit Formaten für Begegnungsräume und Kooperationen mit neu Angekommenen experimentiert, die sich einerseits als Vorübungen 'einer künftigen, transkulturellen Gemeinschaft' (Heeg/Hillmann, 2017) motivierten, andererseits als eitle Posen kritisiert wurden. Matthias Lilienthal erklärte: „Gute Sozialarbeit ist mir lieber als schlechtes Theater" (vgl. Diesselhorst, 2015). Es zeigte sich, dass nicht nur Anspruch und Realität, sondern auch die Anforderungen einer akuten Notsituation und kontinuierlicher Arbeitsabläufe von Kulturbetrieben, und nicht zuletzt die Erfahrung und Bewertung der Prozesse durch die unterschiedlichen Beteiligten oft weit auseinanderklafften.

Auch deshalb schlossen sich im überregionalen Postheimat-Netzwerk Initiativen zusammen, die sich langfristigere Auseinandersetzung und fruchtbarere Kollaborationsstrukturen auf die Fahnen geschrieben hatten.

Gerade bei „nie dagewesenen" Hypes, die etablierte Institutionen erreichen, lassen sich oft viele Diskurslinien nachzeichnen, die auf Entwicklungen in lange marginalisierten Szenen und Vorarbeit durch oft mit wenig Anerkennung belohnten (art-)aktivistischen Akteur_innen verweisen. Wie Stuart Hall schreibt:

> „Es wäre doch eine eigenartige Geschichtsschreibung (...), die nicht berücksichtigte, daß die tiefste kulturelle Revolution durch den Einzug der Marginalisierten in die Repräsentation ausgelöst wurde – in der Kunst, der Malerei, der Literatur, überall in den modernen Künsten, in der Politik und im sozialen Leben im allgemeinen. Unser Leben wurde durch den Kampf der Marginalisierten um Repräsentation verändert." (Hall, 1994, S.59).

Bei dieser Veränderung handelt es sich um aufeinander aufbauende Wirkungsschichten von mehreren Generationen von Aktivist_innen und Kunstschaffenden.

Awni Karoumi etwa hätte sich eine so breite Offenheit, wie die Theater 2015 für die syrische Diaspora an den Tag legten, wohl nicht träumen lassen. Der Schauspieler, Regisseur und Dozent, der in den 1990ern wie viele andere auf Grund der politischen Situation aus dem Irak ins Exil ging, musste sein in Deutschland verbrachtes Leben lang um Räume für sein Theater kämpfen. In der wenig umfangreichen Rezeption seines Schaffens auf Deutsch zeigt sich ein Blick, der seine Arbeit exotisierte und Relevanz lediglich im Sinne künstlerischer Entwicklungshilfe für sein Herkunftsland, nicht aber als Denkanstoß für ein deutschsprachiges Publikum zugestehen wollte (vgl. Haakh, 2019, S.227f.).

Im gleichen deutschsprachigen Kulturbetrieb ließen sich Inszenierungen arabischer Dramatik weiterhin an einer Hand abzählen, selbst Inszenierungen der Texte eines so bedeutenden Dramatikers wie Sa'd Allah Wannous (Haakh 2019, S. 177f.), der als ITI-Theaterbotschafter des Jahres 1996 und experimenteller Vorreiter eines in Damaskus erprobten politisch und ästhetisch radikalen 'Theaters der Politisierung' (vgl. Kassab 2010, Glenn 2018, Wannus/Myers/Saab 2019) eigentlich weitreichende Rezeption verdient hätte.

Die Abwesenheit der Werke von Wannous im deutschsprachigen Kanon zeigt den blinden Fleck, in dem die zeitgenössische Kunstproduktion des arabischen Raums in Europa lange ausgeblendet wurde. Awni Karoumi steht exemplarisch für eine frühere Exilgeneration, bei der sich der scharfkantige Abstand zwischen seiner Bedeutung im arabischsprachigen Raum und seiner Marginalisierung in der deutschen Theaterlandschaft zu Lebzeiten nicht auflöste. 2006 erlag Karoumi auf einer Probebühne der Berliner Werkstatt der Kulturen einem Herzinfarkt – ein Jahrzehnt bevor die Plattform Nachtkritik im Zeitraum von wenigen Monaten – Sommer 2015 bis Januar 2016 – ganze 80 Projekte mit arabischsprachigen Akteur_innen auf den Bühnen des Landes zählte.

Diese rasante Entwicklung war möglich, weil in der deutschen Kulturszene im vorhergehenden Jahrzehnt viel passiert war. Forderungen nach der Reflexion der Sehgewohnheiten der Mehrheitsgesellschaft, der Repräsentation marginalisierter Perspektiven und der Revision des Männerdominierten und eurozentrischen Kanons insgesamt waren so präsent wie wohl nie zuvor. Dies geschah durch Impulse von außen und von innen, nämlich durch die zunehmende Präsenz translokaler, international mobiler, postkolonial bewusst agierender Kunstszenen und den Erfolg der postmigrantischen Theaterbewegung im deutschen Kulturbetrieb.

Bereits während der ersten Jahre des sogenannten 'Arabischen Frühlings' hatte das Interesse an politischer Kunst aus Kontexten unbequemer Dringlichkeit mit dem utopischen Glanz zivilgesellschaftlichen Widerstands zu einer Verdichtung der Kontakte zwischen Kultureinrichtungen und Kunstschaffenden im deutsch- und arabischsprachigen Raum geführt. Künstler_innen wie Rabih Mroué und Lina Magdaliya, Laila Soliman, Meriam Bousselmi oder Mohammad Al-Attar zeigten Gastspiele und Auftragsarbeiten. Hier muss allerdings hervorgehoben werden, dass es sich dabei meist um durch engagierte Einzelpersonen ermöglichte punktuelle Initiativen handelte, meist in Form von Festival- und Residenzeinladungen mit kurzer Dauer.

Der Erfolg der postmigrantischen Theaterbewegung (Sharifi 2016) in Verbindung mit einem zunehmenden Interesse an un-erhörten Perspektiven, sei es durch Neue Dramatik (wie von Sasha Marianna Salzmann, Hakan Savas Mican oder Maryam Zaree), sei es durch Ansätze aus dem Dokumentartheaterbereich (wie sie etwa Rimini Protokolle, She She Pop oder Yael Ronen praktizier(t)en), stieß im ganzen deutschsprachigen Raum eine Welle der Auseinandersetzung von Theaterschaffenden mit und ohne eigene Migrationserfahrung mit einer Diversifizierung der Figuren und Geschichten auf und – wenn auch deutlich zaghafter –hinter der Bühne an. Auf ästhetischer Ebene spiegelte sich dies in der zunehmenden Präsenz von Ansätzen mit Verbindung zu Dokumentartheater oder dem (lange als „Soziokultur" aus dem „Hochkultur"-Kanon, vgl. Kosnick, 2004) Bereich der Kulturellen Bildung.

Die viel gewählte Strategie der Arbeit mit Quereinsteiger_innen und 'Expert_innen des Alltags' bringen allerdings spezifische Herausforderungen mit sich. In welchem Verhältnis stehen die Sichtbarkeit auf der Bühne und die Teilhabe an der Gestaltung des Prozesses und der Früchte erfolgreicher Rezeption? Oft zeigte sich in diesen Projekten eine ambivalente bis problematische 'Ausstellung des Körpers als soziale Tatsache' (Kurzenberger, 1997, S.106f.) und eine Festlegung auf bestimmte Themen mit Tendenz zum 'Autobiographiezwang' (Huggan, 2001).

Diese problematischen Aspekte sind ausführliche analysiert worden – die 'Vermarktung des Andersseins' (hooks, 1994, S. 33), der 'Hype um Hybridität' (Ha, 2005), die besondere Belastung der 'Killjoys' (Ahmed, 2012, 2021), denen als vereinzelte Diversitätsbeauftragte in sonst trägen Institutionen die Verantwortung aufgebürdet wird, notwendige kollektive Transformationsprozesse in Schwung zu bringen.

„Die Konstruktion rassifizierter und prekarisierter Körper von KünstlerInnen of colour findet innerhalb eines Diskurses statt, in dem das Sprechen über 'Vielfalt' und 'Hybridität' Teil eines Prozesses der Kommodifizierung und neuer Formen der (Selbst-)Ausbeutung wird." (Kömürcü, 2010).

Sichtbarkeit und Selbstbestimmtheit oder Mitbestimmung gehen auch in der Repräsentationsmaschine Theater keineswegs Hand in Hand.

Das Post-Heimat-Netzwerk als Mikrokosmos

Bei den Projekten, die sich im Post-Heimat-Netzwerk zusammenfanden, handelte es sich um Projekte mit teilweise langer Kontinuität im Bereich der Kulturproduktion im deutschsprachigen Raum. Sie verfügten über (sehr unterschiedliche) erprobte Arbeitsweisen und ästhetische Interessen, wenn diese auch nicht unbedingt klar reflektiert oder benannt wurden. Nun wurden Kulturschaffende, die den deutschsprachigen Kulturbetrieb als neuen Raum kennen lernten, in die bereits bestehenden Strukturen eingeladen und in den laufenden Betrieb eingegliedert. Das zeigte sich unmittelbar in d den Rahmenbedingungen, die für die Zusammenarbeit konzipiert wurden, und in denen sich die jeweiligen Schwerpunkte der ausrichtenden Institution deutlich:

So akquirierte das Berliner Maxim Gorki Theater, an dem die postmigrantische Theaterbewegung um Shermin Langhoff seit 2013 über die Infrastruktur des Stadttheaters verfügte, für das dort angegliederte Exil-Ensemble in Deutschland exilierte Schauspieler_innen. Durch Deutschunterricht und die Arbeit mit verschiedenen Regisseur_innen sollten sie über den Kontext des Exil-Ensembles hinaus für ihre eigenständige Weiterarbeit im deutschen Kulturbetrieb bestärkt werden. Dabei waren die Überführung biographischer Elemente der professionellen Schauspieler_innen in die Inszenierungen Teil des Erfolgsrezeptes etwa der Hausregisseurin Yael Ronen.

Die Münchner Kammerspiele hingegen holten für ihr No-Border-Ensemble ausgebildete Schauspieler_innen nach München, die in Syrien und den Nachbarländern arbeiteten, und auf die Forderung, sich autobiographisch zu äußern, eher überrascht reagierten.

Das Theater Mühlheim an der Ruhr hatte schon ein temporäres türkisches und ein Roma-Ensemble beherbergt. Jetzt wurde dort das Kollektiv Ma'alouba gegründet, in dessen Rahmen professionellen syrischen Theatermacher_innen, darunter Ikonen des syrischen Kunstszene wie Amal Omran, neue Inszenierungen auf Arabisch entwickelten.

Im Boat People Projekt in Göttingen arbeitet ein freie-Szene-Kollektiv *weißer* deutscher Theatermacher_innen in wechselnden Projektkonstellationen mit einem wachsenden und wechselnden Netzwerk von Künstler_innen verschiedener Hintergründe. Projekte werden mit Laienspieler_innen ebenso wie mit professionellen Künstler_innen realisiert.

Das Hamburger Projekt HaJuSom bezieht sich in seiner Arbeit mit inzwischen eigener Spielstätte und parallel arbeitenden Gruppen mit Jugendlichen und Erwachsenen weiterhin vom Namen und dem Ideal einer Zusammenarbeit auf Augenhöhe her auf die Mitglieder des ersten Ensembles von *Newcomern* in Deutschland.

Das Kollektiv Ruhrorter, das mit nicht-professionellen Performer_innen eindringliche ortsspezifische Performancearbeiten entwickelte, gehörte mit zu den Initiatoren des Netzwerks, schied aber während der Netzwerkzeit aus, weil die (immer wieder neu zu akquirierenden) Projektfördermittel nicht bewilligt worden waren.

Es zeigt sich: Arbeitsweisen, Kontexte und Produktionsbedingungen, Vorstellungen von Ästhetik ebenso wie die Bedeutung, die der Post-Heimat-Auseinandersetzung innerhalb der Ausrichtung der einzelnen Projekte zukam, und sich etwa im Umgang mit Vielsprachigkeit oder dem Verhältnis von Künstler-Persona und Bühnenfigur zeigte, waren schon vor Beginn der Postheimat-Projekte sehr unterschiedlich.

Welche Figuren und Positionen wurden sichtbar? Wo und von wem werden Entscheidungen getroffen, die die Rahmenbedingungen für die Arbeit und die künstlerischen Setzungen betreffen? Welche Perspektiven werden ins Rampenlicht gestellt, was für Rollenzuweisungen fortgeschrieben, welche reflektiert?

Fallbeispiel: 'Die Probe' und 'Cultural Brokering'

SAHAR: (In die Kamera:) Ich bin froh, dass ich hier endlich wieder die Gelegenheit bekomme, in meinem Beruf zu arbeiten... Ich habe schon so viel Welcome-Kaffee getrunken, dass es eigentlich ein Wunder ist, dass ich überhaupt noch schlafen kann. (Nicht mehr in die Kamera:) Aber ich will doch nicht Kaffee trinken, ich will arbeiten. Das Stück konnte ich mir nicht aussuchen, aber das ist hier normal, glaube ich..." (Hamdoun/Dieselhorst, 2017)

Für „Die Probe" (2017) hat das Boat People Projekt in Göttingen die Zusammenarbeit zwischen Anis Hamdoun und der Journalistin und Autorin Sophie Diesselhorst ermöglicht. Das von Hamdoun inszenierte Stück zeigt ebenfalls einen Inszenierungsprozess. „Die Probe" begleitet die Figur Sahar, einer syrischen Regisseurin, bei ihrem ersten Projekt an einem deutschen Theater. Die Figur des Intendanten Gerhardt – „Auch ich habe im Sommer 2015 ein Refugees-Welcome-Plakat an meinem Theater aufgehängt" – hat sich nämlich einen dramaturgischen Knüller ausgedacht: Sahar soll das Brecht-Stück 'Das Leben des Galilei' inszenieren. Der Plan des Intendanten ist, dass ihre Interpretation den Stoff mit einer ihr zugeschriebenen kollektiven Narration in Beziehung bringen wird:

> GERHARD: „Wir leben in Zeiten, in denen ein politisches Theater wichtiger denn je ist. Die Wahlen stehen bevor, die gesellschaftliche Stimmung ist heikel, wie wir alle wissen. Im Theater versammeln wir uns, im Theater können wir uns unmittelbar herausfordern mit den Problemen unserer Zeit. Wer, wenn nicht eine Frau, die vorm Krieg geflüchtet ist, kann uns etwas über diese Probleme erzählen?"

Der etablierte Stückkanon des deutschsprachigen Theaters wird geöffnet, aber unter Einschränkung: Die syrische Regisseurin darf einen Klassiker inszenieren, soll sich dafür aber weniger auf eine eigene Version als auf eine ihr per Gruppenzugehörigkeit zugeschriebene Sprechposition beziehen. Hier zeigt sich eine Dynamik, die als 'Cultural Brokering' beschrieben worden ist.

Die Anthropologin Ruth Mandel prägte den Begriff des 'Cultural Brokering' in ihrer Studie im Berlin der Jahrtausendwende für die ambivalente Situation Kulturschaffender mit türkischem Hintergrund,

> "who often find that in Germany they are accepted as cultural and intellectual elites (artists, writers, musicians, film- makers, professionals, politicians, academics) only if they reinvent themselves as ethnic elites. Many of them willy-nilly become cultural brokers and spokespeople for the workers (...)." (Mandel, 2008, S.186).

Diese Sprechposition geht mit einem ambivalenten Verhältnis sowohl zu der minorisierten Gruppe, auf die sich als Mitglieder einer geteilten Erinnerungsgemeinschaft bezogen wird, als auch zu den hegemonialen Diskursen der Mehrheitsgesellschaft über diese Gruppe einher und beinhaltet das Dilemma "of displacing those she claims to represent" (Sieg, 2010, S.160). Auch wenn die Wortmeldungen, die sich in diesen Zusammenhang stellen, vom Wunsch nach Differenzierung motiviert und somit als Korrektiv intendiert seien, werde darin dennoch oft die Selbst-Festschreibung auf bestimmte Inhalte fixiert. Gerade das Aufgreifen und Wiedererzählen der hegemonialen Narrative gewähre migrantischen Eliten autonomen Raum in der Öffentlichkeit (Mandel, 2008, S.156f, Haakh, 2021, S.86).

> „Die authentische Stimme spricht und sagt das, was die Mehrheit hören will. In diesem Moment verquickt sich ein hegemoniales Zuhören, welches nur das hört, was die dominanten Verhältnisse stabilisiert, mit der Forderung der politisierten Minorisierten für das Recht auf eine eigene, eben authentische Stimme." (Castro Varela/Dhawan, 2006, S.436).

So stehen Theaterschaffende, die als Neuankömmlinge in den Kulturbetrieb kommen, gerade angesichts der großen Zahl von Projekten mit Laiendarstellern, oft vor dem Dilemma, „(...) auf der Bühne primär aufgrund des eigenen biographischen Erfahrungskontexts zu stehen" (Heinicke, 2017, S.43). In seiner Untersuchung von Literatur aus Minderheitenkontexten stellte Graham Huggan fest, dass auch anderen Genres zuzuordnende Werke maßgeblich in der Kategorie der Autobiographie verortete und vermarktet würden und diagnostizierte deshalb einen 'Autobiographiekult' (Huggan, 2001). Die Arabistin Margret Litvin hat auf Grund solcher Spezialkompetenzen, die sich arabische Künstler_innen im europäischen Kulturbetrieb aneignen müssen, den Entfesselungskünstler Harry Houdini als Inspirationsfigur herangezogen, "who made a sensational living getting locked into difficult situations and wriggling out again (...)." (Litvin/Sellmann, 2018, S.46)

In ‚Die Probe' schlägt Entfesselungskünstlerin Sahar eine absurd eigenwillige Re-Kontextualisierung des Brecht-Stücks vor, die nicht nur ihr syrisch-deutsches Ensemble überrascht, sondern auch so gar nicht in den vom Intendanten vorgegebenen Rahmen passen will:

> STEVE: Ich verstehe die Verbindung zwischen Joghurt und [Galileo] G[alilei] noch nicht. ASTRID: Don't worry, du wirst dich dran gewöhnen, an deutschen Theatern Regisseure mit komischen Ideen zu treffen. Sahar passt eigentlich sehr gut hierher.

Nachdem Intendant Gerhard kurzzeitig die Regie an sich genommen hat, kommt durch die Verschwesterung zwischen Sahar und Ensemblespielerin Astrid schlussendlich doch Sahars Version auf die Bühne. Eine Version, die eine eigenwillige Neu-Interpretation des Klassikers anbietet – aber als Einblick in die spezifische individuelle Weltbeziehung der Künstlerin, nicht als Stellvertretererzählung einer angenommenen Kollektividentität.

Fallbeispiel 'Your Love is Fire' und 'Safe Houses' für Kreativität in der Krise

Einen sehr persönlichen und zugleich kollektiv anschlussfähigen Ausdruck für die Situation, zwar selbst in Deutschland, mit Kopf und Herz aber in Syrien zu sein, präsentierte der Dramatiker Mudar Al-Haggi in seinem Stück 'Your Love is Fire' (2017). Rafat Al-Zarkout inszenierte den Text mit dem arabischsprachigen Ensemble des Kollektivs Ma'alouba in Mühlheim.

'Deine Liebe ist Feuer' zeigt als Kammerspiel eine Wohnung in Damaskus. 24 Stunden Sonderurlaub hat Chaldoun (Mohamed Alrashi) vom Militär bekommen, die er gerne mit seiner Freundin Rand (Amal Omran) genießen möchte. Weil aber draußen plötzlich der Beschuss wieder losging, sitzt nun auch Rands Freundin Hala (Louna AboDerhmen) die gerade zu Besuch war, in der winzigen Wohnung fest und verunmöglicht es dem Liebespaar durch ihre Anwesenheit, intim zu werden. Diese erzwungene Wartesituation, in der keine der Figuren weiß, wie es weitergehen soll, nutzt der Autor zu einem Kunstgriff:

(Schweigen über den längst möglichen Zeitraum). HALA: Was hat er denn? Warum hört er denn jetzt wieder auf zu schreiben? CHALDOUN: Nee, der hat nicht aufgehört zu schreiben... Das ist nur Schweigen über den längstmöglichen Zeitraum. (Schweigen.) STIMME DES AUTORS: Nein... ich habe aufgehört zu schreiben. Bleibt einfach so, bis ich wieder anfange (...). Jede Bewegung, die ihr macht, bringt mich durcheinander und dann weiß ich nicht weiter.

Es stellt sich heraus, dass Hala die Partnerin des Autors ist, der gerade die Auffanglager in Deutschland durchläuft und sich in der Sinnkrise des Exilanten befindet, der mit einer unbekannten, wenig gastfreundlichen und letztendlich willkürlichen neuen Umgebung konfrontiert ist. „Und warum ausgerechnet Deutschland?" fragt eine der Figuren schließlich. „Keine Ahnung. Der Autor will es so."

"My imagination was blocked in the two years that preceded the Syrian revolution in March 2011. I did not know what to work on. Syria was too real. (...) I was blocked before the revolution and I was paralyzed in its first two years. What to do? How to express myself?"

So beschreibt die Choreographin Mey Seifan die Herausforderung, die Unterdrückung, Konflikt und Wandel für die Navigation im Alltag und für den kreativen Prozess bedeuten (Seifan, 2016, S.45). Unter den Projekten des Post-Heimat-Netzwerks sticht das Kollektiv Ma'louba insofern heraus, als die in diesem Rahmen arbeitenden syrischen Künstler_innen nach einer anfänglichen personellen Findungsphase am eigenständigsten Projekte entwickeln konnten. Das einzige konsequent auf Arabisch arbeitende und spielende Ensemble hat mit 'My Love is Fire' eine der anschaulichsten und detailliertesten Darstellungen nicht nur der Situation in Syrien sondern auch der Paralyse der Exilierten vorgelegt. Das erinnert an die temporären Schutzräume für die Arbeit an besonders vulnerablen Gruppennarrativen *in progress*, die Mary Louise Pratt als 'safe houses' bezeichnet hat:

> "Where there are legacies of subordination, groups need places for healing and mutual recognition, safe houses in which to construct shared understandings, knowledges, claims on the world that they can bring into the contact zone." (Pratt, 1991, S.40).

Fallbeispiel: 'The Situation' und die Figur des wohlmeinenden Deutschen

Räume, in denen Menschen mit ganz unterschiedlichen Geschichten und unumgänglicher Eingebundenheit in asymmetrische Machtstrukturen einer postkolonialen und intersektionalen Gegenwart zusammenkommen, erfordern von allen Beteiligten neue Kompetenzen. Dabei werden oft die Bewegungen derer, von denen gefordert wird, sich 'zu integrieren', eher fokussiert als jener, die durch ihre Positionierung von Machtstrukturen profitieren.

Als weiß gelesene Menschen sind die Zielgruppe der Illusion von 'Happyland'. So nennt Tupoka Ogette das konstruierte Weltbild, in dem das Leid der (oft rassifizierten) Vielen, das die privilegierte Leichtigkeit der Wenigen ermöglicht, wirkmächtig ausgeblendet werden kann (Ogette, 2020). Auch hierfür ist das Konzept der 'Contact Zone' hilfreich, weil die Partizipation an strukturellen Machtverhältnissen nicht ausgeblendet, sondern das jeweils spezifische Navigieren auf schwankendem Grund (und die möglichen Verbindungen dazwischen) in den Vordergrund gestellt werden. So kann reflektiert werden, wie die Leichtigkeit und Hürden beim Navigieren von der Beschaffenheit des 'unsichtbaren Rucksacks' (McIntosh, 1989) der jeweils spezifischen Eingewobenheit von Subjekten in strukturelle Machtverhältnisse bestimmt werden.

In den Stücken von Yael Ronen hat die Figur des wohlmeinenden, aber unbeholfen von Fettnäpfchen zu Fettnäpfchen schlitternden Deutschen Tradition.

Im Zentrum von 'The Situation', einem der Stücke, mit denen sich das Exil-Ensemble am Berliner Maxim-Gorki-Theater formierte, steht ein Deutschkurs, in dem Nahostkonflikt und Syrienkrieg im Kreuzberger Kiez anhand von Konversationsübungen und grammatischen Konstruktionen von Vergangenheit bis ins Konditional durchgenommen werden.

Regisseurin Yael Ronen steht in der deutschsprachigen Theaterlandschaft stilbildend für autobiographisch inspiriertes Dokumentartheater, das mit radikalem, die Grenzen von gutem Geschmack austestenden Humor vor keinem wunden Punkt zurückschreckt. In ihrem deutschen Debütstück 'Dritte Generation', das 2009 an der

Berliner Schaubühne realisiert wurde (auch dort schon in Zusammenarbeit mit ihrer langjährigen Komplizin, Dramaturgin Irina Szodruch, mit der sie seit 2013 als
Hausregisseurin am Gorki weiterarbeitete) stellten sich deutsche, palästinensische
und israelische Schauspieler einer bitterbösen und oft brüllend komischen Vergan-
genheits- und Gegenwartsbewältigung. Seitdem spielt Ronen mit der Kombinati-
on aus persönlichen Geschichten, dem Handwerkszeug der professionellen Schauspieler, und dem Verschwimmen der Grenzen zwischen Realität und Fiktionalisie-
rung. Zwischen autobiographischem Narrativ und dramaturgischer Zuspitzung ist
oft nicht klar, ob die Stimme auf der Bühne gerade eine_n Protagonist_in oder eine
Figur erzählt.

Nach diesem Prinzip treffen in einem Deutsch-Kurs in 'The Situation' ein ver-
krachtes israelisch-palästinensisches Ehepaar (Orit Nahmias und Yousef Sweid),
zwei Neuankömmlinge aus den palästinensischen Gebieten (Maryam Abu-Khaled
und Karim Daoud) und ein Neuankömmling aus Syrien (Ayham Majid Agha) auf
den völlig überforderten weißen Deutschlehrer (Dimitrij Schad):

DIMITRIJ: I just want to help you.

AYHAM: Why? I don't like to owe people. It's enough you letting me stay at your
place for free.

DIMITRIJ: I don't know, maybe it feels good to help somebody from Syria, it's just
what you should do. And it makes me happy, I don't know. I have this feeling I
can help you. Help you establish something. Something here. I want to integrate
you. Who knows? When they will have the Syrian 'Yad Vashem', I might get a tree.
[Musik langsamer] Like in the Holocaust? For saving.

An der Figur dieses Deutschlehrers wird genüsslich durchgespielt, wie zwischen
Hilfsbereitschaft, First World/Post-Holocaust Guilt und Retterphantasien die pa-
ternalistische Leitkulturrhetorik aufblitzt, die sich in eigenen Komplexen und in-
ternalisierten Kriterien eines gelingenden Lebens verheddert.

DIMITRIJ: Well, I didn't really save you like save you, save you. But you are here. You
came to me. I don't know how you came or what you've been through... but maybe
one day you will tell me. I mean I couldn't save you when you maybe needed me
the most. But now I am here and I want to help you. And I think you should just
learn German. (Musik aus.)

AYHAM: Why should I learn German? I got a permit for 6 month and when it's
finish, I back to Syria.

Fallbeispiel 'Miunikh-Damaskus' und Kollaboration auf schwankendem Grund

Das Open-Border-Ensemble an den Münchner Kammerspielen unter der Intendanz von Matthias Lilienthal warb ebenfalls syrische Schauspieler an, allerdings solche, die sich nicht auf den Weg nach Europa gemacht hatten, sondern in Syrien und den Nachbarländern beschäftigt waren. Die Konfrontation mit semi-biographischem Dokumentartheater führte hier zu einiger Irritation bei den professionellen Schauspielern: Von Beruf her hantierten sie virtuos damit, von Figur zu Figur zu wechseln und sich dramatische Texte zu eigen zu machen. Die eigene *persona* auf der Bühne breit zu treten, waren sie weniger gewohnt waren. In der Inszenierung 'Miunikh-Damaskus', die Mitglieder des Open-Border-Ensembles und des regulären Kammerspiele-Ensembles unter der Regie von Jessica Glause entwickelt hatten, wird das Ringen um Verständigung mit seinen Absurditäten thematisiert:

MAJD: You understand me? MAJA: Ja, I think I do. MAJD: How come? No one understands me back in Syria. I don't even understand myself...

Die Übersetzung bei mehrsprachigen Szenen übernimmt hier einerseits eine „Übersetzungsmaschine" auf der analoge Übertitel per Kurbel weitergedreht werden. Aber auch der kommunikative Ensembleprozess selbst zeigt sich als Suche nach Verständigung, in der verbale und nonverbale Übersetzungsstrategien verwendet werden. Das gemeinsame Nachspielen von biographischen Situationen wird zur szenischen Forschung darüber, im gleichen Bild zu sein – oder eben nicht:

MAJA: Wir machen eine Party. Es ist Donnerstag! Kommt! Wir machen eine Party gegen die Depression. Eine Party, weil wir nicht mehr wissen, was wir machen sollen. Weil die Scheissbomben immer weiterfliegen und wir nichts tun können (...) Tanzen! Immer weiter tanzen. Und dann sind wir nicht mehr hier, nicht mehr auf dem Dancefloor. Wir sind nicht mehr in Damaskus, wir sind nicht mehr im Krieg. Wir sind hier, ja einfach genau hier in diesem Moment! Und das ist für mich der schönste Moment. Und ich denk: Ja! Das ist schön! Wir leuchten! Ja! München! Sowas hast du noch nicht gesehen! (Maja tanzt und lässt sich gehen.) KINAN No. Maja. It is not like this. (Maja ist überrascht.) KINAN We make parties yes, but we are not happy like you. And we don't scream like ayayaaaa....

Die Darstellung des Schreiens aus Lebenslust und Freude bei einer Party durch die *weiße* deutsche Darstellerin Maja wird als unrealistisch kritisiert, ebenso wie ihr spielerisches Angebot eines Entsetzensschreis, als sie in einer späteren Szene die Situation nachspielt, in einem Bus zu sitzen, der plötzlich unter Beschuss gerät:

KAMEL: No, no, Maja, you wouldn't scream. You just sit and freeze. MAJD If you do it. It's more like a sound effect.

Die Inszenierung macht das Tasten nach Ausdrucksformen sichtbar, die die Einfühlung in eine selbst nicht erlebte Situation erproben, ebenso wie die Momente des Affronts und des Scheiterns, des Auseinanderklaffens der Perspektiven und Positionen – und wie diese herausfordernden Erprobungen durch einen wertschätzenden Umgang auf Augenhöhe gehalten werden könnten.

MAJA: Ayayaaaa?! Was? Und was guckt ihr mich denn jetzt wieder so an? Ich hab's doch versucht! Ich übersetze für euch hier die ganze Zeit und dann mach ich einmal einen Schrei nicht ganz richtig und dann guckt ihr mich so an. Neee. Ich mag jetzt nicht mehr.

KAMEL: No, Maja, it is so complicated to understand, we know. We know.

KINAN: Maja, no, please. Inside the party I was happy, of course. Because I don't imagine that I was in Syria, or at war or even in the middle east. But not like this. Imagine it could be like this, that the electricity is off, in a second and there is no way to continue the Party.

MAJA: Ok, ja. Das tut mir auch leid. (...) I am sorry. Mißverständnis. Ok? Let's do the Mißverständnis-Hug-Circle, ja?

MAJD: Ok, I hate it. But ok. And Maja. You wouldn't scream like this, there is always joy and sadness in the scream. Try it.

MAJA (screams.)

In der Contact Zone stehen die Prozesse im Fokus, durch die Subjekte sich in Beziehungen zueinander kontinuierlich konstituieren und transformieren, "(...) not in terms of separateness and apartheid, but in terms of copresence, interaction, interlocking understandings and practices, often within radically asymmetrical relations of power" (Pratt 1992:7). In 'Miunikh-Damaskus' wird einerseits die Unüberbrückbarkeit der (Nicht-)Erfahrung der Extremsituation sichtbar gemacht. Andererseits wird die Möglichkeit der Verständigung im und durch den gemeinsamen Prozess herausgestellt. So erleben wir in der Contact Zone – im besten Falle – das Abenteuer Kollaboration:

„Kollaboration ist etwas ungleich Schwierigeres als Kooperation. Bei Kooperation treffen verschiedene Akteure aufeinander, die zusammenarbeiten und die sich nach der gemeinsamen Tätigkeit wieder in intakte Einheiten auflösen. Kollaboration meint dagegen eine Zusammenarbeit, bei der die Akteure einsehen, dass sie selbst im Prozess verändert werden, und diesen Wandel sogar begrüßen." (Terkessidis 2015:14)

Die Contact Zone zeigt sich als ein herausfordernder Raum voller Risiken und Wunder:

„Along with rage, incomprehension, and pain, there were exhilarating moments of wonder and revelation, mutual understanding, and new wisdom – the joys of the contact zone." (Pratt, 1991, S.39).

Kollaboration in der Contact Zone

Als Contact Zones konzeptualisierte die Linguistin Mary Louise Pratt

"social spaces where disparate cultures meet, clash, and grapple with each other, often in highly asymmetrical relations of domination and subordination – like colonialism, slavery, or their aftermaths as they are lived out across the globe today" (Pratt, 1992, S.4).

Die hegemonialen Machtverhältnisse sind dabei in der Contact Zone keineswegs aufgelöst, sondern wirken weiter fort. Dekoloniale Aktivist_innen und Forschende weisen eindringlich darauf hin, dass diese Begegnungen keineswegs in einem machtfreien Raum stattfinden. Vielmehr geht es um ein Verständnis „der herrschenden europäischen Gegenwart als einem Ort oder 'Schauplatz' der Integration, an dem all diejenigen Gegenwarten, die sie aktiv zerstört hatte, neu zusammengefügt und in einen Rahmen gefaßt werden" (Hall, 1994, S.38). Deshalb ist auch das Risiko, das mit der bewussten Bewegung in der Contact Zone einhergeht, keineswegs gleichmäßig verteilt: Der 'unsichtbare Rucksack' (McIntosh, 1989) struktureller Privilegien und Hindernisse bleibt bestehen. Gleichzeitig wird die Dringlichkeit der umfassenden Dekolonisierung durch die fatalen Folgen der Verquickung von patriarchalen und rassistischen Dominanzstrukturen im globalen Kapitalismus immer deutlicher.

Die zunehmende Bewusstwerdung über die Vielzahl dieser teilweise in eklatantem Widerspruch zueinanderstehenden und sich wandelnden Situationen, Erfahrungen und Be-Deutungen kann mit Momenten akuter kognitiver Dissonanz einhergehen. Zugleich verspricht sie die Möglichkeit einer tiefgreifenden Transformation hin zu einer gerechteren und verbundeneren Menschlichkeit auf individueller und kollektiver Ebene. Der Psychologe und Rassismusforscher Mark Terkessidis ist überzeugt davon, dass gerade die vielfältige Gesellschaft, gerade die Prekarität und Ungesichertheit der eigenen Identität als relationale Positionierung, Kollaboration im Sinne reziprok transformativer Praxis unumgänglich macht:

> „Wir stehen heute alle auf schwankendem Grund [...] und zu akzeptieren, dass wir Wesen auf der Suche sind, macht uns bereit für Kollaboration." (Terkessidis, 2015, S.14).

Fazit und Ausblick: Was bleibt nach dem Hype?

Mit der Verflechtung Syrien-Deutschland ging die Ankunft und Ansiedlung einer neuen arabischen Künstler_innenszene in Deutschland in relativ kurzer Zeit vonstatten. Im Gegensatz zu früheren Diaspora-Generationen konnten die syrischen Exilant_innen auf Strukturen, Zugänge, Diskurse und Sensibilisierung aufbauen, die die postmigrantische Theaterbewegung für das deutsche Theater insbesondere in den zehn Jahren zuvor erkämpft und ermöglicht hatte. Das Wagnis einer auf allen Ebenen des Prozesses praktizierten Kollaboration auf Augenhöhe erfordert aber noch viele weitere Experimente, um zur Gewohnheit zu werden.

Mit der Ankunft der syrischen Diaspora kam es zum ersten Mal in der Geschichte des deutschen Kulturbetriebs zu einem die freie und institutionalisierte Theaterszene, Sprechtheater und Performance, Sozialarbeit und Theaterpädagogik transzendieren Spektrum von Kooperationen von der Freien Szene bis zum Stadttheater. Im Post-Heimat-Netzwerk fanden sich einige davon zusammen.

In den untersuchten Projekten zeigen sich rein quantitativ große Verschiebungen in Zugänglichkeitsmechanismen, während die Ambivalenz des theatralen Selbst- Ausdrucks zwischen Autobiographiezwang und fiktionaler Bühnenfigur als Stein des Anstoßes unterschiedlicher Erwartungen bestehen bleibt – allerdings in einer lingual, ästhetisch und personell im deutschen Kulturbetrieb so noch nicht dagewesenen Vielstimmigkeit (vgl. weiterführend Haakh u.a., 2019).

Eine enorme Entwicklung ist in Bezug auf die zunehmende Gewöhnung an den Umgang mit Mehrsprachigkeit im Prozess und auf der Bühne zu verzeichnen. In Workshops (etwas von *Nawras*) und Konferenzen wächst auch der Austausch auf der Meta-Ebene. Ob mit Übertitelung oder Synopsen, unter Einsatz neuer Technologien oder mit Auftritten von dolmetschenden Personen, als innovatives dramaturgisches Puzzleteil oder als Set-Element – der Umgang mit Vielsprachigkeit und die Ansprache eines deutsch-, arabisch- und meist auch englischsprachigen Publikums haben durch vielfältige Experimente einen Entwicklungsschub erhalten, der weiter andauern sollte – und zwar nicht als leidige Pflichtübung, sondern als weiteres ästhetisches und dramaturgisches Spielfeld der multidisziplinären Kunstform

Theater. Das Magazin Theaterubersetzen.de bietet eine wertvolle Fundgrube für das breite Spektrum möglicher Strategien.

Das Postheimat-Netzwerk zeigt sich als 'Contact Zone', in denen die Gräben zwischen Arbeitskulturen von künstlerisch und prozessbegleitend Tätigkeiten und zwischen Freier Szene und institutionalisierten Stadt- und Staatstheaterapparaten sichtbar wurden und sich nur schwer überbrücken ließen. Im Verlauf der *Encounter* wurde das Aufeinandertreffen unterschiedlicher Arbeitskulturen immer deutlicher: einerseits die auf punktuelle Projektförderung angewiesenen, aber durch flache Hierarchien beweglicheren Initiativen der Freien Szene. Andererseits die staatlichen und damit durchgängig geförderten, aber als Teil eines großen Apparats mit mehreren Entscheidungsgremien trägeren, auch einem höheren Erfolgsdruck ausgesetzten Institutionen.

In den teilnehmenden Projekten und den *Encounters* wurde immer wieder sichtbar, wie träge die notwendigen Veränderungen sich tatsächlich zeigen, z.B. in Bezug auf asymmetrische Machtkonzentration in Entscheidungsprozessen oder die Gestaltung von inklusiven Austauschformaten. Trotz und wegen allen guten Willens und aller Sachzwänge haben ausgrenzende Strukturen eine starke Tendenz, sich zu reproduzieren, die sich offenbart, wenn im Prozess der Schritt in die *Contact Zone* tatsächlich gewagt wird.

Die meisten *Encounter* des Post-Heimat-Netzwerks bestanden aus einem öffentlichen Veranstaltungsprogramm und internen Arbeitsgruppen-Treffen. In den thematischen Arbeitsgruppen sollten Akteur_innen der verschiedenen Projekte (sowohl Spielende also auch hinter den Kulissen im Bereich Produktion, Dramaturgie oder Presse Tätige) mit den begleitenden Forschenden zusammen in Austausch treten. Dabei handelte es sich vorwiegend um diskussionsorientierte Formate. Als Arbeitssprache wurde meist Englisch gewählt. In Abschlussrunden spiegelte sich die ungleiche sprachliche und formale Zugänglichkeit meist in einer wenig paritätischen Redezeitverteilung wieder. Im Verlauf der Treffen schrumpfte die Zahl der Teilnehmenden, insbesondere die der Ensemblemitglieder.

Viele Synergien, deren Früchte sich vielleicht erst in der Zukunft zeigen werden, entstanden wohl am Rande, dort, wo auch am Ende der *Encounter*-Reihe noch ein umfassendes Veranstaltungsprogramm organisiert wurde und die Arbeitsgruppen selbst organisiert weiterliefen, wo ungeplante Begegnungen passieren und Ideenaustausch und Kollaborationspläne selbst gestaltet aus der Erfahrung nicht unbedingt geteilter Herkunft, aber geteilter Blickrichtung erwachsen konnte. Die Möglichkeit, sich anhand gemeinsam erlebter künstlerischer Arbeiten konkret über austauschen zu können, zeigte sich als wertvolles Mittel zum Erkunden inhaltlicher und ästhetischer *Common Grounds* und möglicher künstlerischer Bandenbildung auf Grundlage nicht geteilter Herkunft, sondern ähnlicher Blickrichtung und resonierender ästhetischer Vorlieben.

Die Förderung des Post-Heimat-Netzwerks läuft aus. Viele der teilnehmenden Projekte haben sich als temporär herausgestellt. Dabei sind Kontinuität und Langfristigkeit in den Rahmenbedingungen wohl die vielversprechendste Basis für das im besten Sinne Weltbild-gefährdende Abenteuer Kollaboration. Die deutsche Kulturförderung hat sich in Anlehnung an die EU-Kulturförderung seit dem Beginn des 21. Jahrhunderts ebenfalls zunehmend zu einer an Themenschwerpunkten orientierten Förderung umgestaltet. Ist die Thematik des Postheimat-Netzwerkes für die Kulturszene so nur ein Hype-Thema, das von den nächsten abgelöst wird? Interessiert sich noch jemand für die Weiterführung der Experimente, wenn nun Digitalität, der Klimawandel oder die sich überschlagenden Ereignisse der Weltpolitik die Aufmerksamkeit fesseln?

Die künstlerischen Suchbewegungen der Projekte, die sich im Post-Heimat-Netzwerk zusammengetan haben (sowie zahlreicher weiterer mit ähnlicher Ausrichtung, deren Arbeit vielleicht nicht mit einer Publikation wie dieser dokumentiert wird) sind ein wesentlicher Teil einer der dringendsten Missionen unserer Zeit: Der Suche nach Übersetzung und Verständigung über Differenzlinien hinweg, der dekolonisierenden Reflektion toxischer Machtstrukturen und Privilegien, der Stärkung von Geschichten und Perspektiven, die innerhalb des dominanten Kanons viel zu lange marginalisiert worden sind, und dem Zusammenkommen in mehrsprachigen, multiperspektivischen Räumen.

Nur in Verbindung mit dieser Suche können vielleicht auch die anderen Herausforderungen unserer Zeit gemeistert werden, die von uns allen ein Hineinwachsen in ungewohnte Konstellationen und den Mut für das Spiel mit noch ungeübten Geschichten erfordern.

Inszenierungen

„Die Probe" von Anis Hamdoun und Sophie Diesselhorst, Uraufführung 30. September 2017, Boat People Projekt Göttingen.

"The Situation" von Yael Ronen und Ensemble, Uraufführung 4. September 2015, Maxim-Gorki-Theater Berlin.

„Deine Liebe ist Feuer" von Mudar Al-Haggi, Regie: Rafat Alzakout, Collective Ma'louba, Theater Mühlheim an der Ruhr.

„Miunikh Damaskus" von Jessica Glause und Ensemble, Uraufführung 4. Mai 2018, Münchner Kammerspiele.

Literatur

Adwan, Ziad. 2008. "Making Mistakes in Cultural Representations". Dissertation. London, Royal Holloway, University of London.

Ahmed, Sara. 2000. *Strange Encounters. Embodied Others in Post-Coloniality.* London, New York: Routledge.

Ahmed, Sara. 2012. *On being included: racism and diversity in institutional life.* Durham: Duke University Press.

Al-Yasiri, Jumana. 2014. *Scène(s) exilée(s). Ancrages et déplacements du théatre syrien depuis 2011.* Paris: IETM Arbeitspapier.

Diesselhorst, Sophie. 2015. „Festung Europa oder das Theater mit den Flüchtlingen". *Nachtkritik.* 29. April. Verfügbar unter https://www.nachtkritik.de/index.php?option=com_content&view=article&id=10905&catid=101&Itemid=84

Diesselhorst, Sophie. 2015. „Blog – Empathie-Schulung, konkrete Hilfe oder Flagge zeigen: Wie die Theater sich in der Flüchtlingsdebatte positionieren". *Nachtkritik.* 2. September. Verfügbar unter https://www.nachtkritik.de/index.php?option=com_content&view=article&id=11429&catid=315&Itemid=100078.

Flam, Helena. 2007. *Migranten in Deutschland. Statistiken, Fakten, Diskurse.* Konstanz: UVK Verlagsgesellschaft.

Foroutan, Naika. 2019: *Die postmigrantische Gesellschaft. Ein Versprechen der pluralen Demokratie.* Bielefeld: transcript.

Göckede, Regina. 2006. „Zweifelhafte Dokumente. Zeitgenössische arabische Kunst, Walid Raad und die Frage der Repräsentation". In *Der Orient, die Fremde. Positionen zeitgenössischer Kunst und Literatur*, hg. Alexander Karentzos, Alexander, 185–203. Bielefeld: Transcript.

Göktürk, Deniz. 2011. *Transit Deutschland. Debatten zu Nation und Migration.* Paderborn: Fink Wilhelm.

Ha, Kien Nghi. 2005. *Hype um Hybridität. Kultureller Differenzkonsum und postmoderne Verwertungstechniken im Spätkapitalismus.* Bielefeld: transcript.

Haakh, Nora. 2013. „Banden bilden, Räume schaffen, Diskurse durchkreuzen. Politisch Theater machen wie am Ballhaus Naunynstraße", *freitext Kultur- und Gesellschaftsmagazin 22*, S. 36–42.

Haakh, Nora. 2019. *Layla und Majnun in der Contact Zone. Übertragungen aus dem Arabischen ins Deutsche im zeitgenössischen Theater.* Dissertation, Freie Universität Berlin.

Haakh, Nora, Anis Hamdoun, und Tobias Herzberg. 2019. „Postmigrantisches Theater und seine Strahlkraft", *Nachtkritik.* Verfügbar unter http://www.heidelberger-stueckemarkt.nachtkritik.de/index.php/debatte/postmigrantisches-theater-und-seine-strahlkraft.

Haakh, Nora. 2022. *Muslimisierte Körper auf der Bühne. Die Islamdebatte im postmigrantischen Theater.* Bielefeld: transcript.

Hall, Stuart. 1994. *Rassismus und kulturelle Identität*. Hamburg: Argument.

Heinicke, Julius. 2017. „Verstrickungen zwischen Alltag und Kunst: (Inter)kulturelles Potenzial oder Beschränkung ästhetischer Freiheit?". *Paragrana* 26, Nr. 2, 27. November. S. 42–54.

Huggan, Graham. 2001. *The postcolonial exotic. Marketing the margins*. London: Routledge.

hooks, bell. 1994. „Das Einverleiben des Anderen: Begehren und Widerstand". *Black Looks: Popkultur – Medien – Rassismus*. Berlin: Orlanda. S. 33–56.

Kassab, Elizabeth Suzanne. 2010. *Contemporary Arab thought: cultural critique in comparative perspective*. New York: Columbia University Press.

Kosnick, Kira. „The gap between Culture and Cultures. Cultural Policy in Berlin and its Implications for Immigrant Cultural Production". European Institute, Florenz, 2004.

Kurzenberger, Hajo. 1997. „Die ,Verkörperung' der dramatischen Figur durch den Schauspieler". In *Authentizität als Darstellung*, hg. von Jan Berg et al. Hildesheim. S.106–21.

Langhoff, Shermin, Tuncay Kulaoğlu, und Barbara Kastner. 2011. „Migration deuten und dichten", in *Das Drama nach dem Drama: Verwandlungen dramatischer Formen in Deutschland nach 1945*, hg. von Artur Pelka und Stefan Tigges. Bielefeld: Transcript. S. 399–408.

Litvin, Margaret/Sellman, Johanna. 2018. "An Icy Heaven: Arab Migration on Contemporary Nordic Stages", *Theatre Research International* 43, Nr. 1. 45–62.

Mandel, Ruth. 2008. *Cosmopolitan Anxieties: Turkish Challenges to Citizenship and Belonging in Germany*. Durham, NC: Duke University Press.

McIntosh, Pegy. 1989. "White Privilege: Unpacking the Invisible Knapsack", *Peace and Freedom Magazine*, August, S. 10–12.

Metzger-Traber, Julia. 2018. *If the body politic could breath in the age of the refugee*. Heidelberg: Springer.

Nobrega, Onur Sozan. 2015. "Race, Precarity and Artistic Labour in Berlin". *Prekäre Kunst: Protest und Widerstand*. S. 30–33.

Ogette, Tupoka. 2020. *Exit RACISM. Rassismuskritisch denken lernen*. Münster: Unrast.

Pratt, Mary Louise Pratt. 1991. "Arts of the Contact Zone", *Profession*, S. 33–40.

Pratt, Mary Louise. 1992. *Imperial Eyes. Travel Writing and Transculturation*. London/ New York: Routledge.

Said, Edward. 1978. *Orientalism*. New York: Vintage Books.

Schmidt, Thomas. 2019. *Macht und Struktur Im Theater. Asymmetrien der Macht*. Wiesbaden: Springer VS.

Seifan, Mey. 2016. "My dear audience, stay awake. I'm dreaming". *A Syrious Look. A Magazine about Culture in Exile*. Berlin.

Sharifi, Azadeh. 2016. „Theater und Migration. Dokumentation, Einflüsse, Perspektiven". In *Das Freie Theater im Europa der Gegenwart: Strukturen – Ästhetik – Kulturpolitik*, hg. von Manfred Brauneck. Bielefeld: Transcript. S. 335–439.

Sieg, Katrin. 2010. "Black Virgins✕: Sexuality and the Democratic Body in Europe". *New German Critique* 109:37, Nr. 1 (Winter). S. 147–85.

Skeiker, Fadi. 2020. *Syrian Refugees, Applied Theatre, Workshop Facilitation, and Stories*. London: Routledge.

Terkessidis, Mark. 2015. *Kollaboration*. Frankfurt/M.: Suhrkamp.

Wannous, Saadallah. 2017. "Selections from ‚Manifestos for a New Arab Theatre'". In *World theories of* theatre, hg. von Glenn Odom. New York: Routledge.

Wannūs, Saʻd Allāh, Robert Myers, Nada Saab. 2018. *Sentence to Hope: A Saʻdallah Wannous Reader*. New Haven: Yale University Press.

Ziter, Edward. 2015. *Political performance in Syria: from the six-day war to the Syrian uprising*. New York u.a.: Palgrave Macmillan.

WITNESSING A NEW STAGE IN GERMAN THEATRE

Julia Grime

Walking through a garden designed and planted by refugees starting life anew in Germany, each plant in a suitcase, I head into the related exhibition at the Europäisches Museum, in Berlin's Dahlem.

*da*HEIM: *glances into fugitive lives*[1] explores the migrant experience and forces the visitor to stop and consider the individual humanity of the people who made the art. The exhibition logo, a figure carrying their identity, an outsized fingerprint, on their back. A huge Hiroshige wave transforms the end wall into a sea of people facing borders of bedframes – "my dreams do not end at borders." Among the wrecked beds, ghostly installations of clothes, everyday clothes that anyone might wear, on the walls are drawn detailed maps of convoluted journeys, journeys to find a place to simply have a life. Everywhere, people's voices: "My only possession is time" – "We are people who had to leave in order to have a life" – "I stood at the sea and all I had was my soul, and even that I had to risk in search of a life."

All begging the question; and then what? To quote Austrian playwright, Elfriede Jelinek's play, **Die Schutzbefohlenen (Charges: The Supplicants)**,[2] written in 2013 in response to immigration injustice in Vienna: "who will make sure that we will also be seen as *beings*?" Deeply moved by the exhibition, I wonder how this question might be addressed through my art world, that of theatre, and how this experience might appear on stage. So many questions. How to work with this situation creatively, opening up and finding something new in a wider dialogue that genuinely interests society, without recourse to forced political correctness and imposed guilt? How to develop and sustain such theatre for the future, to embed it in society? What about cultural as well as linguistic translation; how do we know what's truly meant? Can fragmentation and post-dramatic theatre segue into other theatre traditions? How to ensure an independent and equal voice for all? And whose voice is actually heard?

What follows is my witnessing of exile theatre in Germany, primarily made by refugees, between 2016 and 2018. Some of which features on my blogsite, **Outofthe-**

---

1   Kunstasyl, 2016–17. 'DaHeim: glances into fugitive lives'. Europaisches Museum, Berlin.

2   Jelinek, E. 2013. 'Charges: The Supplicants', translated by Honegger, G., 2016. Seagull Books, London, p15.

BlackBox.co.uk, a gathering of shows, people, interviews, meetings – which along with my notebooks, is quoted throughout. [3]

The year before, in 2015, Angela Merkel had thrown open the German borders to Syrian refugees, famously announcing "Wir schaffen das." (We can *do* this). A gauntlet taken up and thrown farther by Shermin Langhoff of Berlin's Maxim Gorki Theater, when she galvanized much of the theatrical response across the country. Theatres across Germany had risen to the challenge, responding with all manner of welcomes – plays, workshops, events, cafes, even direct support for the refugees, connecting people. As Leonie Webb of Gorki's Exil Ensemble observed to me:

> "Shermin's really good at seeing needs, identifying who's not represented already, ideas that people want to think about. It's not just about ethnicity. And we don't just want to speak to one part of the pie."

And indeed, there are so many people, so many groups, that need representation on stage, to have their voices heard. The **Roma Armee**'s playing at the Gorki – an angry howl of young Roma asserting their identity. *"This is what we have in common, our diversity"* they cry, telling their stories, addressing issues within their culture head-on – issues of sexuality, under-age marriage, and modernisation – but also telling of oppression, brutal dismissive treatment founded in prejudice, at the hands of others... *"we have a disappeared history but there will come a time when you beg us to remember."* A sentiment echoed in the discussion afterwards about how people outside of the mainstream of society get treated – *Gorki reminds us of the words of Hannah Arendt: "The community of European peoples went to pieces when – and because – it allowed its weakest member to be excluded and persecuted."*

The particular stage in question is situated in a city that is home to both the Memorial for the murdered Roma and Sinti peoples and now, to Europe's first-ever Roma Institute for Arts and Culture (ERIAC). Berlin – a city of terrible contradictions, but always changing, always moving – is a natural home for this show. Clearly, the ongoing movement of people and the need to cross borders will continue, whether because of war or climate change or even because people want to move around, to try living somewhere else. Far from shutting down, the social debate around migration and borders needs to expand, along with our thinking.

And yet, after the initial enthusiasm and general welcome of 2015, other responses rose. Support had been growing for the far-right wing Alternative für Deutschland (AfD), a reaction against 'the other', not just the usual xenophobic

---

3   Much of the material in this article derives from the author's 2017–18 British Council funded project exploring refugee theatre in Germany. This was reported through a blogsite – www .outoftheblackbox.co.uk – and the various quotations from that site have been included to indicate their source rather than using repeated references.

kneejerk – "they'll take our jobs" – but a deep fear for a notion of traditional German culture, whipped up further with populist politicking. German society divided between those who welcomed its new citizens and the diversity they brought and those who put up barriers, protesting a perceived assault on Heimat, a deeply bedded sense of 'German-ness'. A disturbing new organisation, PEGIDA emerged. German theatre director, Falk Richter, disturbed by the dual fears unfolding in his society – not just the fear of change and the unknown 'other', but more fundamentally, the fear of the associated resurgence of the far-right wing, wrote and directed a play – *Fear*. Staged at Berlin's prestigious Theater Schaubühne, it sparked an aggressive and sustained reaction from the AfD.

And the play? A warning of dream fragments coming home to roost... Dancers shimmering in and out of shadow – is this how fear moves? Images of Nazis, past and present, loom on screen amid huge green zombies and images of AfD politicians. Set in a comfortable middle-class home, the characters explore the rise of the new right-wing, populism, nationalism, and perhaps most importantly, the complacency of their own lives. Europe is possibly sleepwalking into a nightmare.

Really? Had modern German culture become so fixed, so fragile, so fearful? I went to the home of a veritable pioneer of internationalism in German theatre, *Theater an der Ruhr* in Mülheim in North Rhine-Westphalia where Artistic Director, Roberto Ciulli has spent more than 35 years pursuing a vision of a theatre that takes impossible turns.

"A vision for a theatre that would develop intercultural understanding, exploring new philosophies and attitudes from other cultures, taking work across international borders and bringing work back to be seen in Germany... Bringing new ideas and viewpoints, uninfluenced by our western media. The idea was that theatre is about a journey, to travel into new cultures, to be interested in the things you don't know. No-one else was doing this in Germany then." said Executive Director, Sven Schlötcke."

There's not much Ciulli hasn't done in internationalizing the Mülheim theatre – there've been many theatre exchanges, festivals of Eastern Mediterranean theatre, a home for a Roma company and his Silk Road project connecting with countries along the ancient trading routes, finding ways to communicate, circumventing the censors if needed, not unlike staging theatre in the old DDR:

"All our shows feature symbolism and representation over words. Censors only focus on fixed rules. It's like in Iran – men and women are forbidden to touch, but how much more does it say if onstage, they don't touch by only one centimetre..."

More recently, they've supported two refugee companies – *Ruhrorter*, an independent company making site-specific work with refugees in the post-industrial Ruhr landscape, and 'intercultural theatre lab', *Collective Ma'louba*, Arabic-speaking and 'penetrating the taboos of Arabic and European society' – both members of the Post-Heimat network. As Schlötcke concludes:

> "the understanding that flowed from all this was wonderful – transcending language. The language of theatre is universal. The Art itself is the opportunity to communicate. And this travelling insight brought a journey through aesthetic thinking too."

Back in Berlin, I attended a poetry reading by French-Algerian poet, Habib Tengour:

> Chasing a place dream
> Of this place that bears place name
> Crushed in exodus hunger
> A place that is but the expression
> Of the desire to place you there where voice
> Carries away.
> *Aleppo 2* [4]

I'm there on an introduction from the French poet, Pierre Joris, who argues that the future is all about translation, as poets, and people, become more nomadic. Like Ciulli, he sees the importance of exchanging cultures, breaking down barriers, not building them. Reading his blog later reminds me that much of twentieth-century Art is about collage, juxtaposition – the strands of tension between what fits and what doesn't, being key to making it work. German post-dramatic theatre is likewise a collage – mixing genres, texts, interpretation – that can offer a richer, often more thought-provoking experience to the viewer – *"an art-based way of questioning authority, tradition and the establishment,"* to quote one of my interviewees from the Free University's Institute for Theater Studies. Ah, here was a great opportunity for a new kind of theatre within Germany, making it easier to open up, to exchange ideas on a practical as well as a theoretical basis. Well yes, but...,

> "there's a difference between picking up a public conversation and actually committing to fostering a different kind of aesthetic environment that lasts and creating structures that last."

So now, where was the theatre of Germany's new citizens? In whose voice did they speak?

---

4   Tengour, H., 2017–18. 'Already Berlin', www.tamaas.org – accessed 4 June 2021.

I talked with Necati Öziri, who had run the Maxim Gorki Theater's Studio Я for a time – "a place beyond all borders; an art haven for marginalised subjects and ways of thinking, a platform for discussion and creative processes – post national, queer, empowering."[5]

Moving on from defining refugees in terms of their journeys, their terrible experiences, to them expressing themselves as human beings, people concerned with universal issues that affect everyone. A post-migrant approach...

> "The idea was not to talk about 'others', but that 'others' should speak for themselves" said Öziri. Enter... **the Exil Ensemble** – a group of theatre practitioners drawn mostly from Syria, but also Afghanistan and Palestine. With total control over their repertoire and staging. "Their work also gives German theatregoers an opportunity, to see their world through different eyes. Langhoff terms this, 'desintegration': opening up German society to celebrating and preserving transculturalism, rather than the oft-proposed integration, which just homogenises everyone into whatever is meant by 'German-ness'," continued Öziri.

Exil Ensemble's programme ranged across theatrical approaches, tropes, genres, exploring what mattered to them, what matters to anyone. And outside of the Gorki support and branding, they were indeed totally in control. In *Winterreise* they worked with Israeli director, Yael Ronen, on a narrative ensemble-derived piece to present their own experiences and perceptions of Germany through the device of a bus trip around Germany. Another show, ***Skelett eines Elefanten in der Wüste***, written and directed by Exil's Artistic Director, Ayham Majid Agha immersed the audience in a city, a society, upheaved by civil war:

> We feel the intensity of the city under fire – the characters leap up above the walls around us, telling us about their world, the circus, their neighbours, trying to come to terms with their own feelings in this impossible situation. No-one ever knows what's coming. A sniper traces us with his red laser dot. This isn't (relatively) benign CCTV surveillance but the scrutiny of snipers – the danger of the predator. A tiny fragment of a broken society. How can anyone really understand these experiences who hasn't lived through them? Even the tangle of language in the surtitles reminds us of the divisions between people, between lives.

And away from the German-run institutions, lots more was happening – Öziri recommended a visit to ***Club Al-Hakawati***, a grassroots theatre group working at Theater X in Berlin's Moabit.

· 5   Maxim Gorki Theater, online. 'www.gorki.de/en/studio-ya' – accessed 7 June 2021.

"No-one gives us our voice. We take it. We support each other, help each other, raise issues together. It's not enough for refugees to survive, they need to live," says the group's Artistic Director, Ahmed Shah. "It's not the pure form, but we're the hakawatis for the modern age... our stories come from being marginalised... we don't want to be treated as background for a play."

This last point, a reference to a 2014 production of *Die Schutzbefohlenen* which came in for criticism for objectifying the refugee members of its cast. Relegated to the role of a largely non-speaking chorus, they were virtually treated like props. Not at all in line with Jelinek's original intention when writing her 'language artwork'.

"We don't want integration, we want to develop our own voice. We use carnival – no author, many voices, dialect, gender-mixing... all individual stories told simultaneously so you don't know which one to listen to..." continues Shah. Other members of the group chime in:
"I've always lived in Germany – I never saw bombing – but I saw a racist war, an emotional war, a discrimination war."
"My father's a Palestinian... he can never go home, never touch the earth of his homeland. This earth means so much – more than gold – the beautiful red colour, the smell. I was born here in Germany, so I could go... he asked me to bring back an olive tree... and when I gave it to him, it was the most emotional moment of my whole life. He looked so happy, so sad – 'This is the only connection I will ever have with my own land,' he said. We both cried... this earth, it matters so much."

And the theatre? Club Al-Hakawati work collectively bouncing ideas off one another, using all manner of forms – Ahmed again;

"this tradition of poetry in Arabic countries is very strong, so for our new piece, based on Picasso's painting, **Guernica**, we've written in verse, rhymed verse, felt verse – mixing poetry into the movement, the acting. And the movement becomes dance, a universal code for the audience. After all, doesn't movement convey alienation better than words? Do things slowly – there's more power. Bodies speak so much. We're using movement to transcend language...And there's a great opportunity to mix the languages – Arabic, German, English even.

I think about all those shows I'd seen in German with English subtitles and those points at which I sensed that the translation didn't really ring true. All those lifetimes of German culture that would always be partially lost to me, coming from the UK... and likewise Arabic cultures outside of my Eurocentric experience. It's not just about the words. Language is full of unspoken, implied meanings and connections. Is it ever possible to ensure a full translation, to truly communicate what's happening in another culture? And so often, theatrical translation is left till the end as an almost administrative task – although I will learn later about the idea of a Cultural Mediator. . .

I hear about another self-starting theatre group. Originally set up by three teenage refugees in Hamburg – *Hajusom – an ensemble aiming to empower young people to find their own creative expression and helping members to professionalise. Growing through a process of 'each one teach one' they've built a sustainable, cross-generational continuity since 1999. The shows have been post-migrant for years, focussing on themes like teenage love, climate change, posthumanism.* . .

By now, the Exil Ensemble have moved on to interpreting the German canon, as they take on Heiner Müller's **Hamletmaschine,** itself a mashup of Shakespeare's most revered play, through the lens of the Syrian civil war, with German director, Sebastian Nübling. And then it'll be Russian avant-garde writer, Daniil Kharms' **Elizaveta Bam** – a piece of proto-Absurdist theatre requiring the audience to rely on their intuition rather than their intellect. A veritable tumble of work. Working together with German practitioners but always ringing with their own voice.

It's not only people that get displaced – sometimes it's the shows themselves too. Hanane Hajj Ali's one-woman show, **Jogging – Theatre in Progress** at the tiny TAK Theater in Kreuzberg, part of Theatertreffen, is a case in point. That subtitle is literal – Hajj Ali reserves the right to change the play each time she performs it. She lives in Lebanon but no theatre there will stage her work, because of the artistic content. And because she refuses on principle to submit a script to the theatrical censors. So, for theatrical performances, she can only play abroad. Her theme, the search for freedom – of movement, of spirit, of life – almost impossible for a woman in Lebanon. . .

A bare stage. A woman circles the space, jogging slowly. She stops, looks at us and says simply: "I was like salt that had dissolved in water." She tells stories of women, women wanting to bear witness, to scream against the stifling patriarchy that denies them autonomy in their own lives, her own story threaded throughout. Medea's story from ancient times. Two others, more contemporary. Yvonne kills herself and her daughters, not as vengeance, but to save them, not wanting them to "suffer the torment that I endured."

She records a suicide note for her husband, but the words are not hers, they are those of Virginia Woolf, the references crossing cultures. Zahra must grieve for her three sons, all 'martyrs' to war.

Hajj Ali challenges the notion that women's happiness and sense of fulfilment must be defined in relation to men and to family, not in their own independent achievement or decision. And she needs to tell this story. "Theatre cannot die," she says in an interview after winning a major international award, [6] "sometimes it re-

---

6   Greene, A., 2021. www.americantheatre.org/2021/02/09/hanane-hajj-ali-jogging-for-surviv al-in-beirut/ – accessed 9 June 2021.

mains latent, only to explode again like water that can't be trapped by stone. It erupts like justice, like freedom."

The situation of women is a theme in several of the shows that I discover. *The Boat People Projekt* a refugee company in Göttingen in Lower Saxony, presented a collaborative piece, *Nora, from Syrian director Wessam Talhouq, which tells the story of a Syrian woman's dilemma, whether to stay or go – "every time I made the decision to leave, I remembered a hundred reasons to stay. And when I decided to stay, I remembered a hundred reasons to leave."*

Over at Berlin's Volksbühne (under the controversial new management of Chris Dercon – an intriguing story, but one for another day) another play centred around this theme. The actors, all women, specifically Syrian refugees, living in exile in Berlin. Couched as an audition to cast a contemporary version of Euripides' **Iphigenia,** the play was written collectively by the cast and writer, Mohammad Al Attar, himself a Syrian refugee. Answering questions from the Casting Director, the nine women reveal individual experiences of war, the difficulties of starting life anew in a different country, life within a patriarchal society offering a picture of oppression, inevitable suffering but surely somewhere, a shred of hope. This piece, the final instalment of Al Attar's international trilogy referencing the ancient Greeks, the first two, *The Trojan Women* and *Antigone* staged in Jordan and Lebanon respectively – the same issue spread across three countries.

Which brings me nicely to Mudar Alhaggi's *Your Love is Fire* staged by *Collective Ma'louba*. A metaphorical piece about fate, external control, dealing with what life throws at you, in this case, a war. Or more accurately, a playwright...

Alhaggi wrote the play in three different cities as he left Syria to seek a new life in Germany – an experience through which he had virtually no control over his own fate. I ask Mudar; would the play have been different in Syria? And he says; "it wouldn't've happened on the big stages in Syria because it wouldn't fit – this modern idiom, this content." The story belongs to two women, Rand, who stays in Syria because of her relationship with Khaldoun, a Syrian army soldier. And her flatmate, Hala who's leaving for Germany any day now for a new life with, well who exactly? Khaldoun comes home on 24 hours leave but dramatic artifice keeps thwarting reunion – one scene runs three times, each with a different outcome. Slowly the action is subsumed by the writer's own story as he takes centre stage, at one point developing writer's block, his own loss of control, while the characters petition him to free them up to live their lives. Unmoved, he determines that, like him, they must wait, wait endlessly to find out their destinies; "There is no beginning to the music. No end to the walk in the devil's garden."

The dislocated tone as the piece progresses emulates the post-dramatic structure so prevalent in German theatre, but in this case, it's borne of life circumstance rather than aesthetic artifice, the very displacement of the writer, bared on stage.

So much inspiring theatre, art, poetry – so much food for new thought. But at root an unease. How would all this activity sustain as the big Staatstheaters move onto the next issue? Funding in the 'Freie Szene' outside of this sector is insecure, perilous even. How could 'desintegration' be assured and German theatre, and indeed society, remain engaged with these new perspectives and cultural practices?

My final interview was with Anne Schulz of city theatre, Münchner Kammerspiele. Under its new director, Matthias Lilienthal, the theatre had reinvented, putting internationalism and transculturalism at its heart, designating itself as a welcome theatre, establishing a broad programme of events, opening up to all the city's residents regardless of where they came from, what they stood for or how much money they had. Artists from all over the world were invited to stage work there. One such piece, **Der Fall Meursault – Eine Gegendarstellung**, from Iranian director, Amir Reza Koohestani, interrogates a classic text from the European canon, Albert Camus' *L'Étranger*, from an alternative perspective. Playing across a carpeted stage, increasingly buried in sand, issues pile up – issues of identity and the intersection between Arabic and European cultures – through naming the Arabic man that Meursault so casually dispatches in the original. Moving the focus to imagine *his* story. Adapted from a controversial novel by Algerian journalist, Kamel Daoud which on its publication in 2013 had met with both acclaim and hostility.

The Kammerspiele and Ruhrorter from Mülheim, had initiated a meeting of the six companies at the heart of this book – **Post-Heimat Encounter#1** – and Anne invited me along. The name referencing the desire to move beyond 'integration' to embrace a diverse society for all. A moment of consolidation, review – a reboot, a new beginning. The purpose, to consider establishing a network to, in the words of Ruhrorter's Jonas Tinius:

"share successes and challenges, the funding systems, the aesthetic practices, how they're dealing with culture and language together, ensuring that all parties have an equal voice."

Six companies introduced themselves and a fascinating and inspiring picture began to emerge, along with a realisation that this proposed network should be crossing borders far beyond Germany. The work ranged across generations, across cultures, across aesthetics. Committed and ambitious. An ambition challenged by issues of language and cultural translation and by resources and funding but undimmed for all that.

An exciting couple of days at the Post-Heimat conference ensued in which all my previous questions and more started to crystallise. Initially, we addressed two strands – Funding and Aesthetics – the former practical, but vital, stuff around the operation, organisational issues particularly the location of control, sustainability, and the very real difficulties of finding and maintaining funding. The latter, considering audiences and communication, the issue of cultural translation...

"Think about the power that the translator has over the non-Arabic speaking audience – what if it's wrong?" said one participant. "And then there's the audiences – they're a vital part of any theatre piece. How do we get them to engage? And how can we work with the communities that are hostile to diversity, some of whom feel ignored themselves?"

And throughout both discussions; *Everybody agreed that diversity should apply at every level, not just on and around the stage, but from administrative and aesthetic decision-making to festival juries too, but the practicalities of this are complex. And this diversity shouldn't just be rooted in nationality, it should be truly intersectional reflecting all the complex variety of humanity. So much of the funding currently goes to people organising 'the other' rather than 'the other' directly. Much of the work is produced under the umbrellas of established theatres because they have the local understanding. And the resources. However well-intentioned, this must beg a question: where is the power? Whose voice is speaking? And in a truly intercultural group, it's not just about developing training and familiarisation programmes. Ultimately don't we need to find a new idea of what theatre should be, a new aesthetic?*

A public symposium – *Witnessing Transitions and Possible Futures* – brought in another perspective, the notion of visibility, as well as further thoughts on diversity;

"most European theatres are effectively private spaces because you can do what you like on the stage with a complicit audience, so it all stays within the bubble... But what happens when you leave the black box? To regain theatre's importance in our society, we must paradoxically leave the theatre itself." Theatre is the most functional and playful laboratory that we have for trying out what can happen in society at large. But we need to update it with new perspectives borne out of a deeper understanding of each other. The art of translation is crucial, reinforcing the words with movement, the way we create the best space for understanding. Even something quite obvious, a reverse approach – "how about some Arabic-West translation for a change?"

In Germany, the involvement of theatre in social cohesion moved on apace with the Integration Act of 2005. Cultural participation became a buzzword but it mostly remained about the public being audience rather than maker and the same applies to diversity. "The theatres have been bringing in immigrants and calling it 'diverse' for years but until we hand over control, it isn't. We need diversity at every level." And that's where we're at now. A clear recurring theme.

And a play. The Kammerspiele had recently established the **Open Border Ensemble**, with the aim of enabling the continuation of professional life outside Syria for four actors, in a similar way to the Exil Ensemble at the Gorki. Creating their first show, **Miunikh-Damaskus,** on a devised ensemble basis with a German director and additional actor, they had developed a new creative role, that of 'Cultural Mediator' in a bid to transcend cultural and aesthetic division. Aiming to reach out to a broader audience, they had also decided to present the piece away from the theatre in various locations across the city – the symposium in action. We headed off to experience this show first-hand and:

> settled down in front of a 'pop-up' mobile stage outside a community centre... joined at one point by three curious passing children who unceremoniously plonked themselves down at the front, we watched a piece of collective writing, deconstructing cultural stereotypes, exploring how everyday cultural differences between the two cities actually point up the similarities, our core humanity – whether through falling in love, or discovering beer, heading off to a party – simply getting on with living. To quote the blurb: "The memories of two cities and their presence merge into a possibly limitless city. Wait a minute, where are we? Munich or Damascus?"

As I headed home, I passed through the big central square in the city centre. Past a PEGIDA display packing up – aerial views sweep across forests, fantasy castles, German towns interspersed with images of churches and children flickering across a huge screen. Accompanied by soaring choral church music. This was *their* dream Germany, the things perceived as threatened. I wondered what they would have made of what I had just seen. How we might begin to square this circle... and then I thought about the decision of the Munich City Council not to renew Lilienthal's contract, a shutting down of so much possibility...

To find new perspectives, to keep growing as a society, we all need to shift ourselves, to become inwardly nomadic as well as outwardly open. To celebrate who we all are, when we finally find a life.

v. An ne xe

Contributors

Contributors

Azadeh Sharifi ist seit WS 2023 Gastprofessorin im Institut für Theaterwissenschaft an der FU Berlin. Zuvor war sie DAAD-Visiting Assistant Professor am Department of Germanic Languages & Literatures der University of Toronto und Gastprofessorin an der Universität der Künste (UdK) Berlin. Ihre Forschungsschwerpunkte sind (post)koloniale und (post)migrantische Theater und ihre Geschichte, zeitgenössische globale Performancekunst sowie dekoloniale und aktivistische Praktiken in theatralen Räumen. Zurzeit arbeitet sie an der Monographie *Theatre in Post-migrant Germany. Performing Race, Migration and Coloniality since 1945* (Palgrave Macmillan) sowie an dem Lehrbuch *Postmigrant Theatre – History, Aesthetics and Politics of a Theatre Movement* (University of Toronto Press). Sie ist Begründerin des Netzwerks Neue kritische Theaterwissenschaft. Zusammen mit Lisa Skwirblies hat sie die Publikation "Theaterwissenschaft postkolonial/ dekolonial" (transcript 2022) herausgegeben.

Christopher-Fares Köhler grew up in Germany and Jordan. He studied Theatre Studies at the University of Leipzig and at the Free University of Berlin. From 2013 to 2015 he was Falk Richter's assistant dramaturg- for productions like "Small Town Boy" at the Maxim Gorki Theater Berlin. In the 2017/18 season, he worked as dramaturg at the Kammerspiele Munich for Benjamin von Blomberg (Artistic Director: Matthias Lilienthal). From 2018 to 2020, he has been dramaturg of the Exile Ensemble at the Maxim Gorki Theater Berlin and is the Artistic Director Assistant to Co-Artistic Director Jens Hillje and Dramaturg at the Maxim Gorki Theater Berlin. From 2020 to 2022 he worked as a dramaturg at Schauspiel Dortmund (Artisitc Director Julia Wissert). In Dortmund he initiated and curated the Queer-Festival. Since 2023 he is a Dramaturg at the Deutsches Theater Berlin, in the artistic direction by Iris Laufenberg. Christopher has been working as a translator since 2014, primarily for Arabic authors for the Theater der Welt Festival 2017 in Hamburg, for the Zürcher Theaterpektakel, the Theater an der Ruhr, the Boat People Project, the Volksbühne Berlin, Münchner Kammerspiele and the Maxim Gorki Theater Berlin.

Golschan Ahmad Haschemi is a performer, cultural scholar and political educator. Her performance practice, research and teaching oscillate around the intersections between artistic, political and academic discourses on power-relations, highlighting power asymmetries therein and strategies of resistance. Her theory and practice are grounded in the intersectional topics of Queer-Feminism, Anti-Racism, Anti-Antisemitism and Empowerment. As a political educator her critical work addresses both arts and cultural education with a decolonial approach. Since 2019 she works on advancing the Anti-Racism-Clause in German theatres and theatre contracts with artists. As an educational consultant she advises and trains institutions of arts and culture in the implementation of sustainable strategies to combat discrimination.

Johanna-Yasirra Kluhs arbeitet deutschlandweit und international als Dramaturgin mit verschiedenen Kollektiven, Regisseur*innen und Choreograf*innen im Spektrum der Freien Darstellenden Künste. Seit dem Ende ihres Studiums der Germanistik und Philosophie entwickelt sie kollaborative Strategien einer dramaturgischen Praxis. Kluhs war Teil verschiedener Programm-, Preis- und Förderjurys und u. a. Co-Leiterin des Festivals FAVORITEN 2014 in Dortmund. Von 2016–2021 co-leitet sie das regionale Kulturprogramm Interkultur Ruhr. Sie ist Mit-Begründerin der Ost-West-AG.

Jonas Tinius studied social anthropology at the University of Cambridge, where he also completed a PhD on German theatre, migration, and Haltung. He was postdoctoral researcher at the Centre for Anthropological Research on Museums and Heritage (CARMAH), Humboldt-Universität zu Berlin, and scientific coordinator and postdoctoral researcher in the ERC project *Minor Universality* at Saarland University before taking up a position as director of the Berlin-Brandenburg Office for Everyday Culture in the Institute for European Ethnology of the Humboldt-Universität zu Berlin. He was a visiting scholar at the Universität zu Köln, the University of California, Los Angeles, and the Kunsthistorisches Institut in Florenz – Max Planck Institute. He is author of *State of the Arts. An Ethnography of German Theatre* (Cambridge University Press, 2023) and co-editor of *Der fremde Blick. Roberto Ciulli und das Theater an der Ruhr* (Alexander Verlag, 2020). He co-directed the research group of the Post-Heimat network with Ruba Totah.

Julia Grime is a UK-based Arts Producer who has worked for many years in theatre and cinema. She was General Manager of Theatr Clwyd, a large producing theatre and arts centre in Wales for 15 years before moving to Berlin between 2016–18, where she pursued a British Council project exploring German 'migrant' theatre, producing a website of articles, interviews and reviews – outoftheblackbox.co.uk. She was a founder trustee of the Plaza Community Cinema on Merseyside and has sat on various UK Arts Boards. She was a Governor of Wrexham University for 6 years where she is now an Honorary Fellow. In 2021 she co-founded arts company Zwiebelfish

CIC, to explore and provoke awareness of social justice concerns. Its first project Refuge from the Ravens, co-created with over 100 homeless people, was exhibited at Wordsworth Grasmere and the Houses of Parliament. In 2024, Julia completed her Master's degree in Environment, Culture & Society at the University of Lancaster.

Kenda Hmeidan was born in Syria in 1992. In 2015 she completed her degree at the renowned Academy of Performing Arts in Damascus. She appeared in numerous plays in Syria and Beirut and participated in the Damascus Theater Laboratory's workshops. Kenda Hmeidan belongs to the Ensemble at the Gorki, with whom she developed the play WINTERREISE الشتاء رحلة together with Yael Ronen. Currently she's also appearing at the Gorki in ELIZAVETA BAM, AUSSER SICH and Die Hamletmaschine, Die Verlobung in Santo Domingo, Herzstück Heiner Müller, 8 soldiers Moonsick, Alles Unter Kontrolle, Hamlet Shakespeare. Beside her work in Gorki she works in Radio, TV series and Movies .

Krystel Khoury Krystel Khoury is a dramaturg and performing arts researcher from Beirut. Her work, writings and practice are interested in embodied knowledge, body politics as well as collaborative choreographic processes. She holds a PhD in Anthropology of Dance and intercultural dynamics from Auvergne Université in France. Since 2006, she has been collaborating with numerous Europe-based and Arab cultural organizations on designing and conducting artistic exchange programs. From 2017 till 2019, she was the artistic director of the Open Border Ensemble at the Münchner Kammerspiele in Munich. She collaborated as a dramaturg with Lola Arias (AR), Ahmed ElGendy (EG), Benjamin Coyle/ Kopfkino (DE-FR), Youness Khoukhou (MA), Nadim Bahsoun (LB) and Marah Haj Hussein (PAL) – amongst others. She is presently the head professor of the Institut Supérieur des Arts et des Chorégraphies (ISAC) at the Royal Academy of Fine Arts in Brussels and the Grants and Program associate at Mophradat asbl (Brussels/Athens) working with artists from/in the Arab world.

Lynhan Balatbat- Helbock is a curator and researcher at S A V V Y Contemporary where she is part of the participatory archive project Colonial Neighbours. She received her MA in Postcolonial Cultures and Global Policy at Goldsmiths University of London. In her work within the permanent collection of SAVVY Contemporary she looks for colonial traces that are manifested in our present. The collaborative archive dedicates itself to discussing silenced histories and to the decanonization of the Western gaze through objects and the stories behind them. In close collaboration with artists, initiatives and activists, the archive is activated through hybrid forms of practice. She assisted the management for the documenta14 radio program––Every Time a Ear di Soun, SAVVY Funk in Berlin (June–July 2017). She supported the artist Bouchra Khalili with several projects and exhibitions (May

2015–May 2016) and worked on a yearlong research project on Julius Eastman in a collaboration between SAVVY Contemporary and the Maerzmusik festival (Berliner Festspiele, March 2017–2018). In 2018 she produced Agnieszka Polska s commission for the Germany's National Gallery Prize show in the Hamburger Bahnhof in Berlin (September 2018-March 2019). Lately she was co-curating the yearlong research and exhibition program HERE HISTORY BEGAN. TRACING THE RE/VERBERATIONS OF HALIM EL-DABH (2020–2021).

Nora Amin is a resident of Berlin since 2015 where she is a mentor at the LAFT/PAP (Performing Arts Program/Berlin) and at Flausen+Bundesnetzwerk. An expert on Theatre of the oppressed, critical pedagogy and dance/performance. Author, performer, choreographer & theatre director. Founder of the nation-wide Egyptian Project for Theatre of the Oppressed and its Arab network, founder and artistic director of Lamusica Independent Theatre Group where she directed, choreographed and produced 40 productions of dance, theatre and music. Advisor on arts management and cultural policy. Currently member of the steering team of the future Dance Mediation Centre in Berlin, and board member of the German Centre of the International Theatre Institute. Her latest publication is „Tanz Der Verfolgten" (MSB Matthes & Seitz, 2021), an attempt to decolonise the history of Baladi dance from a feminist perspective, linking patriarchy with capitalism and racism.

Nora Haakh is a cultural scientist, dramaturg, lecturer and (visual) performer. While studying Islamic Studies, Political Science and History in Berlin with time in Paris, Istanbul and Cairo, she started working in theatre. She worked with the early postmigrant theatre movement as assistant and dramaturg at Kreuzberg theatre Ballhaus Nauynstraße, resulting in her first book, „Muslimisierte Körper auf der Bühne" (2021). Since then, she has participated in various productions as assistant, surtitler, dramaturg, director and performer. Her PhD Dissertation "Layla and Majnun in the Contact Zone. Transfers from Arabic into German in Contemporary Theatre" was awarded a special award for Culture by the Augsburger Wissenschaftspreis for Intercultural Studies in 2021.

Özlem Canyürek is a sociologist working at the intersection of cultural policy, politics and education. She holds a PhD from the University of Hildesheim, Department of Cultural Policy. Her research centres on marginalised knowledges, narratives and aesthetics in the performing arts field in Germany. Her dissertation Cultural Diversity in Motion. Rethinking Cultural Policy and Performing Arts in an Intercultural Society was funded by the European Open Science Cloud for open access publication. She has examined diversification processes in the performing arts for the German Performing Arts Fund (2021) and in children's and youth theatre for ASSITEJ

Germany (2023), focusing on practice-informed pluriversal approaches to cultural policy.

Rana Yazaji is a researcher, trainer and cultural manager; she serves as the co-director of "Arts and International Cooperation" at Zurich University of the Arts and currently conducting artistic research on contemporary arts and popular culture during and post-war context. She bases her work on combining research and cultural practices focusing on three interconnected levels: creative initiatives, institutional building and policy discussions. In 2011, she co-founded Ettijahat- Independent Culture, a Syrian organisation formed to support independent arts and culture to play their role in social and political transformation. In 2014, Yazaji became the Executive Director of Culture Resource (Al Mawred Al Thaqafy), a regional cultural organisation active in the Arab Region. Yazaji completed a B.A. in Theatre Studies from the Higher Institute of Dramatic Arts (Damascus, 2001), an M.A. in Design and Management of Cultural Projects from the New Sorbonne University (Paris, 2005), and an M.A. in Theatre Directing and Dramaturgy from the University of Paris X (Paris, 2006).

Ruba Totah is an independent postdoctoral researcher.
She holds a PhD from the Johannes Gutenberg University of Mainz in Germany (2021). Her research sits at the intersection between anthropology, cultural history, and performing arts with regional specialization in the Middle East. Her research interests include transnationalism, intercultural and cross-cultural performing arts spaces, and religiosity. Her recent interest in Performing rituals of church communities around Jerusalem contributes to an anthropological approach to analyzing the history of ethnomusicological practices.